Approaching Freedom

Happy days in Havana - 1952. My parents, myself, and Tia Sara with Papi's new government car.

AUTHOR'S NOTE

I have done my best to describe events as they actually took place, but memory is mutable and susceptible to the whims of time.
With the exception of my immediate family all other names have been changed to protect the privacy of individuals.

All photographs courtesy Maria A. Nodarse.

"We must be willing to let go the life we planned so as to have the life that is waiting for us."
Joseph Campbell

Approaching Freedom

An Exile's Quest for a New Self

A Memoir by
MARIA A. NODARSE

Copyright © 2018 Maria A. Nodarse

All rights reserved.

No part of this book may be reproduced, stored in a retrieval system, or transmitted by any means, without the written permission of the publisher, nor be otherwise circulated in any form of binding or cover other than that in which it is published, except by a reviewer, who may quote brief passages in a review. Any members of educational institutions wishing to photocopy part or all of the work for classroom use should send their inquiries to the author.

Published in the United States by Maria A. Nodarse
First Edition November 2018
Camarillo, California
mariaanodarse@icloud.com

ISBN: 978-1-7328929-0-3   Paperback
ISBN: 978-1-7328929-2-7   eBook EPUB
ISBN: 978-1-7328929-1-0   eBook MOBI

Cover design by Brandi Doane McCann
www.ebook-coverdesigns.com

ACKNOWLEDGMENTS

I would like to thank the following friends and professionals for the time and effort they invested in this book: Ronald Eddy, for his enduring support, laser-focus editing, and multiple revisions of my drafts; Pedro Yanes, my lifelong mentor and irreplaceable friend; Beth Medina for offering her home as the venue for our writing club, for her wise editorial feedback, and for her friendship; Timothy Bay for being my buddy and an outstanding critic; Dr. Dennis Kottler for his encouragement during all these long years; Debbie Rudell for her feedback and support; Mary Embree for her editorial wisdom.

DEDICATION

In loving memory of my parents who sacrificed everything so their children could be free.

For Ron, who completes me.
You are my love and my compass.

Chapter One

It wasn't a scorching afternoon, yet the tall scrawny teenager wearing a Western Union cap looked like he'd stepped out of a swimming pool. I was home for lunch. My mother and I were rocking and chatting on the front porch when we saw *el muchacho* open the small wrought-iron gate in front of our house. His long legs had him at the porch in no time. With his eyes fixed on my mother he said, "*Señora, telegrama*" and asked her to sign for it. *Te-le-gra-ma.* He could have punched me in the stomach. I'd seen enough World War II movies to know telegrams were bad news. Mami, briefly upset by the messenger's arrival, pushed herself up from her rocker, scribbled her signature on his pad, and said, "*Espera.*" She didn't bother with her shoes before stepping inside the house. She always enjoyed the coolness of the tile floor. A moment later she was back handing the boy some coins. "*Gracias,*" she said.

As the messenger closed the gate behind him, Mami

slipped two fingers inside the unsealed envelope and pulled out a small yellowish sheet of paper with narrow white strips glued onto it. The typed English words were all caps. I watched her scan the words, but then I always watched her. She was a beautiful, svelte brunette with a round face like Myrna Loy's and deep-set almond-shaped hazel eyes, fluid as a river. I locked eyes with her trying to anticipate what she might ask me to do.

"Puchita, *está en inglés*," she said and although she could sometimes decipher English, she handed me the telegram. Her request made me feel grown up. I was doing a good job translating it until I got stuck on a word: "absconded." I'd never come across it before; no idea what it meant.

"Something about Loren leaving school. But let's wait for Papi," I said.

My father arrived shortly after the telegram. His white-linen *guayabera* clung to his skin revealing a few spare pounds around his waist. As he bent down to kiss her—he was six feet to her five two—Mami said, "We got a telegram from Loren's school but Puchita can't translate it."

"That's so unfair! I just didn't know that one word!" I said.

"Not now, Puchita," my mother snapped as she pushed the telegram into my father's hand. He read it out loud in thickly accented but impeccable English. I'd already read that my brother Loren had run away from the academy but Papi's baritone voice conveyed a level of gravity I hadn't grasped.

After Loren's troubles with several of Havana's private schools, my parents had shipped him off to Georgia Military Academy in the States a year earlier, in 1957. Now, as he was about to finally graduate, he had pulled this stunt. The telegram went something like this:

MR. NODARSE:
YOUR SON LORENZO AND FRIENDS ABSCONDED WITH MILITARY EQUIPMENT TO JOIN CASTRO'S FORCES STOP DESTINATION MIAMI STOP POLICE ALERTED STOP.
GEORGIA MILITARY ACADEMY

Our cook Belén watched this scene from the arched kitchen doorway, her massive black body blocking the door. She'd wanted to tell Papi lunch was ready. Having a sixth sense about things, she hadn't ventured outside her realm yet. There was no need; she could hear every word. I caught her eye, and her look acknowledged what I'd suspected: our ranks destined us to be mere spectators.

Papi read the message again, translating it into Spanish. He wanted to be sure Mami understood what it said. "Lorenzo, we must find Loren and stop him," my mother said, sounding like an army drill sergeant. "I'm not having my son killed at eighteen."

"Águeda," my father said, "I'm not sure we can even find him. What's wrong with that boy anyway? Another couple of weeks he'd have been home with a high school diploma."

"What do you mean? He has to be stopped."

"First, we have to find out where he is. I'll call some parents. Maybe one of the kids called home. Better still, I'll call Georgia."

"Remember our phone might be tapped," my mother said.

"What makes you think they didn't read the telegram?" Papi was right; our mail was regularly opened and re-sealed with tape.

I saw Belén motioning me to come into the kitchen. As Papi placed the long-distance call, Mami stood next to him hanging onto every word he said. I took Belén's advice and headed to the kitchen.

"You better stay here," Belen said.

"Why?" I asked, wanting to be where the action was.

"*Porque el horno no está para galletitas,*" Belén said. Roughly translated, it means the oven was way too hot for cookies.

A few days later my father called collect from a payphone in Miami. I could tell he was with Loren. Good thing too—after the telegram's arrival you could've sliced the tension in our house with a knife.

"No, he shouldn't come back," I heard my mother say. "It's too dangerous." She paused and I could tell my father was explaining something. She listened attentively, frowning and biting her lip. "Let's do that," she said at last. "He's safer in Mexico with Fello."

Just last year we'd been a family of six; now there were three of us left at home, like the storied bears. My grandmother, *abuela,* who'd always lived with us and who I adored had recently died. Fello, my oldest brother, had left to attend medical school in Mexico after Fulgencio Batista, Cuba's present dictator, closed the University of Havana on November 30, 1956.

Batista's corrupt government, the brutality of his police, and the social and economic injustices thrust upon the Cuban working class had fueled years of persistent student demonstrations and riots. Thousands of people had been murdered or had disappeared at the hands of Batista's secret police under the guise of crushing communist sympathizers. As in the rest of Latin America, Cuban political unrest first brewed at the universities. The University of Havana had always been the birthplace of dissent. Numerous student revolutionary groups dedicated themselves to the struggle for liberty and justice for all the Cuban people. Disruptions through demonstrations or sabotage had become daily occurrences in the lives of Cubans throughout the island.

Years earlier, during Gerardo Machado's dictatorial regime, my own father was a Havana University law student. During *el Machadato*, as his regime was referred to in the streets, urban turmoil and terrorism abounded in Havana. The university was a hotbed of political opposition and agitation. The government closed it in an effort to stamp out persistent demonstrations and organized dissent, preventing my father from graduating when he was scheduled to.

Even at twelve I had a good idea of what was going on in Cuba. Exploding homemade bombs and Molotov cocktails were a frequent occurrence in Havana. Bombings were so common that when the nightly cannon was fired from La Cabaña, the old fortress in Habana Vieja, a tradition dating back to colonial times, people would ask, "Was that a bomb or *el cañonazo?*" Since *las bombas* were often hidden in public bathrooms, my mother wouldn't let me use the restrooms when we went to the movies or department stores. But the sabotage didn't keep people from going out. People seemed to be indifferent to the explosions. Once in a while I'd wonder how many bombs it would take to make people stay at home.

Batista's police regularly tortured or shot political opponents who organized demonstrations against his government, even some who didn't. It wasn't unusual to find graphic black-and-white photos of their victims filling the pages of *Bohemia*, Cuba's popular weekly magazine. It was as if all sides wanted everyone to know the cost of dissent and the price of freedom. There were places like El Laguito, a small lake in the outskirts of Havana, where bodies were dumped on a regular basis. In a way, one could say at least the families knew where to look when one of their own disappeared. Rafael Salas Cañizares, Chief of the National Police, got what he deserved when he was mortally wounded in a shootout with rebels on October 20, 1956. His death served to demonstrate that Batista's iron rule was susceptible to attack.

After revolutionary student groups stormed Batista's presidential palace on March 13, 1957, a brutal reprisal followed. I still remember the day of the attack because of the panic it caused among everyone I knew. My family sympathized with the students who charged into the presidential palace hoping to assassinate Batista. While the palace was under fire, student leader Jose Manuel Echevarria and several others commandeered an important radio station, shouting into the microphone of Radio Reloj that Batista was dead. Echevarria was shot and killed by police on his way back to the university. Forty students died during the palace attack. That day prominent people thought to favor the revolution were taken out of their houses and shot.

That was just what was happening in the city of Havana. In the provinces the fighting in the Sierra Maestra kept escalating, and spreading to other provinces, particularly Las Villas. Batista's press releases sugar-coated the fighting in the mountains, but few were fooled. Back then people liked to say, "*Lo bueno que tiene esto, es lo malo que se está poniendo.*" What's good about what's going on is how bad it's getting.

Chapter Two

We visited my brothers in Mexico City the following Christmas. Havana was on the brink of open warfare. My parents decided our going to Mexico was safer than trying to bring my brothers back home.

We had welcomed the New Year at a lovely residence in Coyoacán, near Mexico City, where relatives of Fello's girlfriend lived. It must have been around two in the morning when we returned to the furnished three-bedroom rental where we were all staying. I was in no hurry to go to bed; I was still dressed to the nines in a red taffeta dress, still wearing my first pair of heels. I remember my hair being up that night, I'd wanted it gathered in a French twist so I'd look older. It must have worked since I managed to score several dances with some handsome university students.

My mother was readying for bed, searching the cabinets for more blankets in an apartment that felt like an icebox, when she turned and asked, "Puchita, did you have fun?"

"What a question! Mami, it was my first New Year's Eve party! Of course I had fun."

We heard a knock on the door. *"¿A esta hora, quién será?"* Mami and I said almost in unison.

"Triunfó la Revolución," heralded the wiry young man at the door, one of the building's resident Cuban refugees. The revolution had triumphed. We'd heard celebrations throughout the building, but it was New Year's Eve, December 31, 1958.

"Why do you say that?" asked Papi.

"My uncle just called me from home—Batista's gone," he answered.

We'd left Havana knowing—and hoping—Batista might be toppled during our absence but we never thought he'd abandon the city without a huge fight. Our stay in Mexico would last a few days longer than planned. We were scheduled to leave the following Saturday, but the airlines were suddenly swamped with Cuban exiles trying to get home again. Papi, being something of a wheeler-dealer, had obtained our plane tickets by bartering advertising space in *Campeón*, the sports magazine he published, with Cubana de Aviación. Since we hadn't paid cash for the tickets, the airline kept pushing us to the back of the line. I loved being in Mexico so I was in no hurry to leave.

On the morning of January 9th we caught a flight home. The tension during the flight was palpable; I think everyone on board was Cuban. None of us knew what to expect when we reached Havana. Rancho Boyeros Airport, on the southern outskirts of the city, felt like a war zone. *Barbudos*, rifle-carrying bearded men wearing olive-green fatigues, milled about the terminal. Later everyone would recall the rosaries that hung from their necks. I couldn't peel my eyes away from the armed rebels. They reminded me of the war movies I'd grown up with. On the way home from the airport I spotted dozens of *rebeldes* patrolling the streets in Batista's tanks, trucks, and jeeps.

Billboards, walls, and store windows were already covered with revolutionary slogans: *Patria o Muerte, Venceremos, Viva Fidel, Viva la Revolución, Cuba, Territorio Libre de América, Movimiento 26 de Julio.*

We'd missed Fidel's triumphant entrance into Havana by one day, but it was broadcast repeatedly on television. Crowds had lined the streets for miles as Fidel and his *guerrilleros* marched victoriously into the city on January 8, 1959. Fidel had taken several days traveling the six-hundred mile stretch from Santiago de Cuba to the capital, knowing people's growing anticipation would be at a fever pitch. Not a single bullet was fired to oppose him. I gave it no thought at the time but later I decided Fidel's unchallenged victory march into the capital reflected the people's reaction against the cruelty of Batista, his corruption and greed, and, in a way, against the Americans who had owned Cuba for so long.

Cubans were tired of corrupt politics, of persistent denials of freedom of speech, of the failure of civil resistance, of general strikes. They were tired of the government's indifference to their need for education, medical care, housing, social and economic justice. I think *el pueblo* must have concluded that nothing short of a revolution could stop Batista, so why not throw their support to Castro?

Passing through our neighborhood I noticed a few houses looked vacant. Their front doors were open, no one seemed to be around. Down our block, Nena's two-story house—where I'd spent so much time playing with her granddaughter Gema—was deserted. I worried about Nena and her husband, but my main concern was whether my girlfriend Gema was still around. As if reading my mind, my mother said, "They probably fled with Batista."

"Maybe they went to visit her uncle in Florida," I said.

All the way home on the plane, I kept imagining my telling Gema about my first real New Year's Eve party! About my hair, my shoes, and the handsome boys who'd asked me to dance. I couldn't have guessed she would've left. I'd known Gema my entire life. Our mothers were best friends. Gema's parents lived in a nearby neighborhood, but she spent a lot of time at her grandparents' home. When she was there, we were inseparable.

I never dreamed that just standing in front of my house could make me so deliriously happy or that seeing Belén there, holding the fort for us, could make my heart chuckle. I ran to hug her. She was my Rock of Gibraltar, and when she said "Puchita," and flashed that smile with a gold tooth, I knew I was safe. I asked her, "Belén, do you know if Gema left?"

"How would I know? People who left didn't exactly

say goodbye, you know. Not that they would have told me, of all people. They just disappeared."

"*Caballero*," she said. She always addressed my father with the Spanish word for "gentleman" and my mother simply as *Señora*. "*¿Sabe quién se mató?*" she asked. Looking straight at him she told him. One of my father's closest friends, a judge, had committed suicide, probably fearing accusations of corruption.

"*Señora, ni le cuento,*" Belén told my mother.

What was it she couldn't begin to tell my mother?

Monday morning, fussing more than usual, I readied for school. I couldn't wait to tell my friends about my thrilling holiday in Mexico, about the New Year's Eve party, but mostly I wanted to see and hear what had happened while I was gone. Would Phillips School be just as I'd left it or would it be *revuluciónario* like the rest of Havana? And my classmates, would they still be there or gone like Gema? I still remember what I wore that day, a black-and-brown plaid long-sleeved cotton shirtwaist dress—it was winter—anchored by a wide beige belt. Once a gangly tomboy, I'd recently become keenly aware of my appearance and budding femininity. That morning I found it hard to tear myself away from my mother's full-length mirror. My legs are too long, my torso's too short, my head's too big. I look like a lollipop. "Puchita, hurry up, you're late," I heard Mami say.

As we walked out of the house I asked my father once again, in hopes of wearing him down, "Aren't you ever going to buy a new car?" He drove a pug-nosed, lusterless black 1950 Chevy, and it was 1959!

"They don't make them like this anymore," Papi said.

"I'll say." I shot back.

Most of my classmates' parents drove late-model, humongous, two-toned American cars with huge fins. Cars like the '58 Dodge Kingsway, Ford Fairlane, or Cadillac Fleetwood. It was embarrassing to be seen stepping out of a car so totally passé. Yet to my father that pugged-nosed Chevy was a symbol of his honesty. What other man in Cuba, handpicked by Batista in 1952 to fill a prestigious political post, had the same car when he left office as he had when he had assumed it? As Cuba's *Director General de Deportes,* Sports Commissioner, my father had been assigned an official government car, a two-toned Buick, the latest! And a uniformed chauffeur, a charming, slight black man who much to my amazement smoked cigarettes and chewed gum at the same time.

Papi's political fame didn't last. His lofty ideas of expanding the city's sporting facilities and encouraging the poor to make greater use of them, didn't jive with Batista's plans of extracting cash from Palacio de los Deportes to enrich himself and his friends.

My snotty preoccupations disappeared when I stepped out of the car: What a relief to see the school just as I'd left it, at least outwardly. No banners or telltale signs of *La Revolución,* which is not to say us students were all of one mind. Some kids were openly enthusiastic about the revolution, others weren't, but I don't remember any discussions getting out of hand. A few teachers favored the revolution and now felt free to discuss the corruption that had characterized Batista's dictatorship; it was civics after all. Many of my classmates echoed their parents' "wait-and-see" attitude while others claimed Fidel was a communist, most likely reverberating what they heard at home.

As for me, I found the *barbudos* handsome and virile. I'd be glued to the television watching Fidel give a never-ending speech until I couldn't take it anymore. At the podium, swarthy Fidel, *el comandante,* was predictably accompanied by his brother Raul, by Camilo Cienfuegos, and Ché Guevara. Camilo, tall and lanky and better looking than Fidel, always wore a big Western hat and everything about him, especially his aw-shucks demeanor, reminded me of Gary Cooper. Next to Fidel, Camilo appeared taller, gentler, the real McCoy. I remember tearing out a magazine page just so I could hide a picture of Camilo in one of my dresser drawers.

When the school bus dropped me home for lunch that day I found my mother sitting on the porch, bare legs atop the glass coffee table, *Anna Karenina* on her lap. I bent down to kiss her and noticed she'd been scribbling in the book, something she'd always warned me not to do.

"Mami, what are you doing?" I felt excited to catch her doing something she'd forbidden me to do.

"Writing a list of characters and the dozen names each one has. It's the only way I can keep them straight. There're so many characters to keep track of."

"Back in a minute," I said and went straight to the

kitchen to kiss Belén. Belén never came out of the kitchen to greet anyone. No exceptions. It wasn't unusual for visitors to stop themselves, mid-sentence, and say, "*Dios mío*, I didn't say hello to Belén."

"I was waiting…" Belén was in the habit of saying in those occasions, "…waiting to see how long it would take you."

"*Hola*," I said, and gave Belén a kiss. Did I say she was my second mother, I adored her? That afternoon she wore a burlap skirt, meaning she'd made a promise to San Lazáro. In the past, Mami told me not to ask Belén about her *promesas*. "Private," my mother had explained. I suspected Mami worried I might adopt some of Belén's superstitions and she wanted logic to rule my life. My mother's efforts notwithstanding, I had a schizoid childhood: logic in the living room and superstition in the kitchen.

"I was thinking of getting you a *medianoche* for your *merienda*," Belén said referring to my favorite sandwich, a small egg bread bun with ham, Swiss cheese, pork loin, mustard, and a sliver of a pickle—the perfect size for a snack. *Medianoche,* midnight.

"Will Mami know?" My *meriendas* came out of Belén's pocket. Well, actually, that's not entirely true; Belén did so much wheeling and dealing it was impossible to tell. My mother thought if I ate too much after school I'd lose my appetite for dinner. Belén didn't think time should interfere with eating and my mother knew it. If, come dinnertime, she saw me spreading my food across the plate instead of eating it she'd ask, "Belén, what did you give her?" A straight-faced Belén always said, "I swear, *señora*, not a thing. *Nada.*" I had no doubt God would strike Belén dead any day now.

"I wasn't going to tell her. What do you take me for, a fool?" Belén said.

"Good." On my way out the kitchen I patted her fanny.

"You think I don't know what you're doing, wiping your hands on my butt?" said Belén.

I scurried to the porch where we had the best rockers, upholstered and ample, made from bamboo. I'm what is known as a *sillonera*, a person who loves to rock back and forth, nonstop. Mami, still struggling with the Russians, ignored me so I picked up the *Bohemia* issue lying on the coffee table. *Bohemia*, Cuba's leading magazine, sold millions of copies during the first couple of weeks of 1959, all celebrating the triumph of the revolution.

"*¡Qué horror!*" I shouted, turning away my head in disgust. Sepia-colored photographs of General Batista's mutilated victims, corpses of tortured men on morgue slabs, pictures of torture instruments and torture chambers splashed across the pages of *Bohemia's* revolutionary issue.

"Puchita, don't look at that," Mami said.

"They're real?" I asked.

"Afraid so."

I tossed the magazine on the table, went back to the kitchen. I knew when Mami was interested in a book, she'd rather read than talk.

"Belén," I asked, "do you think Gema's grandfather knew what was going on? Like do you think he knew about the torture and the killings?"

"I don't know for sure," she said. Seeing the

disappointment in my eyes, she added, "My guess is he didn't know."

"I miss her so much."

"Gema?"

"Yes. I miss our walks around the neighborhood. The two of us liked Tito. Gema never admitted it, but I could tell. I don't think Tito liked us. I think he liked older girls." Tito was the brother of a young woman Fello really liked.

"That's because he's older. Thinks you're a couple of kids."

"Not that old," I said.

"Old enough to like women, not girls. Besides your mother never liked his family."

"Are they gone?"

"Don't know. Like I said, *la señora* doesn't like them. Where's Gema? Miami?"

"No, about two of hours away from Miami."

In the pre-Castro days, Gema's grandfather held a government job at *palacio*, as we called the presidential palace. Being a friend of Batista, he secured a diplomatic post for his son in Florida where he'd been living with his wife and two children for some years now. Alina, the daughter, was still my good friend. She came to Havana every summer to spend time with her grandparents down the block from my house. Twice I'd been lucky enough to go to Florida with Gema to visit her.

I couldn't believe the freedom Alina enjoyed in the States. She even went out without a chaperone. I remember us going to a party given by one of her friends and not a single adult was there. The boy's folks had left him the house. In Cuba we brought parents to parties.

Gema's absence hurt deeply. I couldn't accept she could just disappear from my life. Yet I was incapable of working out in my head how or when I'd see her again. She and her family wouldn't be returning anytime soon. I forced myself to face facts—Fidel wasn't going to let any Batistianos off the hook. Quite the contrary, he was thinking of new ways of punishing them. Gema and her family would not return. I couldn't name the emptiness I felt. I had no clue where Cuba was heading, but I wanted the country and the life I knew back.

Chapter Three

Castro's horrors soon followed. The *revoluciónarios* swiftly seized General Batista's *carniceros*, butchers. It was impossible to avoid seeing photos of Batista's atrocities, splashed as they were across Cuba's newspapers and magazines. The masses, oppressed and exploited until now, called for retribution: executions in the name of justice. As photogenic as a Hollywood movie star, Ché Guevara, Fidel and Raul's trusted accomplice, led the revolutionary tribunals that dispatched Batista's collaborators to the firing wall. In addition to Batista's henchmen, a lot of innocent people were massacred at *el paredón*, as often happens when the victors thirst for blood. They televised the executions; complete with a chorus of vengeful Cubans on the sidelines screaming, "*Paredón, Paredón, Paredón*." To the firing wall. Not our finest hour.

My parents tried to shield me from the televised *fusilamientos* but it was tough to know when they would broadcast anything. Apparently the regular TV broadcast schedule had been tossed out with Batista. After school I used to watch *Hopalong Cassidy*, *The Lone Ranger*, and several other westerns. My mother would join me occasionally. When a cowboy got knocked out, punched, shot at, Mami would say, "Watch: now a woman will show up with a bowl of water and a *toallita* (a small towel) and after she places the *toallita* on his forehead everything will be fine. Americans solve everything with a *toallita*." But those days were gone, now you could never tell what would be on TV. Couldn't even count on watching *Perry Mason* or *I Love Lucy,* the revolution's broadcasts ruled.

Nearly ten months after Fidel's triumphant takeover, on the night of October 28th to be precise, Camilo Cienfuegos vanished at sea as he flew his Cessna from Camaguey to Havana.

A search of epic proportions followed. His disappearance was the lead story on every news program day after day. Mami was fond of saying the hunt for Camilo reminded her of the silent cliffhanger movies of her youth. By the time the search was called off, the towering figure of *El Líder* had eclipsed the memory of Camilo. Neither Camilo nor the plane was ever found.

At school, among friends, we couldn't stop talking about Camilo. "He was gorgeous!" I said. "What was he, twenty-five?"

"People liked him too much," one of my classmates said. "That's why Fidel had him killed."

"Twenty-seven," Luis, a friend since kindergarten, said.

"They're friends, Fidel and Camilo," I said. "They go all the way back."

"My parents say Fidel had him killed because he tried to defend a traitor."

"But they were friends!" I insisted.

A nation grieved when Camilo was pronounced dead. All over Havana swaths of black fabric draped Camilo's photographs. People took to wearing mourning bands. At school a girl in a lower grade who'd enrolled right after the revolution tied a black ribbon around her white sleeve.

"*¿Y eso?*" I asked, knowing full well what it was, resentful of this usurper trying to appropriate "my" Camilo, not to mention my school.

"Honoring Camilo."

"That's so tacky," I said, and was sorry the moment it came out of my mouth. That was pretty low I realized. She was much younger than me. The girl turned on her heels and scurried away. There's always been something in me that enjoys the rush of being a little bad. But being discourteous to the new kid was likely to cause me trouble.

For me, Camilo's death was the proverbial straw. When they gave up searching for him, I realized how fed up I was with revolution. Didn't want to hear more slogans, read any more posters. Not one more *Patria o Muerte, Venceremos,* not one more *Cuba, Territorio Libre de América,* not one more *Gracias Fidel.* Done. *Basta.*

The day after I told off the new kid, my teacher summoned me. They wanted me in the office. My only real—and admittedly annoying—discipline problem was that I was a non-stop talker. *Una cotorrita* as they say in Cuba, a little parrot. So as I headed for the office I expected to be reprimanded for never listening, for always having *la boca abierta,* my mouth open.

I stood at the doorway and when I saw the stern look in la Doctora Luisa's face I just about wet my panties. La Doctora Luisa, white-haired and motherly, was the school's assistant principal, and all of us liked and respected her. In the gentlest of voices she said, "Come in and sit down. You've let me down." Nothing could have made me feel smaller.

"Let you down?" I asked. It was just talking after all.

"The fact that you've been here since kindergarten," she stopped again, this time to look straight into my eyes, "doesn't mean you own this school." I wanted to interrupt her during her brief pause, but she'd signaled me to wait. "What you did was wrong. If we don't let other people express their opinions, why should they listen to yours, or mine or anybody else's? You should apologize."

I stared at the floor. "I'm sorry," I said, finally realizing why she was disappointed.

"Don't apologize to me. Apologize to the poor girl you've upset."

"Just don't tell my mother."

"Too late," Doctora Luisa replied. My heart trotted.

When the school bus dropped me home, my mother's

nose was still buried in *Anna Karenina*. I hurried over to kiss her cheek, hoping to quickly dart into the house as if nothing had happened.

"Puchi, you have to learn to be careful. Things are very different now," she said.

Maybe it was watching all those Hollywood movies; maybe it was just being a romantic adolescent; or maybe it was that at school we were studying the French Revolution, who knows? The fact is that in spite of being overdosed with all the slogans, all the propaganda, I thought of Fidel as a Robin Hood figure, a maverick who stole from the rich to give to the poor. I thought Fidel was doing things for the people, for the very poor. I'd seen Havana's slums, full of barefoot parasitic children with distended bellies. That's where my head was when I learned the government had forced land and property owners to lower the rents (by a third or a half), when the Revolution had mandated agrarian reform and when Fidel had signed *la reforma agraria,* amidst *campesinos* and *guerrilleros* in the Sierra Maestra mountains. Talk about staging! The agrarian reform law limited land ownership to 1,000 acres, with the government appropriating the rest, turning Cuba's economy upside down. Agriculture was collectivized and although we didn't own land, many of our friends did. Each week there seemed to be fewer kids in my school. Entire families took off to Miami by the plane-load, their men unable or not allowed to work in the businesses Castro's regime had seized. The Cubans who escaped during the early stage of Castro's revolutionary government, between 1959 and 1962, were probably the best-educated large group of immigrants to arrive in America since the Second World War. They had been doctors, lawyers, business entrepreneurs, university professors. White, educated, refined professionals, they were the poster children in the battle against communism. It was precisely for this reason that Fidel had to put an end to what had become a brain drain. On the one hand, Fidel didn't want the *gusanos* in the country but on the other, neither could the revolution afford to lose the nation's entire skilled workforce. It was rumored Fidel would stop the Havana-Miami flights while there were still some professionals left in the island.

My father had always worked for an American company in Havana and he knew his breadwinning days were numbered. During the revolution's first year my parents worked to be optimistic. They hoped the worst was over and some kind of stability would soon return. Papi's family was still in Havana and his mother's health was fragile. I overheard Mami saying it was time to leave Cuba but Papi wouldn't hear of it. He wasn't leaving his mother behind, and she was too weak to travel. For once, I kept my mouth shut. I couldn't work out what it would mean to live in another country. What about Belén? Would she and her husband come with us? I didn't want to leave; many of my friends were still in Havana at the only school I'd ever attended, a school which was my second home. Mami talked as if it would only be for a short time. Probably just months she'd say. Maybe I'd still be able to celebrate my 15th birthday with my friends. But on the other hand, if we stayed in Miami for a while, maybe I'd see Gema again.

As the sweeping nationalizations continued, my

fathers' job was swept away with the rest. A short time later *abuelita* passed away. Papi had already stopped publishing *Campeón*, the sports magazine I'm sure, given time, would have become a hit. Well known in the world of sports, my father had no problem getting athletes and sports commentators to contribute to the magazine; he even had a doctor write a column on sports medicine, way before it became popular. Advertising revenue had been growing before the revolution but took a big drop afterward. But none of that mattered because the government had taken over everything. So my father left for Miami with a tourist visa, a suitcase, and little else, certain his English skills would help him land a position in Florida. The moment he landed a job and found us a place to live he'd send for us. The significance of his leaving didn't really register with me. Maybe because he'd always traveled for business; maybe because, as people like to say nowadays, I was in denial. What I remember vividly is my mother's growing concern about our getting out of Cuba. Every day the rumor mills worked overtime. In Miami, it was said, the word on the street was Fidel wasn't going to let any more Cubans leave the country, period. No one knew what to believe, or what Castro might do next. Now with Papi gone, and still searching for work, and with no money coming into the house other than the little Loren could earn, my mother was becoming increasingly worried. By early September 1960 Mami decided we should get the hell out of Cuba. Fello was safe, still in Mexico, and she was sure she could persuade Loren to come with us. She misread Loren. He wouldn't hear of it; he was twenty-one and was staying. Once ready to join Fidel in the mountains, Loren's furor took a turn. He was now determined to help bring down Fidel and his cronies. It hadn't taken long for him and his friends to realize Cubans had traded a right-wing dictator for a communist tyrant.

Loren's late hours, his odd comings and goings, led my mother to suspect he'd joined one of the underground organizations aiming to overthrow Castro's government. She wasn't giving in easily. She took his hands, looked into his eyes and said,

"Loren, there is no need for you to get involved. The revolution won't last. Nothing here ever does. Your father and I lived under Machado's dictatorship, and he was much worse than Batista; we've lived under a succession of presidents who lined their pockets with the people's money, and we've lived through Batista's tyranny. In the end they all fall."

"Yeah, but this is different and you know it."

Chapter Four

Belén stood on the other side of the glass wall at Rancho Boyeros Airport. *La pecera,* the fish tank, that's how Cubans nicknamed the waiting room because it separated with glass those hoping to leave from their relatives watching from the outside.

Belén's blackness stood out in the mostly white crowd. She was in her Sunday best: a short-sleeved tailored plaid dress with a wide collar. She wore the gold jewelry—bracelets, loop earrings, a gold pin—that she'd bought on installments with her hard-earned money. Her hair was the same, straightened with a hot comb, parted in the middle, and covered with a black hairnet; and she wore her bifocals. Our eyes locked, and I realized she'd been crying. "*Para que me recuerdes,*" she said right before we got separated, handing me a miniature leather-bound copy of Kemphis'

An Imitation of Life that I still keep in my night table's drawer. I blew her kisses across the glass wall and said as loudly as I could, "*Volvemos pronto, Belén,*" believing I'd be back in no time. At fourteen I didn't doubt I'd always see the people I loved again.

"María de los Ángeles," I heard. My mother called me Puchita unless she was upset. Then it became Maria de los Angeles. I whipped my head towards her. She was surrounded by *barbudos* in crumpled olive-green uniforms, rifles slung over their shoulders. A gruff-looking *miliciano* opened her suitcase, battered and mostly covered with blue Pan-Am stickers, and pulled out my mother's neatly folded underwear and stockings. "*Su cartera,*" he said. Without looking at the young man she handed him her boxy patent leather bag. He took out her wallet and counted the money. "Is that all you're carrying?" he asked.

"Yes," she said, lying; I knew she had money inside her brassiere. And there were the medals as well. Papi had dozens of gold medals and just as many silver medals, all won at tennis tournaments. The medals, mounted on black velvet in a gold, glass-encased frame, were my father's pride and joy. Mami had removed them from the frame and put them in a brown paper bag she rolled and buried in her suitcase. She knew she was taking a chance, they could get confiscated, but she wanted to surprise my father.

"*Su cartera,*" he said again, this time addressing me. Mami took a small step toward me. I remember getting a whiff of *Femme*, her preferred perfume. *El miliciano* opened my handbag but not my wallet and then took his time checking me out. I feared he'd want my *dormilonas,* the small diamond studs I'd worn since I was an infant.

"How much money are you carrying?" he asked. I tried to think of what was in my bag, but before I could answer he said, "Next" and stretched his hand towards the person behind me, "Identity papers" he said. I snapped my handbag closed while Mami quickly gathered her clothing, stuffing it back into her suitcase. I knew she was fuming, but no one could say a word. The man standing behind me reminded me of my godfather Marcelino. His straight silver hair, combed back, was resplendent with Brylcreem. His white linen suit, heavily wrinkled after the long wait, called attention to his elegance. Unlike my *padrino* this man had that haughtiness of the upper class.

"How long do you intend to stay in Miami?" one of the *barbudos* asked him.

"*Un mes,*" he replied. "*De vacaciones.*"

Traveling was a big deal back then, especially air travel. Well-dressed, well-heeled men and women filled the lobby: men in white linen suits or *guayaberas*; women wearing make-up, jewelry, and stockings; gussied-up little girls and suited boys. Moving through the airport the difference in appearance between the would-be passengers and dozens of armed, scruffy young *barbudos* hit me like a brick.

As my mother and I approached the stairway of the Cubana de Aviación plane, the passengers ahead of us looked up to the airport's crowded second-floor wide terrace and waved one last goodbye. I spotted Belén in no time, blew her kiss, took a few steps, turned around and blew her another. My mother also searched the wide terrace, her eyes darting from one young man to another. "Look, there's Loren," she said. My movie-star looking brother would have been conspicuous in any crowd. That morning he'd worked his shift at Cubana de Aviación's ticket counter. He looked striking in his blue uniform. His decision to stay behind had broken my mother's heart.

Reaching for my seatbelt, I asked my mother when we'd be back. *"Pronto,"* she said.

"¿Qué es pronto?"

"Seis meses, más o menos." It was September 26, 1960, which meant we wouldn't be back for Christmas. I'd never been away from Belén for that long.

"Where am I going to school? I hope it's where my friends are."

"I don't know, Puchita. I know we won't be able to afford a private school in Miami and I don't know how public schools work."

"I hope they're not lousy like in Cuba."

"I doubt it."

"They look good on television."

"I'm sure they're fine."

The moment the stairway was pulled back, the plane began moving to the runway. As the plane left the ground, my mother stared out the window, fixing her eyes on the landscape, on the copper-colored soil and verdant royal palm trees that like giants towered over the island's lush vegetation. Climbing up through the tropical clouds the plane bounced and shook like an old jalopy car. I was glad the flight was barely an hour. Many of the children started to whimper and cry. The little boys looked cute but awkward in their tiny suits while the girls, cradling their favorite doll, appeared more at ease in their fancy dresses and shiny black shoes. Elegant mothers dabbed their tears with white, embroidered linen handkerchiefs. As I remember it, there were fewer men than women and children, and I recall their gravitas. The aircraft's atmosphere was solemn and foreboding. I wanted to ask my mother a few more questions about what lay ahead, but I felt so wretched that like most passengers, I kept to myself. We were at the tail end of the first wave of refugees to hit Miami. Like all others who left Cuba early on, my family and I were certain that Fidel's government wouldn't last and that our stay in Miami was temporary.

With my big eyes about to pop out I inspected the terminal as we descended the stairs to the tarmac at Miami International Airport. The waiting crowd was large, and we were still too far away to be certain, but I was sure I'd caught sight of my father waiting for us near the gate. It looked like he was talking with another man standing beside him.

Papi's hair had turned jet black. I, not one to like change, decided he looked better with his salt-and-pepper hair. And besides, this contrast drew attention to his ever-deepening widow's peak which I didn't know back then was a neat thing to have. At just over six- feet tall, long-limbed, with an athletic build, and still a good-looking guy for his age, my father would have been hard to miss at any airport.

"*Gracias a Dios,*" he said with an ear-to-ear smile, his white teeth—polished and even, like piano keys—flashing against his dark olive complexion. He was nervously excited. We Cubans are superstitious and Papi never talked about anything good without giving God his proper due. "Now all we need is Loren here *con el favor de Dios.* Let me introduce you to Chiquitico," he said, turning to the swarthy man by his side. He liked to sound like that, formal. "We're extremely fortunate to have him as our neighbor. He kindly drove me here in his car to pick you up," he said.

Chiquitico's hair matched my father's, but since he was younger, he looked pretty hot with that jet black mane. Had they used the same Clairol number? Had they helped each other with the coloring?

Chiquitico had the looks of the quintessential Hollywood Latin lover— earthy, sultry, and vigorous. He went to get his car while Papi helped us find our luggage. We followed Papi out of the terminal to the sidewalk curb where he ushered us into an old blue Ford sedan. It made Papi's 1950 Chevy look like a limo. "I paid thirty-five bucks for it," Chiquitico said with no small amount of pride. To keep the right front door closed he tied it with a rope to the back door.

"Careful," he said when I stepped in, pointing to a hole in the floor. "Lets you stick out your foot when the brakes don't work." He broke up with laughter. As we left the airport he said, "I'll drive down Flagler so you can see it."

We'd been to Miami several times before. It was a

popular vacation spot with my family. I was happy to see that Walgreens, home of the world's best soda fountain, and Burdines, showplace of the coolest fashions, were still there. When we headed southwest, or *El Sagües,* to use the Cuban pronunciation, I realized this wasn't the Miami I knew. Southwest Eighth Street *(Calle Ocho)* was flooded with signs like *Batidos, Café Cubano, Envíos a Cuba, Sándwich Cubano, Medianoches.* This surrogate Miami looked and sounded—Cuban music pulsing from storefronts—like a sham replica of Havana. Cuban men huddled in front of insignificant cafes, smoking and drinking espressos from dainty pleated white paper cups, gesturing operatically, talking in loud voices at machine-gun speed, no plurals, no word endings, words chewed out at a frenzied speed, to their very marrow—*mijito, venpaca, nomedigatu,* as opposed to *mi hijito, ven para acá, no me digas tú.*

I'd wanted to feel like I was in the United States, not in Fake Havana. "Well," I said as I looked out the car window with a face as long as the peninsula itself "at least Burdines and Walgreens are still here." I wondered how the Americans felt about their city becoming unfamiliar. Ignored once more. "Papi," I said, determined not to be deterred, "how far is your apartment?"

"It's not my apartment, Puchita. It's our apartment. It's not far," he said.

"Puchita, just look out your window," Mami injected. "We'll be there soon."

I realized Mami had barely spoken a word since getting off the plane. The car turned on Tenth Avenue and somewhere in the neighborhood of Second Street,

Chiquitico parked his thirty-five-buck car, got out, and untied the rope holding my door closed.

We followed Chiquitico down the sidewalk. He turned up a walkway leading to a faded yellow two-story apartment building. A few Cubans hung out on the front porch. We're not going to live here, are we? I knew better than to ask.

"Move on, Puchita, I'm tired," Mami said. When we left home that morning my mother had looked stunning in her hunter green and black dress and high heels. But that was before saying goodbye to her son, to Belén, and the neighbors who were staying; that was before encountering the *revolucionarios'* insolence at the airport. Now she looked like yesterday's corsage. Ignoring her exhaustion, my father focused on his recent acquaintances, dragging us from one person to another saying, "Let me introduce you to my wife and daughter." He was always like that, he tended to disregard what others wanted, certain he knew best. Mami and I had met everyone; could we go inside now?

"Mami," I said, in an effort to cheer her up, "smell the coffee?" We climbed up to the second floor and Papi opened the door to a matchbox-sized apartment. I didn't want to go in. In Havana people had maid's rooms larger than this. Was this really to be our living room, dining room, and kitchen? There was a separate bedroom with a double bed that left almost no space to move around it. I felt claustrophobic just looking into the bathroom.

"*Espero que les guste*," my father said. Was he crazy? He expected us to like this? I must have looked miserable because he quickly added, "When I get a job we'll get a bigger place."

"It's fine," my mother said, "it's fine." She was beat.

"So, Puchita, what do you think?" Papi asked. I said nothing. As a kid I had grown antennas to pick up on Mami's moods. It was safer that way. My mother shook her head a little. I realized this was not the time to say how horrendous the place was. Mami could barely stand up. Papi wanted us to like it. And I didn't want to get in trouble.

"Where am I supposed to sleep?" I asked. Papi pointed to a daybed covered with a flaming flamingo-themed bedspread.

"It's only for a while," my mother said.

I reached down and grabbed my suitcase and popped it open. "Where do I hang my clothes?"

"I guess we're all going to share the bedroom closet," my mother said.

The aroma woke me up. Mami had made coffee. She'd remembered to bring *la tetera*, a fabric coffee-making contraption shaped like a cow's teat attached to a metal hoop with a handle. I looked around the sorry-ass apartment—dinette set, stove, refrigerator, kitchen sink, all right in front of my eyes—and wanted to shriek, but there was something so matter-of-fact, so domestic and assuring in the way Mami went about making coffee that watching her and getting a whiff calmed me. We're really going to live here. I longed for the privacy of my bedroom.

"Puchita, we need to find a store. We have nothing to

eat," she said.

"You want me to ask someone where the closest store is?"

"We'll have to walk, so we won't be able to carry much." I rushed downstairs to the super's apartment. Anything to get out of there. I couldn't stop thinking of the only home I'd known. I kept seeing it the way we'd left it, as if we were going on an errand: armchairs and sofa facing the TV, diplomas hanging in the hallway, the porch's four rocking chairs parked around the bamboo coffee table, waiting for a conversation to begin. I'm sure even the frog was at its usual place, at the bottom of the yellow ceramic pot centered on the coffee table. Funny, how well I remembered the frog.

"*Ayyyyyyyyyy*" I'd screamed when I saw the frog jump inside the water-filled pot.

"Puchita," my mother had said, "What's that all about? It's only a little frog. What could something that small do to you?"

"Blind me," I said.

"Blind you? How?"

"Peeing in my eyes. Belén told me that if a frog pees in my eyes I'll go blind."

"Puchita, use your head. How can a frog possibly pee in your eye? Think."

I shrugged my shoulders.

"Belén!" Mami called.

Now Loren and the frog had the house all to themselves. Belén would come and cook for him. "*Señora*," Belén had said, "I've been cooking for that boy all my life and I'm not about to stop." I wished I'd been Loren's age in the old Cuba, wished I'd been able to go to Tropicana, Sans Souci, Montmatre, wished I'd had the opportunity to see all the famous people who came to Cuba to perform like Edith Piaf, Xavier Cugat, and Carmen Miranda. If I'd been Loren's age, I'd have danced the night away and then, like so many *exilados,* I could have said,"*Que me quiten lo bailado.*" "Let them take all those dances away from me."

To fall asleep at night, I came up with this trick of recreating my house so as to stop worrying about how my father would get us out of this hole. I'd start at the sidewalk, open the small wrought-iron gate, walk the red tiles and climb the five steps up to the porch, walk past the goddamned frog without fear, walk into the living room, the dining room, and the kitchen. I'd see Belén in the kitchen in her burlap skirt and wonder why she never wore an apron. But after getting to the kitchen I'd grow melancholy and then I'd decide to stop there and start imagining the club.

That first week it poured, and I'd stare out the rain-streaked apartment window feeling sorry for myself. Every September since kindergarten I'd gone back to the same school, with the same classmates, same principal, same janitor even. Now I couldn't even go to school—any school. Until late 1960 Miami's Dade County schools would only accept exiled students who were not permanent residents if their families paid tuition. We didn't have the money, so I was stuck with my mother all day long in that two-room pissy apartment.

One morning Mami sat over her *café con leche*, her mind a thousand miles away.

"You okay?" I asked.

"I was thinking about Loren. It worries me he's still in Cuba. I hope he doesn't get into any trouble."

"You mean because of what he did in Georgia?"

"I mean because he's a rebel and I don't want him doing anything he shouldn't be doing. They can do anything they want to him. Throw him in prison and let him rot there."

"Mami, nothing is going to happen to Loren."

"Now you're starting to sound like your father."

"So, that's it, Loren?" I asked.

Mami looked at me and nodded. "Thank God Fello's in Mexico. I hope he doesn't have to interrupt his studies."

"You think he'll be able to finish?" I asked. It was difficult to worry about Fello. He'd always been a hard act to follow.

"We have to hope for the best. He's frugal, not like Loren."

When Loren was at Georgia Military Academy, he'd draw dollar signs on the margins of his letters. Fello, on the other hand, would sometimes tell my folks he didn't need money yet, he had some left over.

"If anybody can do it, it's Fello," I said. He was my hero in those days.

"I don't know, Puchi," Mami continued, "whether he'll be able to finish. We're running out of money. I don't know what's going to happen if Lorenzo doesn't get a job soon. We'll be out of money in two months."

"In two months?"

"We can pay rent for two months; we can get by for two months. That's it."

"What happens after that?"

She looked at me and shrugged her shoulders. Since arriving in Miami I hadn't heard her complain once. She hadn't griped about moving into a matchbox; she hadn't mentioned how she wished her sons were with her and not abroad. She saw me grinding my teeth. "You shouldn't do that Puchita. It's bad for your teeth. Don't worry; Lorenzo will have a job by then. He's a lawyer. He knows English. He's a fast typist. He worked for an American company for twenty-five years. Why wouldn't he get a job?"

What I heard my mother say was that we might starve to death in two months' time. Boredom was already making me eat too much—dresses didn't fit, pants wouldn't zip, shirts looked about to pop open, but I didn't want to talk about it. "*Te estas poniendo gorda,*" my mother would say as if I didn't know I was getting fat. What else could I do but eat? We didn't have a television. I was the only teenager in the building. It was either boiling hot or pouring rain outside. Not a word out of me. What's the point? Instead, I helped myself to some cottage cheese and strawberry jam, stuff I wouldn't have touched with a ten-foot pole in Cuba.

"Mami, is there room here to make *arroz con pollo*?"

"*Claro,*" she said, which means of course.

"*¿Flan?*"

"Puchita, can you think of something else besides

food? That's all you talk about. You're not getting fat, you ARE fat. You eat all day long."

She was right; I was storing food for the lean times ahead, for that empty-cupboard day.

"Belén's apartment was bigger than this." I wanted to complain about the size of our apartment but she wouldn't bite.

"About the same."

"Guess so," I said, remembering the day I went home with her. She'd needed something from her apartment and I went along. Belén lived in a charcoal-colored building in El Cerro, one of Havana's oldest neighborhoods. The apartment was minuscule—and immaculate. When I walked into the living room, the first thing I spotted was a large altar devoted to Santa Barbara, a bright red glass votive candleholder to each side of the saint's statue, a ripe crimson apple in front. Belén lit the candles and a ruby-red light flooded the room. I wanted to ask her about the offering, I wanted to say, "Belén, you really think Santa Barbara will eat that apple?" But I knew better because I had said something like that once as we drove past the Chinese cemetery in El Vedado. When I saw *los chinos* offering food to their ancestors I'd asked, "They think they're going to eat it?"

"And do you think your grandmother will smell our flowers?" my mother replied.

My first lesson in tolerance.

Chapter Five

Mami wanted to conceal the pots and pans that sat on three pitiful plywood shelves above the kitchen sink. I guess she had to make the place feel like it was hers. "Do you want to go to *El Tencén* and see what we can find for these shelves?" she said. That's what Cubans called the dime store, *Tencén*

"Claro," I said.

In Cuba, we went to the big Woolworth dime store in Habana Vieja practically every Saturday. Back then nothing made me happier than to sit at the long soda fountain bar and wolf down a huge banana split while Mami sipped on a malted. I can still see the front of the two-story Woolworth facade with its protruding massive gold letters, all caps, set against a fire-engine-red background. Now I was ready to jump at the chance to go to the grocery store, the hardware store, the pharmacy, anything to get out of that crappy apartment.

The afternoon felt like a humidity festival; my clothes were drenched in sweat in no time; even my hair weighed me down. It was roughly a ten-minute walk to the nearby five-and-ten. "Feel that air-conditioning," Mami said as we entered Woolworth's. When I didn't see an escalator, I wondered where the rest of the store was. I noticed the fabric section at the back of the store. From where I stood it didn't look like much of an assortment but my mother plunged ahead. She picked up a red-and-white checkered oilcloth and said, "It's not what I had in mind, but it's cheap, and we won't be looking at pots and pans all day. Tell the clerk to give you two yards." Most sales clerks in Miami only spoke English back then. Mami grabbed some thumb tacks and a pair of scissors and headed for the cashier. I was in no hurry to leave. I wanted to sleep at Woolworth's; it was so cool in there.

We left the store reluctant to face the torpid humidity we'd briefly escaped. I was about to say something to that effect but as we crossed the street, we smelled the wet soil and with a sudden clap of thunder, the rain poured down with typical tropical temper. We dashed for the cover of a nearby store awning but Mami stopped abruptly, gasping for air.

"*¿Qué pasa?*" I asked, worried there might be something seriously wrong with her.

"*No nos vamos a encoger*" she said and laughed. It's not like we're going to shrink. But I could see she'd run out of breath. Now that I was with her all the time it was hard to miss how easily she got tired. Mami used to have women help with the housework in Cuba. Besides Belén, who really ran the house, there was always a cleaning woman/washer and ironing lady. But why was she so tired when we lived in a place you couldn't take more than five steps at a time? Nerves maybe. The rain stopped as unpredictably as it had started. Miami was a lot like Cuba: in less than half an hour the sun would dry the streets and sidewalks and you wouldn't be able to tell it had rained at all.

What little we had in that apartment came from Woolworth's; the clunky sea-foam coffee mugs and cereal bowls we used every day could have survived a missile strike. Anything that came with the apartment was useless, particularly the cooking pans, thin as onion skin. Mami's first purchase in Miami had been a large cast-iron frying pan.

"Isn't the frying pan too heavy for those shelves?" I asked as she stood on a dining room chair pleating the oilcloth and tacking it to the edge of the wooden shelves.

"*Quizás.*"

She stepped down off the chair to examine her creation and then picked up the leftover cloth—she could have bought half a yard less—and shaped it like a bow, then stuck it in the middle of the top shelf. "*Muchísimo mejor,*" she said with pride.

As it turned out, we wouldn't starve. But not because Papi had landed a job. We started getting boxes of surplus and donated food from the Catholic Relief Services of Miami. Powdered milk and eggs, vegetable oil, institutional packaged cheese, tins of spam, and jars of peanut butter we never figured out what on earth to do with. I think it was Chiquitico's wife who came up with a recipe for a mouth-watering flan using powdered eggs and powdered milk. My mother became popular in no time. Women would knock on the door and ask to borrow her cast-iron frying pan, "Águeda, *¿me puede prestar el sartén?*" She and Chiquitico's wife seemed to be the only ones in the building who knew how to cook. I remember women dropping by our apartment and asking, "Águeda, *¿cómo se hace el arroz?*" Rice, really! Mami would brew them "*un cafecito,*" and at those times with those women I saw her smile.

One late October afternoon we were both sitting at the dinette table almost whispering so as not to wake up Papi, who was napping in the bedroom after hitting the pavement all morning when we heard a knock on the door. "*El sartén,*" I said, thinking out loud about the frying pan, our great investment. Mami had always been generous; besides, we were all in the same boat. She wasn't the only one lending stuff; I recall an ironing board on the second floor making more rounds than a Greyhound bus.

"*¡Dios mío, Loren!*" my mother screamed at the door. "*Ay Lorencito, no te imaginas.*" Nothing, not even my father landing a job, could have surpassed the joy she felt setting her eyes on her son. Loren bent over and hugged her.

"You'll break her in two," I said and jumped up to hug my handsome brother. At five six, I was just the right height.

"Lorenzo," my mother shouted, "Loren is here!"

"How did you get out?" Mami asked.

"I had a *Cubana de Aviación* ticket, a vacation pass, and an American diplomat who owed me a favor got me the visa."

Papi came out of the bedroom. "*Bendito sea Dios.* Now we can sleep again."

"Loren, I was so worried about you," my mother said. "We heard Fidel's locking up people in prison with no good cause."

Loren ignored the remark, apparently uninterested in discussing Fidel, and ran his eyes over me. *"¡Qué gorda te has puesto!"* You got so fat! To make his point across, he puffed his cheeks like a blowfish.

Criticón. That's what everyone in my family was good at: criticizing. Would it have killed him to say "I missed you?"

"Gracias," I said. "You staying?"

"Of course I'm staying. If anybody's crazy enough to want to travel to Cuba, I'll give him my return ticket." Loren said, pleased with himself. "Papi, how's the job hunting?"

"Bad. I think they don't want to hire Cubans. They don't think we're white enough. Besides, the rumor is Fidel won't last long and they say they don't want to train people who have one foot in Cuba."

"So you haven't found any work?"

"Just a painting job."

"Painting?" Loren asked. My father had never done physical work in his life.

"You hear about a job and no matter how early you get there, there's a long line of Cubans ahead of you. There's a bus drivers' strike, so if Chiquitico is not free I have to do a lot of walking."

"This place is like a closet," said Loren. "Are you sure you have space for me?"

"What a question!" answered my father.

"Loren, tell me about Belén," I said.

"I almost forgot," Loren said. He picked up his suitcase and put it on the loud Floridian bedspread, took out a box, and handed it to me. *"De parte de Belén."*

I grabbed the box and found my favorite treats inside: *boniatillos, guayaba, torticas de Morón*. I grabbed the *torticas de Morón* and stuffed my mouth with shortbread cookies.

"She sent you a note," said Loren, "and photos."

Belén only made it through second grade, but she was innately intelligent. *Inteligencia natural* my parents liked to say. Papi had taught her to calculate percentages when she'd started running a loan business out of our kitchen. Afterward, neighborhood maids paraded up and down the side yard corridor that led to the kitchen door. Belén held court at the pantry's Formica dinette set. She'd do her calculations on the red Formica table in front of the washer and dryer while her customers sat on the vinyl-upholstered chairs with aluminum legs that matched the aluminum band bordering the table top.

"I don't want to do this," I'd heard Belén tell a customer more than once, "but if you don't pay what you owe, I will have to send my lawyer to collect it." The lawyer was Manolo, Belén's six-foot, two-hundred plus-pound mulatto husband. We had so many maids up and down that corridor that Mami called the pantry "Belén's office."

> "Puchita," her note began, "Thank God we're well here and I miss you with all my heart. Manolo won't get on a plane so I guess we're staying. I'm sending you the food I know you miss. And also some pictures. Don't forget me. God bless you. Always love you.
> Belén"

I heard the sound of her voice and my heart scrunched up like a paper ball. I spread the photos on the small dinette table. I wanted to be alone with Belén; I wanted the photos tattooed in my mind. I was no longer the girl in those pictures and I got scared of losing her. *Voy a perder todo lo que era antes.* There was my first communion picture. White dress, white veil, white flowers, like a child bride. A picture of a birthday party at a park with all my Phillips School classmates, a white-boxed *merienda* in front of us, a classic Coca-Cola bottle next to it. What were we? Eight? Nine? A picture of Mami and Papi standing next to me by the swings at the Havana Yacht Club. We weren't members, so why were we there? A photograph of my neighbor Maria Elena, in her white, starched Baldor school uniform, with her new Dachshund puppy, plus more pictures of me petting dogs, in the park, at our neighbor's house, in the street.

The next morning, after Papi, Loren, and Chiquitico went out looking for work, I spread out the photos on the dinette table once more. "You know, Mami," I said, "it must have been *dificilísimo* for Belén to part with these photos because that's all she had left of us. I really miss her."

"You think Belén loves you more than I do because she spoils you?" was her reply. Where did this come from? I wondered. Is she jealous? Had she been jealous all along?

"Belén loves me."

"I know Belén loves you, but Belén doesn't know what's good for you; I do. I give you what you need and Belén gives what you want. Belén spoils you and I don't. You think I didn't know the junk she gave you before dinner?"

"It wasn't junk."

"It ruined your appetite."

"Wish someone would ruin my appetite now," I shot back, always needing to have the last word.

Why wouldn't Belén spoiled me; she had no children of her own. I was her baby—the youngest of the three—and the only girl. I was sure I was her favorite, but that wasn't Mami's problem. Mami feared Belén was *my* favorite. She knew I had adopted a mother—a loving, superstitious, indulgent black mother—but what she didn't realize was that I had two mothers. Maybe it was time to tell her.

The news spread like wildfire throughout Miami. On October 19, 1960, in the aftermath of Cuba's nationalization of all large companies, the United States imposed a trade embargo on exports to Cuba (except for food and medicine). That day our building danced to a different beat, a conga rather than a tango: *"Ahora sí se cae Fidel! Ahora sí."*

"Fidel cannot endure *el bloqueo*," as Cubans called the embargo. "Cuba cannot subsist on its own," Papi said.

Mami didn't like hearing him talk that way. When he used highfalutin words like "dipsomaniac," she'd ask him, "Why can't you say 'drunk' like everybody else?" But she didn't pick at him now. You'd think they would argue more now, stuck as they were in this foxhole of a Miami apartment, but these days she let him get away with all sorts of things. In Cuba, she'd never hesitated to put Papi in his place. In Miami I think she felt sorry for him, like that early evening when he dragged his bone-tired body home after painting a house with *Chiquitico*, hunched over and drenched in sweat, looking more like a beaten-down boxer in an old Hollywood movie than the lawyer she'd married. I know it broke her heart. Then there was the day he confessed he'd lied, claiming to be fifteen years younger when he applied for a job at a wholesale liquor distributor, only to be caught in the ensuing lie-detector test, not an uncommon practice in those days. "Shouldn't have lied," he kept saying. Exile so crushed Papi that he had to believe we'd be going back to Cuba any day now.

Mami, who'd always had her feet firmly planted on the ground, decided we both should get Social Security numbers so we could work, as if there was enough work to go around in Miami those days. Off we went, only to find the Social Security Administration office packed with Cubans. Classified as political refugees, Cuban exiles were allowed to apply for a social security card and encouraged to find a job. After a long wait we each got a form and a short pencil and searched for a space on the long tables to work in. I wanted to figure out on my own how to fill out my first U.S. application.

"My name doesn't fit, Mami," I whispered. "I counted *los cuadritos* (little boxes), and it doesn't fit."

"Just write your name and initial," Mami said.

"Which name, Maria or Angeles?"

"It's your name, you decide." Really, since when do I decide?

"It's not my name if I have to cut it in half," I whined. Nonetheless, I filled in five *cuadritos* with "Maria," then in *el cuadrito* for a middle initial I grudgingly wrote "A," when it should have been, "d, l, A," as in "de los Angeles." Maria A. Nodarse, a practical name for a practical country.

"Why did we have to leave?" I asked my mother while we waited to hand in our applications. She signaled "lower your voice."

"Because *Fidelistas* were about to lock your father in prison. Because your father worked for Batista. Years ago. But that wouldn't have stopped them. Because the government stole all the American businesses. Should I go on?"

I wanted to be back in Cuba, with my full name or my nickname, "Puchita." I blamed my parents for my not being home with Belén, not being at Phillips School, not being able to swim in our club's Olympic pool.

"Besides," Mami said, "he didn't have a job anymore."

"And he doesn't have a job now."

Mami looked at me. "It's not for lack of trying."

"Well, maybe if he'd stayed home that night, we'd still be there, at home with Belén."

But even as I said it, I knew there was no "there" anymore. Besides, I was proud my father hadn't stayed home the night Fidel gave a speech at the Ciudad Deportiva's Coliseo, a sports complex built in the late '50s by Batista's brother-in-law, my father's convenient replacement. In his speech, Fidel announced the revolution would ensure that Cuba would have its first honest sports commissioner. I'd been sitting on the couch with my parents watching the televised speech. When Papi heard Fidel say all previous sports commissioners were crooks, he jumped up from the couch.

"I was the first honest sports commissioner in Cuban history," Papi said. He had a very high opinion of himself and without giving the matter any further thought he said, "I'm not letting him get away with calling me a crook." He grabbed the car keys.

"What are you doing?" Mami asked, furrowing her brow.

"I'm going to clear my name."

"Don't be foolish, Lorenzo; he's not going to let you do any such thing."

"We'll see about that."

In what felt like seconds my father was out the door, speeding away in his old black Chevy. There was nothing Mami could do. She picked up a white box of *Regalias El*

Cuño and her lighter, went out to the porch, and lit a cigarette. "Puchita, call me if you see your father on television."

Didn't happen; no one could get that close to Fidel. Accustomed to being recognized from his days as a tennis champion and a sports commissioner, my father assumed he could just walk past Fidel's guards. Some ego, to think you can take a microphone away from Fidel Castro. If we are to believe his version as he approached the podium Fidel's guards pointed their guns at him. That's when a boxer he knew from his sports commissioner days came to his rescue. *"Docto,"* he said—in Latin America everyone is a doctor— *"No vale la pena."* Not worth it. So goes the story.

My family, 1951

Belen

Maria, Fall of 1958

Chapter Six

As I walked in the door after retrieving our nomadic frying pan from a downstairs neighbor Mami announced, "Roberto's coming to live with us." Roberto was Loren's closest friend. Never mind I was on the cusp of womanhood, I still had no say in what happened in my own life. Next she's going to tell me I have to give up my bed. The night Roberto arrived I slept on a borrowed *"pim-pam-pum,"* (as Cubans call folding beds for the noise they make when opened) while Roberto slept on a mattress on the floor smack in front of the bathroom door. Everybody was snoozing, and I was thinking about sanitary napkins. Where would I keep them? What would I do with the soiled ones? Roll them in a ball and carry them out of the bathroom? And then what? I couldn't have Roberto seeing them.

Roberto and Loren hit the pavement every day except Sunday when everything closed. Loren, always volatile and quick to assign blame, had no doubt that Miamians discriminated against Cubans. "People in Miami are allergic to Cubans," he'd say. I ignored his complaints. Get a job so I can go to school, so we can get out of this shoe box, so we can buy a car. Bus drivers were still on strike and looking for work without wheels in a sprawling city like Miami got the better of him. He'd filled out applications at airline companies, department stores, banks, and, so far, *nada.*

"Roberto," Loren said, "we need to look for work somewhere else." He'd been cracking his knuckles for a while, a habit that drove me crazy but apparently annoyed no one else. "We're wasting our time here."

"I've got a cousin in New York," Roberto said.

"Well, that settles it. We'll go to New York. There's gotta be work in a city that size." Loren always jumped into things with both feet. Even as a teenager I knew that much about him.

Mami overheard him. In an apartment that size privacy could only be found in the bathroom. She asked him, *"Te vas a ir tan pronto,* Loren?" *"Acabas de llegar."* "You're leaving already? You just got here."

We'd come to the States at the height of the electoral brouhaha. In Cuba most of the time we knew before the first ballot was cast who'd be our next president, but not here. Cuban refugees couldn't vote, but that didn't stop them from backing Richard Nixon despite his not being simpatico. Being simpatico is a number-one priority with Cubans. However, Nixon had the credentials. He'd been one of Senator McCarthy's aides before Eisenhower picked him for his VP, and had proven himself to be a rabid anticommunist, something of huge importance to us displaced Cubans. The election was a hot topic in our building. All our neighbors thought the next American president would decide Cuba's future. For me the day was significant because it was the day I turned fifteen, *quince*. Little else mattered. In pre-Castro Cuba, upper- and middle-class girls celebrated *"Los Quince"* with a fancy coming-out party, usually held at a private club or one of Havana's famous nightclubs. But with the emergence of socialism, my group of friends—and countless other middle-class Cubans—found little reason to celebrate. Not wanting undue attention from governmental authorities, some families gave up celebrating *Los Quince*; others marked the occasion on a much smaller scale with a *misa y desayuno,* a mass and breakfast.

It was at a *desayuno* earlier that year at the Havana Yacht Club—Cuba's oldest and most prestigious country club—that I discovered one of my closest friends was no longer in Havana. I'd asked a mutual friend if Ileana had arrived. *"Se fue,"* she replied. She left.

"What do you mean, she left? She went home already?"

"Her family left Cuba."

"No! When?"

I couldn't believe she'd do that. I was hurt, and, yes, mad. When I got home I told my mother, "She left without calling me, without saying goodbye, without even telling me how I can get in touch with her. Mami, I've known her all my life." I'd known Gema all my life too.

Two of my closest friends had left without telling me. At least I'd been in Mexico City when Gema left.

"Everybody's scared, Puchi," my mother said. "It's got nothing to do with you. She probably couldn't tell anyone." But at fourteen everything is about you. Except Mami was right. Not long after she left I got a letter from Ileana explaining she wasn't allowed to say she was leaving. We exchanged a couple of letters but soon lost touch.

Fifteen was no different: some birthday! I was feeling like the only animal Noah left behind when a Cuban *muchacho* who often frequented the building surprised me with a bottle of *White Shoulders*, my very first perfume. I hadn't heard of the brand then and had no way of knowing what a financial sacrifice he'd made. I hope I showed my gratitude. His gentle gesture touched my heart and showed me romance was still a possibility. I'd wanted to see more of him, but my mother disapproved. He was in the habit of visiting Caridad, Cari for short, a young neighbor whose husband was away training for what would later be known as the Bay of Pigs Invasion. Early in 1960 President Eisenhower, who viewed Fidel Castro as a threat who had to be disposed of, authorized the CIA to recruit Cuban exiles and train them in Guatemala so they could invade Cuba. Cari, an attractive brunette—petite, slender, and effervescent—had been left on her own and had found ways to amuse herself. Mr. White Shoulders liked to keep her company part of the time, and the building's residents, who had way too much time in their hands, liked to gossip about it. Rumor had it she'd let the super into her apartment one day while wearing nothing but a sheer negligee. Mami didn't want me spending time with her either.

"Mami, can I watch the election at the super's apartment? I want to see what Jackie's wearing." I had a crush on the Kennedys, Jackie more than Jack, but living in a Republican building I kept my pleasures to myself.

"A Democrat in the White House will not endeavor to liberate Cuba," Papi liked to say. "At a time like this we need Nixon, a bona fide anti-communist, not *un niño lindo,*" (a pretty boy).

At a visceral level I understood that communism had upended our lives, and that Nixon was the gung-ho right winger, *el más anticomunista,* but I still favored the candidate with the good looks, the charm, the impeccable diction, not to mention the glamorous wife.

I'd been back in our apartment for only a short while when the super knocked on the door and said *"Teléfono. Larga distancia."* Like many of our neighbors, we didn't have a phone and Papi had asked the super if he could give the building's number as his. *"Enseguida,"* my mother said.

"Puchita, come with me."

My mother always dragged me along whenever she suspected people would speak English. A Cuban man she didn't know was on the phone. We shared the receiver. "My name is Ignacio," I heard him say. "I'm a friend of Marcelino." He paused and Mami and I exchanged looks. "I'm so sorry to have to tell you," he said somberly. "Marcelino died last night." He went explained that he and Marcelino worked as dishwashers in the same dinner club in Hackensack, New Jersey. "He got pneumonia,"

Ignacio added, "and was hospitalized two days ago. Last night he had a heart attack and died."

"*¿De pulmonía?¿Se murió aquí de pulmonía?*" My mother asked in disbelief. She couldn't comprehend how, in 1960, her brother could die of pneumonia in the United States.

Besides being my favorite uncle, Marcelino was my godfather, my *padrino*. Mami was well aware Marcelino was something of a lapsed Catholic when she asked him to baptize me, but of all her brothers she loved him the most. She made the right choice.

Marcelino could be outrageous, but he was more of a *padre* to me than a *padrino*. He'd left Havana for Miami some months before us. When he couldn't find a job there, one of the charities helping Cuban refugees offered to relocate him to somewhere with better employment chances. He got a second-hand winter coat, a plane ticket, and a small amount of cash. Shortly after arriving in New Jersey he found a job washing dishes. The last time I saw him was in Havana, the day he left. I'd missed him immediately. He used to lunch with us practically every day, and whenever Mami insisted that I eat red meat or some other source of iron I detested, Marcelino would fix his green eyes on me and move his ears up and down to make me smile. I had last seen him healthy, elegant, and funny, so how could I believe he was dead now?

I stopped thinking about myself when I saw my mother weeping. Up to that phone call she had been unfaltering, so much so I'd never stopped to think how difficult it had to be for her to leave behind, at forty-eight, the only life she knew. If she had any regrets about coming to this country, I hadn't heard them until Padrino died. Back in the apartment, I sat at her side as her lustrous deep-set eyes swelled with tears she wouldn't acknowledge. I could see Padrino in my mind's eye, puffing out his cheeks and blowing out air the way kids blow out their birthday candles. *"¡Qué calor! Esto es un infierno, por Dios,"* he'd say when he walked into the house. Marcelino was finicky about his appearance. Right away he'd change into a cool sports shirt, carefully hanging up his damp *guayabera* where the breeze would refresh it. He'd take off his two-tone spectator shoes and check them for scuff marks, white shoe polish by his side. Often he'd dip a Q-tip into the liquid polish so he could get into the white decorative perforations. Before returning to work he'd dab Brylcreem onto his hair, comb it straight back, and splash cologne on the back of his neck. My godfather had everything going for him: looks, charm, intelligence, wit, a disarming smile. I chose to remember him as a sales agent in Havana—a job that fit him like a glove—not as a dishwasher at some country club in New Jersey.

"I have this image of Marcelino dying all alone," Mami said. "How could anyone understand what he needed when he couldn't speak English? How could he explain what ailed him?" She couldn't stop crying.

"Remember how *Padrino* could make his ears go up and down?" I asked. It was a dumb thing to say at the time but it was so typical of him I couldn't help it. Mami looked up at me with liquid eyes and smiled.

Later that day I heard my parents arguing in the bedroom. My mother wanted to go to the funeral but my father wouldn't hear of it.

"*Tú estás mal del corazón,* Águeda," he said, despite knowing she didn't like to be reminded of her heart condition. "I'm going, Águeda, I'll find Loren; I'll be with him. We'll take care of the funeral arrangements."

The next morning my father headed to one of several philanthropies devoted to helping Cuban exiles. I can't remember which one specifically since by then Miami had more Cuban refugees than it could handle, and more charities were pitching in, helping exiles relocate north. New York City, Union City, Jersey City, and Chicago topped the list. I recall my father returning with an airline ticket and a winter coat. It amazed me how heavy the coat was. Later that day Chiquitico drove him to the airport.

That evening Mami told the super's wife, "I'm sorry for being such a nuisance but Lorenzo is in New Jersey and I'm expecting his call." I was sure by then the whole building knew she'd lost her brother and my father had gone to bury him.

"It's the least we can do, Águeda," the super's wife replied. "I only wish we could do more."

When my father finally called that night he said Loren and Ignacio had picked him up at the airport. "Ignacio knew Marcelino had offered to take Loren out for dinner the night he died," Papi said. "So he drove to Loren's boarding house to break the news to him in person." Papi was phoning from Roberto's cousin's apartment, where he and Loren would spend the night. "I'll call again when I know more about the funeral arrangements."

The following evening we were back at the super's apartment. "Águeda," my father said, "we just got back from the funeral house. Ignacio knows a lot of Cubans here. I guess the funeral director understands what we're going through because he won't be charging us for the service. And the local Catholic Church is donating the plot. Loren won't make it to the funeral because he has to work. He landed a job as a typist with the Railway Express Agency in Long Island City. After we bury Marcelino, I'm going to apply for a job myself."

Only my father, Ignacio, and the priest were present at Marcelino's funeral. A plain, white wooden cross marked his grave. He was the first of us to die in the United States.

When the following day I heard the super's wife scream, "Long distance, Águeda," I was so embarrassed by how we were intruding into these poor people's lives I could have just about died. If I made no mention of what a pain in the neck we'd turned out to be it was because I could tell Mami didn't need more grief.

Papi was saying, "You won't believe this, Águeda, because I can't believe it myself. I went to Railway Express to apply for a job and the gentleman who interviewed me didn't even bother to read my application. I told him about my position in Havana, but he didn't even listen. Never in my life did it occur to me I'd be treated like this. I was offered a job in the warehouse."

"And what did you do?" asked my mother, holding her breath.

"What was I supposed to do? I took it."

"It's only temporary, Lorenzo. I'm sure something better will come up. It's probably all they can offer right now. I'm glad you took it."

"Loren wants to talk to him. He's really upset. He thinks the way they've treated me is inexcusable. He wants us to exchange jobs; he wants me to have his typist job so he can do the warehouse work. I told him it's too risky. I told him there was a chance we'd both end up without a job."

"That was sweet of him," my mother said. "Like I said, Lorenzo, I'm sure it won't be for long."

"We're moving again?" I asked my mother when we got back to the apartment. "To New Jersey? Or is it New York? Not again, Mami! We just got here." Moving again meant there would be no way for me to hook up with my friends from Phillips or the club. All we needed was money for me to enroll in a Miami high school and I'd have friends again. Up North I didn't know anyone. Not to mention we were getting farther and farther away from Cuba.

"Puchita," my mother said sternly, *"Tú papá aceptó un trabajo de estibador, así que yo estoy preocupada con otras cosas."* My father had just accepted a job as a stevedore?

Chapter Seven

The day before Thanksgiving, on a glacial afternoon when the sky was a sheet of gray steel and the wind a razor blade, my mother and I landed at Newark airport. I saw my breath turn into haze. "Look, I'm smoking," I told my mother as we walked across the tarmac. She didn't smile; she'd already suspected I smoked behind her back. Why is it so dark already? I took stock of the dreary surroundings—what a dump! ¡*Dios mío, qué frio!* The second-hand woolen winter coat I wore felt as restricting as a straightjacket and as itchy as a rash. I spotted Gema's aunt, Carmela, at the gate. I'd forgotten how short Carmela was. We hadn't seen her or her family since Fidel's takeover. My mother's face lit up when she saw her; they'd always been close. I loved Carmela like my own aunt and seeing her lifted my spirits.

"Is Gema still in West Palm Beach?" I asked Carmela.

"Yes, in high school."

"Águeda," Carmela said, as we waited for our bags, "I'm taking you to Union City. You can stay with Carlos and Luisa in Union City until you find a place to live." Her brother Carlos had left West Palm Beach and moved to New Jersey after the revolution. I didn't even ask about Union City. What was the point? I sat in the back and looked out the window as Carmela drove. I looked at those pitiful trees, not a leaf to call their own.

"Tomorrow when you come over for Thanksgiving you can see whether you like Ridgefield Park," Carmela said, her eyes looking straight ahead. She sure knew her way around. "We love it there; it's great for the kids. It's not far." That's the first time I'd ever heard of Cubans celebrating Thanksgiving, *San Givin'* as it was pronounced. I looked out the window as Carmela drove down Bergenline Avenue, the main drag in Union City, a lively working-class city. I noticed some Cuban storefronts and a sign that read *"Se venden muebles"* caught my eye. I didn't know whether we'd be buying furniture. I knew of some Cubans who lived with the barest necessities because they were certain Fidel wouldn't last. I kept mum.

The apartment building where Carlos and Luisa lived was small and narrow. It faced a busy avenue; it might have been Bergenline but I'm not sure. Later I'd learn the apartments in those buildings were called railroad apartments. With no side windows, they were very dark. I don't think we stayed long at Union City; I remember little about it. Cold, gray, Spanish-speaking, working class, that about sums it up.

White-as-Wonder-Bread Ridgefield Park—the birthplace of Ozzie Nelson—was the quintessentially quaint American town. Carmela lived above one of the mom-and-pop stores that dotted Main Street, right across from The Rialto, the town's only movie theater. In Cuba, Carmela had lived in a spacious two-story home. Now she, her husband, and three kids crammed into a compact two-bedroom apartment.

That Thursday, Carmela's only concession to the American holiday was the baked bird. No mashed potatoes, no cranberry sauce, no sweet potatoes or corn graced the table. Instead, the turkey came with black beans, white rice, ripe fried plantains, green fried plantains, and yucca in a garlic-drenched mojo powerful enough to reach the moviegoers at the Rialto.

"Carmela," Mami said, "Where do you get all this stuff?"

"Right where you're staying. In Union City you can find a lot of Cuban *mercados*. Ask Luisa to take you. You'll be amazed. Union City is like Miami's Little Havana, only smaller."

"Lorenzo," Mami said. "You're working now; do you think we can afford to live around here?" She must have been starving for a friend.

"Maybe; we can start searching next week," Papi said.

Had anyone asked me—imagine *that*—I'd have chosen pewter-hued Union City. There I could walk to Cuban stores, listen to machine-gun-speed Spanish, maybe have a mango milkshake, feel a bit at home. Instead, we moved to Ridgefield Park where Papi rented the first floor of a two-story Cape Cod forest-green house owned by a young Portuguese couple, Berta and Manolo. Originally designed for a single family, they had remodeled the house to turn the ground floor into a rental. The dining room, separated from the living room by a heavy oak pocket door, became my parents' bedroom. I slept in the living room on a Hollywood bed while Loren used the sofa bed. Loren couldn't get out of his New York slum boarding room fast enough.

"Mami, Berta is sooooo white! I imagined the Portuguese darker." I thought all milk-white people looked tubercular.

"I think it makes her jet black hair even more striking," said Mami.

Berta, petite, dynamic, and young, quickly took to my mother and asked her to consider babysitting her two small kids in exchange for rent when her maternity leave expired. Most of Berta's family was still in Portugal. With Loren and my father employed, Household Finance Corporation gave Papi a modest amount of credit at an immodest rate to be used at its local furniture store. No one knew how much I didn't want us to buy furniture. Of course we needed beds, chests, the works, but that wasn't the point. For me, buying furniture meant accepting we wouldn't be returning to Cuba. And even if I had wanted us to buy furniture, I didn't want to buy it *there*. The stuff was so crappy; we had much better furniture in Cuba.

Good furniture: wood, not Formica; upholstery, not plastic. But by the time we left, Mami had opted for a caca-colored sofa (better than the plaid one), two aquamarine fake leather side chairs, a pair of two-tiered Formica end tables with aquamarine lamps, a two-tiered Formica coffee table, a Formica-topped gray bedroom set, and—the best part—a small black-and-white table-top TV. And it could all be delivered the same day. Later the week, Carmela took us to the Hackensack Salvation Army store where we found an Early American kitchen table and four chairs with the white paint peeling off of them.

"Do you think we can paint them?" my mother asked.

"I don't know, Mami. I don't like them; they're old-fashioned. They don't match the style of the other furniture," I added, as if the other furniture had style.

"Águeda, I have a can of red paint you can have," Carmela said. "Should I call my friend to haul them home?"

"Let's get them," my mother said. I rolled my eyes.

The kitchen now had red chairs and red gingham café curtains. Why this penchant for red? We had nothing red in Cuba. Besides, it was the color of the revolution, of communism. It reminded me of that scene in *The Lady and the Tramp* when they're eating a bowl of spaghetti. Mami had loved that movie, so maybe... Even so, the gingham café curtains were cute as a button. Those sheer, ruffled Priscilla curtains that covered the living room windows must have also been inspired by an American movie because usually there was nothing frilly about my mother's taste. A later addition to 36 Euclid Avenue was a Britannica Encyclopedia set my father bought, at great peril to his life, from a door-to-door salesman while my mother and I were out grocery shopping one Saturday afternoon.

"We can hardly pay the bills and you bought an encyclopedia set?" my mother asked. "Maybe we can eat it since we have such little money for food."

I disappeared into the bathroom. When I came out my parents weren't talking to each other, an oppressive state of affairs in a place that size. My mother acted like she was reading *Selecciones*, Reader's Digest in Spanish, and my father was fussing with the encyclopedias.

¡*Dios mío, qué lío*! What a mess! My main concern remained where to hide. Suddenly, laughter. Mami would sometimes crack up when you least expected it.

"He must have been one hell of a salesman," she said when at last she stopped laughing. "Got to give him that. Selling an encyclopedia to penniless Cuban refugees. Now *that* takes talent."

The encyclopedias came with a bookcase which helped fill an empty spot against a living room wall. Then one winter morning we washed the ruffled Priscilla curtains in the bathtub and hung them outside to dry. When we went to fetch them we found triangular ice sheets, practically capable of standing on their own. After they thawed, Mami dried them with an old iron she'd picked up at the Salvation Army store.

In December Fello flew in from Mexico City to spend Christmas with us. It didn't bother me to sleep in the living room with both my brothers because, *al fin*, we were all together again. Neither Fello nor Loren complained about how cold it was, probably a macho thing, although Loren claimed he'd gotten used to freezing his butt off in Milledgeville, Georgia. I liked to sleep late; I wasn't in school, so no reason to get up. Fello and Mami always woke up at the crack of dawn and made coffee right away.

I'd once been close to Fello, or as close as a nine-year difference between brother and sister allows. Before med school in Mexico, he often took me to matinees at a neighborhood movie theater. I swooned over Paul Newman in *Cat on a Hot Tin Roof* and was checking him out as he came out the shower when someone in the audience screamed, *"Agarralo, que está limpio."* Grab him; he's clean. Fello smiled but said nothing. Asking questions while we watched a movie with Fello was taboo, but had a good idea what was going on. I'd always looked up to my big brother. When he left for Mexico, I took it hard. I was twelve and felt he'd abandoned me.

Since he was a kid—although I suspect he was thirty at birth—my brother Fello knew he wanted be a doctor. By 1957, after studying in the University of Havana's Medical School for three years, Fello calculated that, considering the constant disruptions, he'd been able to attend classes for a year and a half at most. The violence at the university—the students revolting against Batista, his henchmen cracking skulls—scared my folks. They were already paying for Loren's education in the United States so they couldn't afford medical school in the States, but they could afford it in Mexico.

Unlike Papi and Loren, Fello didn't talk about

returning—our leitmotif—didn't start sentences with *"Cuando se caiga Fidel"* or *"Cuando regresemos..."* If Fello mentioned Cuba it was to talk about Belén or his *madrina*, Tía Sara, or to ask what had happened to people he knew. Fello abstained from the exile's elixir, and I wanted to know why.

"I'm not going back," he said.

"Because you want to be a doctor in the States or because you want to live in Mexico?" I sometimes wondered if he could have been adopted. Unlike every other Cuban I knew, he rarely elaborated. I needed a corkscrew to pull out his words.

"En Cuba hay demasiados cambios." "Too many changes," said the Cuban *pragmatista*. I was taken aback because he'd always been so predictable. At home he walked through the door, went straight to his bedroom, emptied his pockets, and stacked his coins on a catch-all plate according to their denomination. There were few surprises in his life; of course he knew what he'd be doing next.

Fello didn't want to answer my questions; instead he told me he'd made a list of New York City's landmarks. "One never knows," he said.

"Never knows what?" I asked.

"Whether another opportunity will come along."

"Another opportunity for?"

"To see the sights."

"Ah."

"So I want to make sure I see certain things. You can come along if you want to," he said.

"Where?"

"The Statue of Liberty, the Metropolitan Museum, St. Patrick's Cathedral, the Empire State Building, the Cloisters. I'm going to New York tomorrow."

"Si, Of course I want to see all that stuff. You kidding?" "Are you going to wait for the New Year at Times Square?" I'd watched the ball drop on New Year's Eve in old black and white Hollywood movies.

"And have some drunk puke all over me? No thanks."

"So where are we going tomorrow?" I asked.

"Trying to decide."

I felt a sense of relief; I'd wonder whether my brother had dropped me. My fear wasn't entirely irrational. In Cuba the three of us used to spend the bulk of our summer vacation at the club—and understandably so. The club had swimming pools, squash courts, a basketball court, a baseball field, a bowling alley, all the trappings of a vacation retreat. One day when Loren and I went to the club Fello stayed behind. I think it took a few days for Mami to realize Fello had stopped going to the club.

"You haven't been going to El Tennis," Mami said.

"Not interested," Fello said.

"Why?"

"Just not interested."

Mami thought Fello was going through a stage and let him be. However, Fello only went back to the club one more time, the day Loren played in a Big-Five baseball game, and he used the stadium's entrance. Papi had asked all his friends at the club if they knew whether Fello had had some kind of disagreement; he'd asked the coaches whether Fello had been slighted in some way, but no one could come up with an explanation for his boycott. Fello bought a set of weights and began exercising in our backyard. End of story.

Chapter Eight

I was dead to the world and wanted to stay that way, but in my dream someone was poking me in my side with a stick

"Puchita, ven a ver esto," I heard Loren say as he rousted me from my slumber with an annoying finger in my side.

"Leave me alone," I told Loren, swatting his arm.

"Puchita, Puchita, ¡*Mira!*"

I raised my head and saw him pointing out the living room window.

"What is it?" Anything to be left alone.

"You gotta see it," Loren said.

"Okay! Okay!" I growled. I pulled myself up and peered out the window. Overnight the purest white powder had draped our walkway, trailing atop the entrance like a bride's train on her way to the altar. Everything in front of me was veiled in a sugary white, so it was impossible to tell where the sidewalk ended and the street began. Exhausted tree branches struggled to support clumps of snow. Kids played outside, throwing snowballs at each other.

"Oh my God! I've never seen anything so beautiful in my whole life. I'm going out."

I rushed to dress and with gloved hands held onto the rail next to where I imagined the stoop was. I took one Braille step after another, with Loren right behind me. Neither of us had winter boots or galoshes, only plastic rain boots. We approached the walkway as apprehensively as two kids on ice skates but soon the allure of the spectacle, the beguiling sight of seventeen inches of snow, freed us from all caution and we flung ourselves into the drifts. Giant snowflakes settled on Loren's Elvis-look-alike hair and, without exchanging so much as a word, we both stuck out our tongues.

"It doesn't taste like anything," I said to Loren.

"I know, it dissolves the moment it hits your tongue," he said.

As though spellbound we watched dogs frolic in the snow, kids pull sleighs, dads pitch snowballs. Unable to resist, Mami, Papi, and Fello joined us. Manolo stepped out of the house with his two kids, their eyes about to pop out. Linda was so bundled up she looked like a UPS parcel. Manolo took pictures of his son and daughter to send to his family in Portugal.

"Lorenzo, would you like a picture?" Manolo asked. I still have it; I call it *Los Cubanos en Siberia*. Whenever I look at the picture, I can't take my eyes off Papi's countenance. Manolo had captured my father's scarred emotional and psychological pain. Leaving Cuba, struggling to build a new life for his family, facing unsurmountable odds had all but crushed him, and his expression in that photograph attested to his defeat.

Fello left too soon for my liking. Honoring his invitation, he'd taken me along on all his sightseeing trips. He whizzed through exhibits at the Met, where he knew exactly what was worth seeing and what was not. He spent just as much time looking at medieval armors as he did looking at famous paintings, but hey, I was grateful. Of all the things we did together that Christmas break, I'll never forget his taking me to a matinee of *My Fair Lady*. When the curtain came down, my cheeks were wet with tears. I applauded until my palms burned. I wanted Fello to stay with us; he was the family's Rock of Gibraltar, but his career was ahead of him.

I clung to the inevitability of our return. Why make plans when we had one foot rooted in Cuba? In Havana I'd dreamed of becoming an architect; in New Jersey I was content being a nanny, temporarily anyway. I enjoyed caring for Berta's kids; they were a welcome distraction. I could ignore those around me grappling with the daily challenges of adapting to life in America. I'd decided, in the way adolescents do, that I'd keep doing it until Fidel was overthrown.

Actually, I didn't even like to leave the house. "It's freezing out there, Mami," I'd say when asked to join my parents in one thing or another. Alone, I ventured only as far as the backyard so I could smoke cigarettes when no one was home. I wore a woolen cap so my hair wouldn't stink of cigarettes and I wore my winter coat. No worry there since in the '60s all winter coats smelled of cigarettes. In Cuba I'd watched a movie called *El Último Cuplé,* with Sarita Montiel, and I'd found her to be sexier than Marilyn Monroe. Shortly after watching the movie, my mother bought me the soundtrack. I had played it over and over again back in Cuba. One of the movie's hit songs was about a woman chain-smoking while waiting for her man to return to her: "*Fumando espero al hombre a quien yo quiero.*" Now, in our backyard hiding from life, I smoked and sang songs softly so Manolo and Berta wouldn't hear me. I was fantasizing of a world far from this one, obsessing on what and whom I'd lost. Even as I playacted, I knew there was something wrong with me. Why did I need to behave like someone else? Because something was missing. I had lost my sense of footing. Unlike other exiles I had no phenomenal material losses to complain about. My losses had taken permanent residence in my psyche and in my heart. I often, way too often actually, wondered whether staying in Miami would have mitigated the devastation I felt. In Miami I'd been able to count on the support of my friends. In Ridgefield Park I was nobody, *nadie*, no one. My consciousness of identity, tied as it was to my language, my culture (of which Belén was a most significant part), my childhood friends, my sense of belonging, and my *cubanismo*, my Cubanness, had all vanished. I felt like sliced Gruyere cheese.

The irony escaped me then. In Cuba just about everything I was interested in came from the States. I grew up on a diet of American romantic movies, starring exquisitely handsome blond teenagers like Sandra Dee and Troy Donahue, romping about in picture-perfect California beaches. When I watched TV with my brothers, it was usually war movies or westerns: *Gunsmoke, The Lone Ranger, Have Gun - Will Travel*. My mother and I never missed an episode of *I Love Lucy, Rin Tin-Tin,* or *Lassie* because the two of us thought dogs were better than people. In Cuba, my idea of a perfect outing was to sit at Woolworth's soda fountain, devouring a bacon, lettuce, and tomato club sandwich and a banana split, before watching the latest Hollywood double feature at a fancy movie theater. I longed to live in a house with a white picket-fence and an eat-in kitchen like the Nelson family. In my mind, I could see myself serving dinner as my handsome husband flew in the door of our picture perfect home. Now, sitting at one of the four fire-engine-red chairs, a *café con leche* in front of me, I yearned for Belén who, truth be told, let me get away with murder. Loren told me they all knew when Belén came out of the kitchen with her famous croquettes and announced "three apiece," I'd already had my extra shares in the kitchen. Daydreaming of the life I'd left behind I forgot about the *café con leche*. I got up, put it in a pan and warmed it over the stove. Just then my mother walked into the kitchen.

"It's time for you to go back to school," she announced.

"No, no, Mami. I'm not going back to school. I don't know anybody here." I knew Christmas break was over. I'd seen a lot of neighborhood kids walking to school with their friends, but I hadn't expected I'd be told to join them.

"You are going back to school," *la jefa* said.

"But…" I started to say. I stopped myself. My mother had a temper; she was not the kind of woman who put up with mouthy teenagers. She pressed her lips tightly enough to make them lose their rosiness. I noticed her left eyebrow was slightly raised. My mother's laser-like stare left me no doubt she meant business. I pictured myself in a school full of strangers and started to cry. I kept crying. I heaved. I vomited. I sobbed and sobbed. She wasn't heartless; she said, *"Okay, mañana."*

The next day she said, "Get dressed. I'm taking you to school."

Like on cue, I sobbed and vomited again.

"Get dressed," she said, indifferent to my performance.

"If you force me to go to school," I said, "I'm going to kill myself."

"No seas ridícula."

Ridiculous? Did I have to swear I would kill myself to convince her of my earnestness? *"Mami, te lo juro. Me voy a matar."*

She opened the kitchen drawer and pulled out a large knife, turned it so that the handle faced me and said, *"Toma."*

Threatening to kill myself wasn't as much of an act as she thought. I was very depressed and thought anything, even death, was preferable to going to a school that wasn't Phillips. I knew this wasn't normal, knew there was something wrong with me. I can't think of a time either as a child or a teenager when the magnitude of my reaction to a disagreeable event wasn't abysmally disproportionate to it. I became aware of this über-intensity early on. When I was twelve, I had an appendectomy. Weeks after surgery I still walked around like the Leaning Tower of Pisa, certain that if I stood up straight, my incision would split open. Not even *la jefa* could get me to walk upright. She took me to see my surgeon, a handsome, elegant, friend of the family. Dr. Armstrong asked me to stand with the side of my body against a wall in his office.

"Now Puchita," he said in the softest voice, "push your hip against the wall."

With great trepidation I straightened up against the wall.

"*¿Ves? No pasó nada,*" he said when I stopped being bent out of shape. He was right, nothing happened.

Now, just because I was being taken to a new school I kept vomiting, and that wasn't normal, and I knew it.

"*Tápate las orejas,*" Mami said after I pulled on my coat. She gave me a glass of water and said, "*Vamos.*" Had she no soul? Did I also have to cover my ears?

"Please Mami, I can't wear that," I said. No teenage girl wants to cover her ears with some crochet contraption that likened her to an old lady playing bingo in a church basement, but I knew as they said in Cuba, *que el horno no está para galleticas.* This was not a time to push the envelope, a phrase that makes as much sense to Spanish speakers as the cookies in the oven to English speakers. All this I had to learn.

A wind more vicious than my current disposition flapped my coat against my legs as Mami and I walked the five blocks to the high school. I had nicknamed my winter coat *El Colador,* The Sieve. The idiotic contraption covering my ears made no difference whatsoever; it was crocheted, for crying out loud. I stood in front of a dated two-story, red-brick building with frozen ears, watery eyes, drippy nose, and cracked lips. The words Washington High School were chiseled into the stone at the top of its grand rotunda, which was supported by four massive columns. A pair of large wooden doors sat beyond the columns.

"I'm freezing," I said, in between my sniffling. "I thought we were going to Ridgefield Park High."

"*¡Basta ya!*" my mother said. Enough already.

Mami looked like she was considering whether we were at the right place. The high school was huge! Took up an entire block. I couldn't imagine so many students in one place. In Cuba our school consisted of three converted residential houses.

I followed her up the icy steps leading to the main entrance, eager to get indoors. We stopped in front of a receptionist and Mami looked at me while motioning towards the woman seated at the desk. I explained why we were there and she pointed down a hallway, saying "You'll need to see our counselor." I can still see myself walking down the sparkling clean linoleum hallway. We stopped in front of a door marked "Counselor." A secretary behind a small desk greeted us and asked us to come in and take a seat. We hadn't waited long when a petite, personable woman in her early forties came out to greet us. Well-coiffed, she wore a tailored jacket, pencil skirt, and black pumps. I felt like an indigent in my hand-me-down coat. She introduced herself and we all shook hands while I told her I'd have to translate for my mother since her English was poor. We went inside her office and sat across from her desk. I hadn't even warmed the seat when Mami said, "Tell her why you didn't go to school in Miami."

I explained I hadn't been able to go to school in Miami because we didn't have the money to pay the fee required for non-residents. At that, she raised her eyebrows. I could tell she didn't believe me.

"So she's missed a whole semester of school?" She asked my mother, looking into her eyes with the characteristic empathy of a high-school counselor. "Then I think she should start as a sophomore."

I translated her words, but before my mother could respond I turned back to the counselor, quickly saying, "With your permission," thinking of the Spanish *con su permiso*. "But school in Cuba is much more difficult than here." The moment I said it I realized I'd made a major mistake. Nothing in Cuba could be better than in the United States. "What I mean to say," I said, trying to take my foot out of my mouth, "is that it's not like high school here. It's called *bachillerato,* and it's longer and harder. It's like a combination of college and high school. That's why I think I should start as a junior."

"Do you really think that's a good idea? You're only fifteen" she said. It was probably meant as a rhetorical question but I was feeling empowered. And I certainly didn't want to spend any more time at this place than I had to.

"Yes. I'm sure," I said. "What's the worst that could happen?" I added. "If I fail, I can repeat junior again next year. I finished the second year of *bachillerato*." Still thinking in Spanish, I argued my case on the fly; I hadn't anticipated any of this so I had no game plan.

"All right, but only on a probationary basis."

"Forgive me, I don't understand."

"Only on the condition that if you don't do well this semester, you'll be retained."

"Retained?" I asked.

"You won't be promoted to the next grade. There's something else you need to decide now, though. You need to choose a curriculum that prepares you for college or one that prepares you for the business world. I strongly suggest you choose the college prep curriculum."

"Tell her I want you to get a job right after graduation," my mother said after hearing "business." I translated.

The next morning I headed off for school, feeling like a lone Gary Cooper walking down Main Street in *High Noon*. My clothes let everyone know I wasn't from here; they weren't American teenage clothes. I wore a bulky sweater from Sears and one of my mother's skirts, which looked like what it was: an altered woman's skirt. I had gained twenty-five pounds since leaving Cuba, all in my belly, and I stupidly thought the bulky sweater would camouflage *mi panza*. Instead, I looked pregnant. The other kids looked so cool. Many girls wore red V-necked boyfriend cardigans with the school's initials in white. They had piles of thick hair on their heads, laboriously teased and combed into a beehive, with tons of hairspray so it could stay in place. What I remember most about those girls now, besides the heavy black eyeliner, was how they scratched their scalp with a pencil because there was no other way to reach it. I looked like the alien I was. I was determined not to like any of this.

My homeroom teacher welcomed me, "I understand you're not from this country. Where are you from?"

"From Cuba," I said proudly.

"I see. We've saved a seat for you."

I glanced around my new classmates. I realized the classroom was like a small community where all the students knew each other. Like the students from my old school, they'd probably grown up together. I was trespassing.

The teacher stood up, and I assumed she was about to start a lesson. I took out a loose-leaf binder and a pencil. Instead of teaching, she announced, "Let's do the pledge," a phrase I'd never heard before. All the kids stood up, so I followed my mother's advice, "When in doubt, imitate." Then I heard the kids say, "I pledge allegiance to the flag of the United States of America…" I didn't know what allegiance meant. I stayed mum. I was an intruder. That wasn't my flag. They weren't my people. Although I understood English, it wasn't my language. I didn't feel Cuban as much as I felt foreign.

After lunch my homeroom teacher pulled me aside and

said, "I noticed you didn't pledge allegiance this morning. May I ask why?"

"I didn't know how…didn't know what it was. And it's not my flag."

"It is now. Make sure to join us from now on." And so I did, acutely aware of being the only foreigner in a high school where even the Spanish teacher was American. My fellow students had never come across anyone with pierced ears. Silly me, I thought all girls had pierced ears. "Doesn't it hurt?" they'd ask. I thought I'd put their fears to rest if I took off an earring and put it on again but I could tell it grossed them out.

In Ridgefield Park, Cuba meant *I Love Lucy's* Ricky Ricardo and his bongo drums. I'm sure they meant well but for small talk they'd ask, "Did you have televisions in Cuba?" "Did you wear shoes in Cuba?" "Do you speak Cuban?" What was wrong with them? None of my Havana schoolmates thought you spoke American in the United States. I wanted to tell them that not everything was better here. You think I'm a peasant? I used to go to a country club; I used to go to a private school. You think in Cuba we spend our days singing *Babalú* and playing the conga drums? But I didn't say any of these things; instead I did what all newly arrived immigrants do: I smiled.

I remember walking through those hallways crowded with students who were members of academic clubs and sports teams, who were cheerleaders and thespians, and feeling like I was trespassing; I didn't belong in that school. It's not that I didn't want to join in their extracurricular activities; I was one-hundred percent certain they wouldn't have me. While there might have been some ostracizing on their part, as I look back now I see a frightened girl who, petrified of being rejected, self-segregated. The entire semester was like that, a living hell. Fortunately, I'd guessed right about belonging in a junior class as opposed to sophomore, and since Mami had insisted I take a business curriculum, the entire semester was a cakewalk. On the last day of my junior year, tired of feeling like a bird without a branch to stand on, I announced to my mother the moment I got home, "I'm not going back next year."

"*Veremos,*" she said. We'll see.

Maybe I'd get lucky, and we'd be back in Cuba by then. Not once did I think I might find Cuba unrecognizable. Or that Phillips School might have changed. We Philippians found out later that the Phillips School we loved had ceased to exist two years after the revolution when the government confiscated all private schools and implemented a new revolutionary curriculum. Fear gave way to extraordinary rumors, the prevalent one being that Cuban children would be Castro's next victims—brainwashed and sent to reeducation camps in Russia. The radio station Voice of America validated this notion. Another link gone.

Chapter Nine

The front door slammed shut. "Puchita!" Loren said, trying to rein in his excitement, tugging his coat off and tossing it over the living room's pathetic aquamarine chair, "Do you know where people from El Tennis get together on Sundays?" He answered his own question: "At St. Patrick's!"

"And you know this because?"

"I was at El Liborio El Liborio," Loren said.

"Since when do you have money for El Liborio?"

"Once in a while Raul and I stop there for a drink. The bartender is Cuban, and he lets us sit at the bar and nurse a beer until it turns flat." In Manhattan, Liborio was the name of a pricey Cuban restaurant in the west forties. New Yorkers seemed to like eating *lechón, plátanos, frijoles negros,* enough not to mind paying a fortune for peasant food. French or Italian food I could understand, but Cuban?

Meeting at St. Patrick's Cathedral sounded really weird. "Who came up with that?" I asked.

"I don't know. Who cares? Want to go or not?"

"What do you think?"

Saturday night found me in bed with my hair rolled around empty Tropicana juice cans. Between the discomfort caused by the faux rollers and the anticipation of seeing fellow *exilados* the next day, I barely slept. Sunday morning I took my time putting on makeup, getting the black eyeliner just so, with a little upward curve at the outer corner of the eye, in Spanish called *un rabito* (a little tail); in English, cat eyes. The crowd of Cubans gathered outside the cathedral blew me away. I didn't want to move away from Loren but I couldn't stand being out in the open. As if freezing to death weren't bad enough, people in this crowd were almost whispering. Cubans, as a group, are loud. Being loud is about the only way Cubans get heard. This bunch, I later learned, had been warned to keep it down. Most were a little older than I, but I knew a lot people in the group, either as Loren's friends or from El Tennis. They were an elegant crowd, with everybody decked out. I sure was glad I'd taken so much pride in my appearance. All the men wore jackets and ties under heavy black coats; the women wore gloves, hats, and polished boots. Winter had its privileges; you couldn't look this classy in Havana's heat. When mass was about to start the women began drifting into the church; most of the guys didn't bother. Mercifully, my brother headed toward the cathedral's doors, which was fine with me. Saint Patrick's had been included in Fello's places-to-see list, so I'd already admired its beauty. This time I needed to warm up.

After mass many of the women formed small groups, greeting and kissing each other on the cheek (we kiss only one cheek) while the men huddled in several small clusters. Something was going on. *Los muchachos,* the young men, spoke in muted tones. If I hadn't been so cold, I'd have sworn I was inside a funeral parlor, all that hushing in black coats and ties.

I joined a group of young women roughly Loren's age, twenty or so. It wasn't long before some decided it was too cold to stand and talk and they started to leave. I wandered over towards to the group of guys Loren was with. He was talking to some friends from the club; and what handsome friends he had. *"La invasión,"* I heard him say. We'd known from living in Miami's Cuban ghetto the CIA was recruiting young exiles to invade Cuba. Two of our first cousins in Miami had signed up for *"la invasión."* Men with duffel bags kept disappearing, and everyone knew somebody who had a cousin, an uncle, a friend who'd gone off somewhere to fight for Cuba's freedom. In Miami, rumor-mill central, every Cuban knew the CIA was training volunteers at secret camps in Central America.

"They've opened a recruiting office here in New York," one of Loren's friends was saying. He must have noticed the excitement in my brother's eyes because, he added, "It's a few blocks away from *Puerto Arturito*,"

Ay Dios mío, no. God, don't let him join. I don't want to be left alone again.

Chapter Ten

The view alone made the bus ride worthwhile.
"¡*Qué maravilla!*" my mother said at the sight of Manhattan. Across the Hudson River, right before being gulped by Lincoln Tunnel's black mouth, a panoramic view of Manhattan's skyline emerges—and electrifies. Colossal skyscrapers shoot forcefully from an almost perfect grid. From our perch across the river, the breadth of the island looked impossibly narrow, famed streets ending right after they began.

"Mami, let me read the directions," I said. I'd taken a day off from school to serve as her translator. This bus only took us to the city; I was looking for the subway line for the Bronx. My mother had an appointment with a heart surgeon on the staff of Montefiore Hospital in the Bronx. Fello had set up her appointment during his Christmas visit. He'd insisted she keep it, saying that this doctor was one of the best heart surgeons in our area. When Mami told me she wanted me to come with her, I remembered that her cardiologist in Cuba had told her she'd probably need surgery after arriving in the States. To be honest, until now, I had paid little attention. I often found her short of breath, but until moving to the States, I'd never spent so much of my time around her. She rarely complained, to me anyway, but her breathing difficulties were getting more worrisome. Whatever the problem was I was happy to be with her and not at school. I never passed up a chance to head into Manhattan.

Since that Friday after Thanksgiving when I'd first set foot in Times Square I'd been enraptured with New York City. Papi had the day off work, so he treated Mami and me to a day in Manhattan. My parents were fond of the city, having made many trips to it over the years, but this was the first time for me. Right away I felt waves of energy in the air; it was everywhere. I was smitten. That night, blinded by masses of neon signs bathing Broadway in floods of primary colors, I was like a moth to a flame, I couldn't resist, I couldn't get enough. An enormous Camel cigarette billboard, it must have been fifty-foot or even taller, dominated Times Square. With his mouth gaping open, the Camel man blew gigantic puffs of real smoke. In circles, I'm pretty sure. Clouds of vapor escaped the subway grates. We must have stood in front of a pizza parlor window for ten minutes watching a man in a white apron toss the dough in the air. The news-ticker on the Times building moved too fast for me to read. Newspaper and magazine stands displayed headlines in foreign languages. Hordes of determined hasty people, all rushing with a sense of purpose, pushed me out of their way.

"So ladies," Papi said, "should we find us a juicy steak for dinner?"

"What a question!" Mami said. She was a true carnivore, my mother. Papi knew of a local steakhouse chain that served a charbroiled sirloin steak, a baked potato and garlic bread for $1.19 so off we went.

"Mami, we're the only ones wearing seamed stockings," I'd said after eyeing the women ahead of me.

"No, we're not."

"Look," I said pointing to an old gray bearded man holding a placard: "The end of the world is near. Repent now."

"He's just crazy."

Ben Hur, two words I didn't recognize, flickered on a movie marque. A long queue of people were waiting to buy tickets for the movie. Pencil-yellow taxis dropped people in front of the theater, all the while fin-tailed cars, pug-nosed cars, and fumy city buses honked non-stop. A noise parade.

And look at me now, taking my mother to a doctor in the Bronx, not a moment's hesitation. After morning rush hour it took a half hour to get from Ridgefield Park to the Port Authority of New York and New Jersey Bus Terminal, *Puerto Arturito* to us. During the winter months *Puerto Arturito* lodged the homeless. Men with pints of liquor sticking out of their dirty coat pockets laid about, either sleeping or passed out, hard to tell. Bag ladies of all ages, their meager belongings always within arm's length, found refuge in the terminal for days at a time.

Mami and I walked out of the terminal, pulled our scarves tighter, and headed east on Forty-Second Street, all the while cursing Fidel, *el monstruo*. That's what Papi always called him. It was because of Fidel we had to contend with this arctic weather. Old black-and-white movie scenes flashed through my head. I was here, right where so many of those old movies had been made. That was a time when every teenager dreamed of stepping off a bus from nowhere and into stardom. Not now. Now there was no hint of glamour here, just one block west of Times Square. The once stately theaters that had lined the famed street were now home to one-dollar movie houses or porno shows. Sex-shop windows sold sordid trappings: crotch-less panties and brassieres with painted nipples poking out of holes. An occasional pizzeria mingled with the dilapidated theaters and sleazy sex shops. I was fascinated and repelled at the same time. From the corner of my eye I'd check whether Mami noticed my meandering gazes of all this red and black forbidden stuff. She had elected to act as if the stores didn't exist, looking straight ahead, head up high. Reaching the subway stairs took an eternity. At long last we went underground. I've long wondered what she was thinking while her teenage daughter escorted her through that sordid maze.

We'd hardly sat down in the surgeon's waiting room when a nurse called my mother. After asking a lot of questions, by way of me, and examining her, the doctor told her he needed to run more tests but more than likely she'd require heart surgery. He explained how he would enlarge her heart valve and I translated the procedure for my mother. I was busy finding the right words, so it didn't really hit me she'd be having major surgery. They attributed Mami's condition, mitral stenosis, childhood rheumatic fever.

"Ask him if I will have a normal life after the operation," Mami said.

"I doubt it," the doctor replied. "But tell her that if she doesn't have surgery, she'll get worse."

Back in the subway, she said, "I don't remember having rheumatic fever as a child, but I'm told that's what caused my heart problem. Back then, who knew? I don't know how I'm going to tell Lorenzo," Mami said, referring to my father's troubled state. He'd been walking around the house like a zombie. She wasn't the only one worried about him. I'd noticed his fixed empty stares and vaguely remembered them; it had been so many years.

I was eight when my father had his first nervous breakdown. Right after being forced to resign as sports commissioner he became a different man, taciturn and apprehensive. During his brief tenure my father had tried to take advantage of his extensive sports contacts and athletic experiences to bring sporting activities to children from all walks of life. He procured access to baseball fields, tennis courts, and swimming pools for disadvantaged kids of all ages. He negotiated with local businesses to donate milk, chocolate, and snacks so the kids could have *merienda*. His childlike optimism intact, he was certain he could work miracles. But his high-minded plans failed to take Batista into account. Like previous Cuban presidents, Batista didn't give a damn about the poor. Papi's stubborn refusal to face reality was his armor; anybody else would have feared dismissal, but he never saw it coming. Being unexpectedly sacked left him so devastated he ended up undergoing electro-shock treatment. Despite being so young, I can remember how crest-fallen and anxiety-ridden he was after his discharge from the hospital. His usual charismatic, outgoing personality gone, he could remember very little of what had happened. For a while I thought his memory had stayed behind in the electroshock room. *Problema de los nervios,* they called it back then.

The doctors who treated him recommended a *descanso,* a rest cure, and so we went to San Miguel de los Baños, a *balneario* in the interior of Matanzas province, a place where people took mineral baths to improve their health. Being a young habanera, el campo enthralled me, by the verdant, lush countryside with palm, ceiba, mango, and banana trees. The rustic cabin where we stayed was at the end of an avenue lined by flamboyant trees. It was a novelty to be awakened by roosters and to see chickens freely wondering all over the place. Perhaps my memory of the town is not entirely reliable since I was so young. But of this much I'm certain: the mineral baths stank like rotten eggs, and we went to *el balneario* every day believing that taking the waters would improve my father's health. "Mami, do you remember San Miguel de los Baños?" I asked.

"*Claro que sí,*" she said. "Your father had lost so much weight. He had no appetite, you see. Couldn't sleep at night. He was in such bad shape."

"And he got better?"

"A little better. And what made you think of it now?"

"Nada." I replied. I didn't want to talk about my obsession with illness, hers and Papi's. An onslaught of conflicting emotions was turning into a panic attack. I couldn't confront the possibility of losing both of them. What if my father didn't recover from his current depressive state? Maybe he'd end up in a mental hospital. How long before he'd recover? What would I we do for money? And now Mami. I loved her more than I loved myself. Would surgery really help her? It was very risky. If something happened to Mami would they expect me to replace her? But, wait a minute; wasn't I really panicking about me? About how I'd survive without her? About whether I would I even want to? I resented being forced to face such overwhelming distress. My wall of denial was seriously cracking. The silence dragged out the ride into Manhattan until I bore no resemblance to the self-reliant girl who'd taken the same line earlier that morning. Mami was lost in her thoughts, and I, well I couldn't say a word, afraid I'd lose my grip.

By the time we reached *Puerto Arturito* I was an emotional wreck. I kept replaying my translation, wondering if I'd been accurate. In the past I had liked translating for my mother—it made me feel important, useful. Today, sensing her embarrassment and defenselessness, I'd been able to put myself in her place. How powerless she must have felt, sitting beside me without a voice while the doctor talked about her life as if she wasn't there. Mami and I had reversed roles—with me acting like the parent, with her treated as a child. As if reading my mind she asked, "Puchita, you're not hiding anything from me, are you?"

"No, Mami. I'm like you; I tell it like it is."

She smiled, pleased with herself.

The way I see it all families develop a strategy to deal with crises—a method, a *modus operandi* as it were. Faced with medical adversities, my family's *modus operandi* comprised consulting my oldest brother and waiting for his guidance with an eagerness usually reserved for the coming of the Messiah. When my father became immobilized by yet another bout of depression, and my mother faced a catheterization in preparation for heart surgery, it fell to Fello to make the arrangements at Manhattan's Mt. Sinai Hospital.

I took another day off to accompany my mother to the hospital for pre-admission tests. Once at the hospital we were instructed to go to the lab where my mother was given a plastic receptacle and shown where the bathroom was. I escorted her to the spacious restroom and when she got into a stall to do her business, I waited for her by one of the sinks. Two other women came in, one of them holding a plastic container, and walked into separate stalls.

"*Ay, no puedo,*" said the woman who couldn't pee.

"*Claro que si puedes,*" her companion replied. Of course you can.

"*No, no puedo,*" said the one who came in with the plastic cup. "Here I'll pass you my cup and you can lend me your piss."

"*¡No!*" shouted Mami from her stall. "*¡No puede

hacer eso!" I'm thinking, Mami, it's none of your business, but she went on to explain that if she was ill, the doctors wouldn't know about it and they would treat her for what was wrong with her friend. I covered my mouth to keep from laughing, and that's the only thing I remember from that period that doesn't hurt. I'll skip the details but Mami's catherization was disastrous, and it took some time for her to bounce back. My father wasn't doing so well either. The medications "*para los nervios*" left him so dazed he could hardly talk; he looked like a man headed to the crypt. This was familiar ground for Papi. Over the years he had succumbed to depression on several occasions and at those times he was either medicated with anti-depressants or subjected to electro-shock treatments. Like most families, we didn't talk about it but we sure gave it a lot of thought. Perhaps this current depression was triggered by Mami's pending surgery.

Well, at least they were in the same hospital. Papi was on one floor, Mami on another, and the three of us kids would take turns visiting each of them, sometimes bumping into each other in the elevator. I hated seeing my mother in that long hospital ward, surrounded by strangers. For me it was humiliating. In Cuba she'd have had her own room, and there would be an extra bed for *la familia*. Reaching her bed I pulled the curtain around us for some privacy. She'd been thumbing through *Selecciones,* the Spanish Reader's Digest. I thought she didn't look as pasty as she had before, and I wanted to believe she was getting better.

"How do you feel?" I asked.

"Stronger," she said.

"Good. You look better, you know. Should I get you some more magazines?" I said. At which point the curtain flew back revealing a squad of interns doing their rounds. I headed downstairs to Papi.

My father could barely acknowledge my presence. He was heavily drugged, and I didn't understand why. No one had explained to me how antidepressants work, how they need to accumulate in your system before they take effect. Looking back, I'm certain he was overmedicated, but I had no way of knowing. I needed to be reassured. I wanted to hear his storytelling and laughter, his never-failing optimism. Papi was the kind of man whose force of personality had always drawn people to him, and here he was, not even a shadow of his former self. I sat on the edge of the bed and tried to make conversation.

When I returned to Mami's ward the doctors were gone. I squeezed past her IV pole and sat on the edge of the bed, waiting, bored, the silence pressing on me like a load of bricks. At home after you did something wrong no one would speak to you. In my house, silence was punishment. All these years later, silence is no friend of mine.

"Do you still have beans?" she asked to break the silence. Before going into the hospital she had cooked a big pot of black beans and a pot of rice. Not knowing how long she'd be gone, she showed me how to cook some simple dishes like white rice and *picadillo*.

"Mami, do you know what happened yesterday?" I said by way of a reply.

"Tell me," she said.

"We missed the bus. *Puerto Arturito* was freezing, and

we waited forever for the next bus. The platform was an iceberg. Anyway, we got home tired and starving. "

"What happened?"

"Well, I realized we didn't have enough rice, so I made some the way you taught me, except it didn't come out *desgranado* like yours. I served it with the black beans and the *picadillo* you left us. Guess what happened?"

"¡Puchita!"

"Okay. Loren scooped rice onto his plate and then asked Fello, 'Want a tennis ball?' That's how sticky the rice was. And then they both started laughing at me."

"Not at you, at the rice."

"Same thing."

"No, at the rice, Puchita. It's not the same thing. You always overreact."

Here I was looking for sympathy, and what did she do? Take my brothers' side. Why hadn't she shown them how to cook rice? Why me, the youngest? I decided not to reply. She was lying in a hospital bed, for heaven's sake. The vacuum of silence sucked me in. I didn't tell her about bursting into tears and throwing myself on her bed sobbing. I didn't tell her Fello had followed me into the bedroom and said, *"No seas tan dramática."*

"No estoy siendo nada. Yo soy así." I'm not being anything; this is who I am.

Chapter Eleven

Dinner was a simple affair. It was just the three of us in the house. Fello had returned to Mexico and Papi was still at the hospital. Loren couldn't stay still, cracking his knuckles, grinding his teeth, and tapping one foot, while Mami and I cleared the table. "What's the matter, Loren?" Mami asked. She'd been home from the hospital for a couple of days. "You've hardly said a word all evening."

"*Nada*," Loren said.

I was rinsing the plates in our sink but kept the water low because I knew something was cooking. After another few minutes Loren sat down at the table, cracking his fingers, again.

"Mami, I need to talk to you," he said at last.

"Come, Loren." Mami got up and headed to the bedroom. Loren followed her and closed the door behind him. I got a knot in my stomach and my heart started racing. Here I am, on the other side of the door, excluded again. I couldn't hear a thing, but I knew nothing good ever followed those I've-got-to-talk-to-you conversations. I don't know about other people, but when someone tells me "I've got to talk to you," every dubious thing I've ever done comes floating through my mind.

I heard some movement and walked away from the door. Mami came out first, not looking pleased. She picked up a towel to dry the dishes. Loren followed her out and said, "I told Mami I'm joining the invasion."

"When?" I asked.

"Next week."

"Did you know already, Puchita?" Mami asked.

"No, of course not," I said. "No one tells me anything. When are you telling Papi?"

"Tomorrow, when I see him." Loren said.

I couldn't speak, the panic rising up my spine took my voice away, but I was thinking, what about me? You can't do this to me. Not now. Doesn't anybody here give a shit what happens to me? *Por Dios* Loren, Mami and Papi are really sick. Fello's away doing his Doctor thing. And now you're off to the invasion? I'm just fifteen, for Christ's sake. You're all the only family I have in New Jersey.

I felt Mami's eyes on me. "It's his life. If he thinks that's what he ought to do, then he should do it," she said.

Really? Since when? Since when have you allowed your children to do as they please? My panic turned to fury. I seethed as I envisioned the prospect of being left alone with sick parents. *¿Y qué soy yo, un moco?* Falling silent, I once more pushed my rage back down inside. I didn't say a word. What's the point? It was clear that what mattered in my family were the needs and aspirations of my brothers. What I wouldn't have given to have been born a man.

My father's psychiatrist had warned us it would take a few weeks for the antidepressants to kick in, and by the looks of him that March afternoon, they taken effect. A smile crossed his face as we entered his mini-ward. One of the nurses had shaved him and when I bent down to kiss him I detected a hint of Old Spice. Loren told Papi about his plans. I sat at the foot of Papi's bed, my eyes wandering about the room, still mad, intent on not listening to this shit again.

"I'm sorry I have to leave while you're in here," Loren said. "I know the timing couldn't be worse, but I can't wait. As a matter of fact I barely had time to join up; they almost didn't take me. The next plane leaves for the camp very soon."

"I'm proud of you, Loren," Papi said.

I'll be damned. Proud of him? Now I'd heard it all.

"You don't need to worry about money. The people who run the camps promised to send you a check for $225 every month while I'm gone," Loren said.

I looked at Papi, expecting to see him shed a tear or two or least show some sign of regret, but a small smile had gelled around his mouth. He looked a tad envious, wishful even. *"Entonces va a haber tres Nodarses en la invasión."* Pride, that was it. Papi was proud to be his father. His son would fight side by side his two nephews in the great invasion to rid his country of *El Monstruo's* tyranny. Three Nodarse men; that's what my father had said. How very macho. Papi deemed Loren selfless; he was after all willing to risk his life for his country's freedom. Selfish is how I saw it, leaving me alone to care for two sick parents in a foreign county with no money to speak of. It's a good thing Papi was getting paid sick leave, otherwise I don't know what would have happened to us. Already, Loren's paycheck was stretched to the max.

A week later, Loren got his call to report for duty. My father was still in the hospital. Mami, Loren, and I went to Mt. Sinai together when it was time for him to say goodbye to Papi. Leaving the hospital, we took the Fifth Avenue bus, got off at 42nd Street, and walked crosstown to *Puerto Arturito*. We had a bit of time left and sat at the terminal's Walgreen's soda fountain, sipping our Coca Colas, wishing we knew what to say. We wanted to make every moment last, every sentence count. When Loren's time was up Mami said, "Loren, you're always cracking your fingers."

"And?"

"Well, stop doing it because if you're in hiding someone might hear you. I read it in some detective novel."

Loren looked at her and smiled. He kissed her cheek and headed for his bus.

Chapter Twelve

On April 17, 1961, the day of the Bay of Pigs Invasion, President Kennedy became the second most hated man in our house. Young men we'd seen grow up were killed that day as they landed in a marshy spot of the Cuban coast, Bahia de Cochinos. *Muchachos,* as Papi would say. Trained by the CIA, the exiled Cuban volunteers had been promised air cover, but President Kennedy backed off. He would deny any complicity in the invasion. Those who made it to shore found Fidel Castro's military waiting for them, having been tipped off by spies who had infiltrated the exile groups.

Two or three days after the invasion my mother entered the hospital for her scheduled heart surgery. She had no clue whether her second son was dead or alive. Days later, when the Cuban government started releasing casualties and prisoners' names, *El Diario* and *La Prensa,* New York City's Spanish-language newspapers, printed the list in their daily editions. Loren's name was never among those captured. I was afraid he was dead, but didn't dare say it. My two first cousins were on the list, so we knew they were imprisoned. Every day we hoped to read Loren's name. Even now I can hear Papi saying, "Águeda, no news is good news," trite stuff like that to calm her down, except all it did was piss her off, even with all those tubes coming out of her. Between Mami's drawn-out recovery, and not knowing whether Loren was dead or alive, minutes stretched like rubber bands. Fello, here for the surgery, was on top of all things medical. Afraid of being left alone, I kept asking Fello, "When are you leaving?" He said nothing—the only Cuban who doesn't talk. And if I asked my father, he'd say, "Ask Fello."

Fello left the day after Mami's health stabilized. Then, on the evening of April 28th, Papi and I were alone in the house, thinking of what to do for dinner, when the phone rang. I heard Papi say, "Yes, I accept the charges." It was a collect call from Cuba, from Mami's cousin Aydee. She'd worked as a doctor at the former Palacio de los Deportes when my father was sports commissioner in 1952. Back then *el palacio* was at the end of Calle Paseo, right next to the ocean.

The building where *los habaneros* watched boxing matches and basketball games, and kids enjoyed Ringling Bros. circuses was demolished three years later to enlarge the Malecón. The old sporting venue was replaced by a huge sports complex called Ciudad Deportiva in El Cerro, one of the poorest municipalities in Havana. Batista's brother-in-law was sports commissioner and as in all public projects on small islands, the power brokers and politicians were better for it.

"Lorenzo, I saw Lorencito," Aydee told my father. "Couldn't talk to him but I saw him. He isn't wounded or anything. He's fine." *Está bien.*

We wanted to tell Mami right away, but she was in a semi-private room, and we decided not to disturb her fellow patient so we waited until the following day to break the news.

Over a thousand Bay of Pigs prisoners were being held at Ciudad Deportiva in El Cerro. The prisoners called themselves Brigada 2506, the number assigned to Carlos Rodriguez Santana, a recruit who'd died in an accident at one of the training camps. The *brigadistas*' fate was anybody's guess. Since the United States had severed diplomatic ties with Cuba, there was no direct access to the prisoners. Everyone expected Fidel to use the prisoners to his advantage, but then Cubans were always making up stuff about Fidel. Almost no news was coming out of Cuba. No one knew anything.

"Águeda, *¿no te lo dije?*" Didn't I tell you? Papi said at the hospital the next day. My mother, with an intravenous needle in her left arm and looking like it was an effort to keep her eyes open, didn't immediately reply. "Lorenzo," she finally said, *"¿y ahora qué?"* Now what? Like Papi, I'd given no thought to *"¿y ahora qué?"* Thrilled knowing Loren was alive, I hadn't thought about what lay ahead.

Papi ignored her question and said, "I knew he'd be fine." I can't think of a reason my father continued to believe he had the power to influence my mother's thinking, all evidence to the contrary.

"Lorenzo, in Cuba our son is considered a traitor, how good can it be?" She paused.

"The Americans know they're responsible for this debacle. I'm certain Washington will take whatever action is required to free the prisoners." Papi said, sounding more like Radio Free Europe than a concerned father. He couldn't help it. It was his coping mechanism.

"Mami," I said, trying to change the subject, "Why did Aydee stay? She's not a communist is she?"

"No, Puchita," she said. "Aydee is not a communist. She waited too long to leave and then she couldn't. We were lucky to leave when we did." I sensed this wasn't a good time to contradict her, but I sure didn't think we were lucky.

Chapter Thirteen

A teenager smoking was no big deal back then. Once I'd turned the street corner, I'd light a cigarette on the way to school. This blustery winter morning I was having trouble lighting up and as I cupped my hands to give it one more try, I spotted a girl walking alone like me, a bleached blonde with a beehive, white as milk, in a pencil skirt. With cherry-red lips and a smile from ear to ear she walked up and said, "Hi, I'm Diane."

In school I didn't get this "hi" stuff. I didn't understand why saying "hi" once wasn't enough, why you had to say "hi" every time you saw someone. Was it every time though? Or was it at particular times like after recess, lunch, P.E.? Was I kind of being left out because I didn't say "hi" when I was supposed to?

"Hi, I'm Maria."

"What are you?"

"What?"

"Sophomore? Junior? Senior?" she asked.

"Oh, I'm a junior. And you?"

"Sophomore."

"Too bad."

"You new?" she asked.

"Yes. You?"

"Yeah. Moved from Palisades Park. Can't stand this place."

"Me too."

Dislocation and loneliness brought the two of us together. I knew why I didn't fit in—I was the only foreigner at the school—but I didn't know why Diane didn't make friends with her classmates. She lived in a dimly lit, grungy-looking, Stephen-King-like house on Route 46. And yet I loved spending time there. She had her own bedroom on the second floor and we could smoke one cigarette after another up there. We'd sit on the bed, look at movie magazines, pine over Paul Newman, envy Elizabeth Taylor, and wonder about Rock Hudson. It seemed strange that her mother never peeked in to find out what we were doing up there, that she trusted her daughter so much. Her father was not like mine. He didn't try to socialize, barely said "hi." What struck me was that my only friend came from a working-class family, from a house that stunk of cigarettes, where people didn't care much about appearances, not to mention manners.

"I'm in love with my priest," Diane said soon after I started spending time in her bedroom.

"The one here?"

"No, no. The one in Palisades Park."

"Does he know?" I asked.

"I'm pretty sure he loves me too."

"He told you?"

"Nah. He won't admit it. He can't, you know. But I can tell."

I took her at her word. It was such a relief to have somebody to walk to school with; I wasn't about to second-guess her. Not going to school alone meant more to me than our comradeship up in her room. Weekends and holidays we didn't see each other because our families weren't friends. We hung out together until the end of the semester, and when our daily routine changed we gradually stopped seeing each other.

Gema, my neighborhood friend from Cuba, was spending the summer in Ridgefield Park. She stayed with her aunt, Carmela, of Cuban-San-Givin' fame. Gema and I spent much of our time walking up and down Main Street, our noses up. We acted as if we couldn't be bothered, as if we wouldn't waste our time talking with the locals. I realize now we made ourselves inaccessible for fear of being rejected. We discovered a new Cuban family had recently moved to town. They were renting an apartment in an old building right off Main Street. A couple in their late thirties, *Los Forment* (I've no idea why we always called them by their last name) had two young kids, a son and daughter. In Cuba he had worked as an accountant. Now he was a bookkeeper for a Manhattan small business, and a part-time salesman at Macy's. Not unlike me in Miami, he and his wife were obsessed with food, and everything he bought with his Macy's employee discount was destined for the kitchen. I found them amusing and, hey, they were. Whenever his son misbehaved, he'd look at me and say, "Herod was a great man."

Academically, that one semester as a high school junior turned out to be too easy. In Cuba, I'd been readying for college, although I'd fared poorly in algebra and geometry; here the business curriculum required none of that stuff. To this day I regret not having taken physics or chemistry although I doubt I could have handled either subject at the time. Taking another Spanish class my senior year didn't exactly tax myself that year either. But, for the record, I also took French.

Had it not been for her height, Miss F., my Spanish teacher, could have stepped out of a Japanese print. With her long jet black hair coiled around her face, chalky white complexion, and ruby-red lips, her face reminded me of Hollywood's stereotypical geisha. Tall, slim, elegant, single, and well-educated, she was the type of woman I aspired to be. When I asked her why she lived in Manhattan, she smiled seductively and said, "I'm a city girl." Luckily for me, Miss F. delighted in having a native Spanish speaker to converse with, and we got into the habit of chatting briefly before and after class. She'd spent time in Spain and spoke with a Castilian accent I'd have killed for. On an otherwise unremarkable fall afternoon she asked me at the end of the period whether I'd met the Cuban girl yet.

"¿Hay otra cubana?"

"As of today there is," Miss F. said with a grin. "Just saw her heading that way,"

One look at her and I knew the girl was Cuban. She walked alone, her big, brown, prominent eyes cast down. Like me she had abundant curly chestnut hair; unlike me, she was voluptuous, curved like a guitar—definitely Cuban. She saw me approaching and tried to smile. I could tell she felt lost, like me.

"Hola. ¿Tú eres cubana?" I asked, straight to the point.

"Sí."

"¿De dónde?" Where from I asked.

"De Sancti Spíritus ¿Y tú?"

"Mi mamá nació en Sancti Spíritus. Yo soy de La Habana". I couldn't wait to tell my mother the new girl was from where she was born.

"Silvia," she said and extended her hand. No "Hi" from her. Yet.

"Maria," I said, and went on to tell her how it used to be Maria de los Angeles or Puchita.

"Puchita?" she asked.

"That's my nickname," I explained as I tried to contain my joy. *Se me abrió el cielo*. I was in heaven.

As it turned out, we were in three classes together—P.E., American History, and English—and although we didn't know what "having a crush" meant we were certainly infatuated with our English teacher, wedding band and all. Thirty or so, tall, lanky and bespectacled, Mr. Gerstenblatt had the girls swooning. It wasn't his appearance that was hard to resist; it was his personality, his sense of humor. I think Silvia's accent—so thick you could have sliced it—and reticence prevented him from picking on her, but he picked on everybody else, including me. He would stand by my desk and sing, "Maria, I just met a girl named Maria," and since he sang it in jest and I'd never heard the song before, I thought he'd made it up for me. That's how insular my life was. When I later heard Richard Belzer belch out the song at a theater in Times Square I practically lost the will to live. I still remember Mr. G's note on my paper on *Macbeth*. He called my comments original, intelligent, and insightful. He liked to tease me about my English. "When you came here you spoke perfect English," he'd say with a straight face. "You said 'yes' not 'yeah.' I hope this trend doesn't continue." Then he'd do something to let me know he was pulling my leg. I now had two reasons to get up in the morning: Mr. G. and Silvia.

Silvia hadn't gone to an American school in Cuba, and her English was very limited. Besides the senior English class where she and I pined for Mr. Gerstenblatt, Silvia took other English classes where she got a lot of flak, the same crap I had to put up with: "Did you wear shoes in Cuba?" "Did you have televisions in Cuba?" "Do all the kids in Cuba pierce their ears?" Silvia couldn't wait for the end of the day so she could tell me about her experiences, and I'd feel as insulted as if I were the targeted aborigine. What's wrong with them? This is Ridgefield Park, less than forty minutes away from Manhattan. Where have they been?

Roughly a month after Silvia's arrival they called me to Miss P.'s office. "You know," she said, in her softest counselor voice, "several students have complained about you and Silva speaking in Spanish behind their backs."

"We're not talking about them. You know Silvia speaks almost no English." I'd assumed all along they were suspicious of Silvia and me because we were, after all strangers, and I got that.

"Nonetheless," said Miss P., now in a more authoritarian tone, "it's very rude to speak in a language people don't understand. So I'm asking that from now on you speak in English at all times."

"But...."

"You're in America now and you should speak English."

I felt she was asking me to give up my identity, my national pride. Probably, like most Americans, she was monolingual and couldn't understand that speaking to Silvia in any language other than Spanish would make me feel like a phony. Miss P.'s request had rendered Silvia and me speechless. But only for a while. Little by little Silvia and drifted out of earshot, lowering our voices, and speaking Spanish. If anyone approached, we'd switch to English.

Weekends I'd visit her. She lived on the other side of town with her sister, brother-in-law, brothers, and baby niece. Silvia's sister had met her husband while studying architecture at a Catholic university in Cuba. I found him hilarious, but it was hard to find him there, busy as he was working two jobs. He intended to get as many family members out of Cuba as he could, and I became used to seeing strange faces in the small apartment. In Cuba, Silvia's parents awaited authorization to leave, any day now. Although I imagined how difficult it must have been for Silvia to leave her parents behind, I also thought it was neat to be brought up by someone as young as her older sister, someone not as uptight as my mother. I liked joining in for neighborhood walks, pushing the baby carriage. Whenever we could, Silvia and I headed to a nearby diner, not the soda fountain on Main Street where all our classmates hung out. "American coffee is like *agua sucia*," dirty water, I'd say and then we'd talk about Miss F. and Mr. G., about the girls with bouffant hairdos (like Jackie Kennedy) and about the boys who didn't know we existed. Neither of us was ever asked out on a date, forget about the senior prom.

Sometime in March Miss P. called me to her office. As I walked there, I reviewed my recent actions, trying to determine what I'd done to get in trouble. Surely, talking to Silvia in Spanish couldn't be it, but that's all I could think of.

"I need to talk to your mother," said Miss P. "I know she'll need you here to translate for her so I suggest meeting after school ends. Ask her if she can be here at 3:15 on Thursday."

"Did I do something wrong?" I asked.

"On the contrary," she said with that counselor smile.

I waited for my mother by the counseling office. The fact I'd been told not to worry didn't keep my heart from racing.

"Do come in," Miss P. told my mother while she held the door open. "Please, sit down."

"Is a problem?" my mother asked right off the bat.

"Quite the opposite," Miss P. said. "I'm sure you know your daughter is a very bright young lady. Her teachers and I think it's a pity for her not to go to college." My mother tried to interrupt but Miss P. signaled her to stop. "I'm almost certain I can get her a scholarship to Jersey City Teachers' College. If she doesn't want to be a teacher after she finishes college then she can switch majors, but she'll have a college degree under her belt."

I translated all of this. I knew my mother, not acquainted with the American higher education system, had no clue what majoring in something was all about, but she wasn't about to ask either. "Tell her," my mother said, "that you'll be going to secretarial school after you graduate." This was news to me. I stared, mouth opened, at Mami's eyes, unsure of what I'd just heard.

"Tell her, Puchita."

And so I did, while wondering where the hell did that come from?

"I don't mean to be rude," Miss P. said, "but I believe you're making a big mistake. Your daughter is college material."

"Thank you," my mother said. She got up, shook Miss P.'s hand and headed to the door.

Outside the school Mami turned and said, "Puchita, I want you to learn how to earn a living. Your father and I have been saving for you to go to a secretarial school in New York. I know you'll get married and have kids but this way you'll have something to fall back on in an emergency."

"Fine," I said.

All the way home I thought why? Why am I the last to learn about the decisions that would affect my life, my future? Where's this business school? How did they find money for that? Why wasn't I asked, or at least told about it? We'd never had any discussions at home about what I wanted to do next. Had no clue someone had already decided. When we got home, my mother asked me to follow her into her bedroom. She went straight to her gray chest of drawers, pulled out the top drawer and fished out a savings book with the name of a local bank on its front cover. Handing me the open passbook she pointed to an amount that, if I remember correctly, neared $500. "Your father and I have been saving money for you to go to secretarial school," she told me. Something in me said I should feel ashamed of myself for doubting her intentions. But why couldn't I have been part of this decision? Why the secret?

After I heard Miss Prim mention it I'd hoped for a scholarship to Jersey City Teacher's College. I could see myself teaching; it was a profession I looked up to. I still remembered Doctora Reboredo, my history teacher in Cuba. My grandmother was proud to have been a teacher. But it would take me four years before I'd be earning a living, and my parents needed additional income pronto. I didn't say a word; what was the point. My future had been decided. But would they ever realize it was my life? Was my future forever to be tethered to my family's wellbeing? I'd seen young women in Cuba still living at home, attending to their parents' needs. I'd wondered if they had ambitions of their own. They seemed to be all but invisible women.

I felt this hole in my stomach sucking my spirit in. My mother let me down. Big time. She should have spoken up for me in there, should have told Miss P. something like, "I know she's bright but we don't have any money and we need her to go to work." If she'd said that I'd have felt validated. Instead, she talked about my being a secretary as if that was all I was capable of. I couldn't understand why she'd lost faith in me. She'd believed in me in Cuba, had enrolled me in *bachillerato*, had sent me to *La Maison Francaise* on Saturdays, had gotten me a tutor for algebra. I felt sold out.

Silvia and I graduated on June 21, 1962. I was sixteen at the time. As luck would have it, Gema's school year in Florida had already ended so she could make it to my graduation. Silvia had heard so many stories about Gema she couldn't wait to meet her. I'd told Silvia about how Gema and I climbed up mango trees at her grandfather's *finca*; how if a tropical rainstorm caught us there, we'd be allowed to go outside and get drenched; how Gema and I started smoking together in Florida while visiting her uncle in West Palm Beach. When Silvia finally met Gema, I could tell she liked her. The first thing Silvia told me was, "My God, she's so beautiful!" That had been my problem with Gema all along. Her looks would upstage every girl near her, me included. In Cuba a girl with dark golden hair and great big green eyes stood out like an emerald shining in the tropical sun. Wherever I went all the attention and praise went to Gema. "You look like Grace Kelly," people would say. Even before marrying the prince, Grace Kelly embodied every young girl's dream. My jealousy made me look like a fool one summer night when my brothers, who'd treated me like a mascot, were discussing movies with my parents. Mami said, *"La Ventana Indiscreta (Rear Window)* now that was a perfect movie."

Not one to be left out, I said, *"To Catch a Thief* was better. I like looking at the French Riviera, not a brick wall, and Cary Grant is so much handsomer than James Stewart."

"Gema looks like Grace Kelly," Fello said. Was there no end to this?

"I have a better body than Gema," I said, and boy, did that remark crack them up. "But I do," I said again. Apparently, my insistence was even funnier.

Mami gave them her Medusa look. "Puchita, you shouldn't have said that. It's in poor taste for people to praise themselves. Besides, the word is *figura* not *cuerpo*. You say somebody has a good figure, not a good body."

I hadn't wanted to knock Gema; I'd wanted them to say something nice about me. Let's face it, beauty is about standing out, and in Cuba I didn't stand out.

If Silvia's remark was any indication, not much had changed for me since the 1954 release of *Rear Window*. Gema was the star, but I'd learned my lesson: I didn't tell Silvia I had a better figure.

I have a black-and-white photograph of Silvia, Gema and me standing in front of the caca-colored sofa. I'm wearing a lovely organza spaghetti-strap dress my mother had sewn for the occasion; Gema wore a printed blouse and white pleated skirt, and Silvia a beautiful flowery dress, a string of pearls gracing her neck. When my parents bought me flowers, they forgot we didn't own a vase, so we had to stick the bouquet in a percolator. Mami had pissed off the three of us right before the shot. Well, I don't know about Silvia; it's hard to piss her off. My mother had previously told us we could go to New York to celebrate my graduation but just before taking the picture she had announced, "It's too late to go to New York." I kept saying it wasn't fair, that she had promised, but that just made things worse. The photo shows three young ladies all dressed up with no place to go.

With Gema I dared go to places my high-school classmates frequented as a group. I had avoided the Main Street soda fountain where the other kids hung out. But with Gema I worked up the nerve. I was drinking my first egg cream and couldn't decide if I liked it. I'd never even seen anyone have an egg cream in Woolworth's Havana soda fountains. Nope, I didn't like it. "My parents will let us go to New York during the day," I told Gema as I hesitantly sipped on my egg cream, "but we'll have to come home before dark."

"What are we going to do in New York with no money?"

"Do you know *la gente del* Vedado Tennis meet at St. Patrick's Cathedral on Sundays?" I said.

"You're kidding."

"No, I went with Loren several times."

The night before our adventure Gema slept on the sofa bed where Loren used to sleep. She and I had rolled our hair in big rollers, a step up from the Tropicana frozen juice cans, but it still felt like sleeping on cinder blocks. After I turned off the light Gema asked, "Who do you think will be there?"

"I don't know. Most of the guys are in jail."

I wish I could recall what we wore. I remember wearing the requisite thick black eyeliner, with that upward curve at the corner of the eye, *el rabito*. Lots of eye makeup, blue eye-shadow, and white lipstick, very early '60s.

As I'd feared most of the guys were gone but I told Gema maybe we could find some guys at El Liborio and we decided to check it out. How much could a Coca Cola cost? People we knew from El Vedado Tennis sat at a round table and gestured us to join them. The conversation was lively and loud. I glanced around the room hoping to spot more acquaintances. That's when I noticed a debonair, dark and handsome young man smoking a pipe. I looked, he looked; I liked, he liked. Very Hollywood. My friends at the table wanted him to join them too. He approached the group radiating self-confidence, pulled up a chair and sat next to me—not the girl with the emerald eyes and quill-like lashes. Everybody seemed to know him. He must have started coming after Loren left—I'd have noticed him otherwise.

In those days most Cuban families didn't trust young men who hadn't gone in the invasion but I could tell at once Toby was different. His intellectual guise set him apart from my brother and his friends. Right away I knew he didn't belong in the battleground but in a library, knee deep in books, preferably sunken in a supple leather chair.

After giving thought to his being shorter than me, I overlooked his height and focused on his haunting saucer-like eyes with lashes that fanned and on his fleshy inviting lower lip.

Later, after Gema returned to Florida, Toby asked me out. I thought I'd found love but I'm not so sure about him. He said he loved me and since, to see me he had to take the subway from Queens to Port Authority and then a bus to Ridgefield Park, I interpreted the sacrifice as devotion. But once in Ridgefield Park what was he to do? He had no car, and the town had as much life as marble. I remember Belén telling me, "Puchita, when you have a *novio* make sure he's not a *rompesillón*," referring to those boyfriends who sat on the porch for so many years that the rocker's cane seat gave way. Toby was twenty-five, and I was sixteen so he'd have been condemned to a long courtship in the living room, with audience participation.

In fairness my parents allowed us to meet in Manhattan in the early afternoon, as if sin, like Dracula, were incompatible with sunlight. Sometimes we caught a matinee. I remember going with him to the Paris Theater, the movie house facing the Plaza Fountain, the water fountain where one evening Zelda Fitzgerald took a dip. More often we visited museums, mostly the Met or the Modern, sometimes the Frick. Toby was an art connoisseur. I had loved art since third grade when an art speaker, a hefty and disheveled American lady, walked into my class with a handful of cardboard reproductions of Impressionist paintings. My memory of that morning—of the Van Gogh landscapes with tulips and windmills and canals, with brushstrokes the likes of which I had never seen—is as vivid now as it was before I left Cuba. On a Sunday afternoon I went with Toby to the Museum of Modern Art. We stood in front of Turner's *The Burning of the Houses of Parliament 1835* while I told him about the art lady and he looked at me and smiled. Fascinated by Turner's ball of light I said, in my naïveté, "Before this exhibit I'd thought artists replicated reality toward the end of their careers."

"Frequently, artists venture into abstraction after mastering realism," Toby more or less said. He might have said it better but what impressed me was how he loved to educate.

But, alas, what I viewed as sophistication my parents regarded as affectation and it relieved them to see him go—Toby's choice, not mine. He'd always been a true gentleman, had always treated my parents with utmost respect, so I'm led to believe the reason they didn't grow fond of him had to do with politics: they probably felt he should have been doing time with Loren. When I asked my mother why our breakup pleased her she said, "I don't like his hands, you can tell a lot about people just by looking at their hands."

"Really?" I said, "I never knew that."

In retrospect, my reaction to that breakup, emblematic as it was of my emotional fragility, should have alerted my parents. There was nothing unusual about our splitting up. My boyfriend and I had an argument, and I hung up on him. I didn't hear from him for a few days and when he called, asking to meet in neutral territory, I knew he'd end it. He was my first boyfriend, and that's the only excuse I have for behaving so shamelessly. When I saw him I begged him to give me another chance—begged—until he told me he didn't love me. The one and only time I begged for anything. After the breakup I sank into a depression. I refused to eat. My mother wasn't about to tolerate the antics of a teenage girl. "You're being hysterical. Pull yourself together. You should be ashamed of yourself, carrying on like this for a man who doesn't love you. Have you no pride?" snapped my mother. I ate, and I cried, and I vomited. She failed to see that like all depressed people, I didn't believe the hurt and pain would ever go away. I'd left Cuba with the certainty I'd always see the people I loved again. That belief had been replaced by a pervasive sense of loss: I lost people. I lost people all the time.

Chapter Fourteen

Fidel wasn't so hard to read after all. A month after the invasion he offered to exchange the Bay of Pigs prisoners for 500 bulldozers. Kennedy favored the deal—he still had egg on his face from the fiasco—but Congress wouldn't support him. So he prodded outstanding citizens like Eleanor Roosevelt and President Eisenhower's brother to establish the Tractors for Freedom Committee. Problem was, Fidel kept changing his demands at the very last minute and his unpredictability led the Committee to be dissolved in June 1961. Afterwards the prisoners were relocated to Castillo del Principe, a nineteenth-century dungeon on a steep hill overlooking Havana, where their living conditions worsened. When the Committee disintegrated, I heard my father tell my mother, "Águeda, *es una piedra en el camino,*" a bump in the road. That might have been the case for him but for my mother it was a brick wall. Certain she'd never see her son again, she behaved irascibly, and it reminded me of how I'd walked on eggshells during my grandmother's lengthy illness back in Havana. Belén had served as a shield back then. How I wished I could have her next to me now!

That summer Mami and I discovered American soap operas which, unsurprisingly, didn't begin to match the ones we watched in Cuba. Sugar wasn't as sweet here either. Mami would have preferred reading a good book, or even a lousy book, but back then everything in the town's library was in English. Even though I had to explain in Spanish what passed for a plot, things moved so slowly in the soaps we didn't miss a thing. We were watching *As the World Turns* in the living room when the phone rang.

"*Oigo,*" said my mother. That's how Cubans answer the phone, saying "I hear."

"Yes, collect is okay."

I jumped up. Only people from Cuba called collect. I stood next to her by the mini-hallway's wall phone.

"¡Belén!, ¡Belén!" I heard my mother say.

"Mami, *¿es Belén?*"

"Shhhhhh."

I tried to listen in. It was a poor connection, but I could hear Belén saying, "*Lorencito está bien. Está flaco pero está bien.*" Belén had seen Loren and other than finding him skinny he was fine.

"*¿Tuvieron visita?*" my mother asked.

I could picture Belén climbing up the hill to El Castillo del Príncipe, flogged by the Cuban sun while standing in line on visiting day. I could see her with one hand on her waist, wearing a burlap skirt for San Lazáro and a blouse that barely contained her bountiful breasts. She would talk to everybody who'd listen, finding out their *vida y milagro* and making them laugh, even in that scorching heat. I remembered how whenever she told me a story and I asked her for specific names she'd say, *"Se habla del milagro pero no del santo."* You talk about the miracle but not the saint." I loved the way she talked.

"Puchita, say hello to Belén but don't take too long."

How could I not take too long?

I grabbed the phone wondering when the last time I'd written to her was. The guilt prevented me from enjoying the call. I didn't hear her laughter; I heard *Mea Culpa, Mea Culpa, Mea Maxima Culpa.* I knew we lived in different countries now, but had our souls moved as well?

"Belén, I know I haven't written, but I still love you."

"*Sinvergüenza*," she said, "shameless."

"Really, Belén, it's not because I don't love you."

"*Anja.*"

After I hung up the phone Mami said, "It took great courage for Belén to visit Loren. She might be blacklisted or punished in some way."

"Punished how?"

"With her ration card or stuff like that, not physically. Don't worry."

"I bet Loren was thrilled to see her."

"I'm sure he was."

I couldn't get her out of my mind. I've let you down, Belén. I should have called, should have written. I pulled out my treasure chest of memories and chose our trips to *el mercado.* Rows of stalls covered with multicolored improvised awnings flaunted *plátanos, mameyes, anones, malangas, and boniatos. Plátanos* were either green, bright yellow, or black with age; small or humongous. In Cuba they were all *plátanos*; here they're either bananas or plantains. Belén worked the stalls the way a politician works a crowd. *"¿Y la reuma? ¿Cómo va?"* she asked the white-haired black man who suffered from rheumatism. She knew all the vendors by name, knew their ailments, and knew how many kids they had. *"¿Cuánto?"* she'd ask pointing to the item that caught her eye. It was never cheap enough. *"Por Dios, chico. Tú crees que es pa' la señora, verda'? No chico, es pa' mí y pa' Manolo. ¿En cuanto me lo das?"* She claimed whatever she wanted to buy was for her and her husband's dinner that night, not for us who didn't need to save a penny here, a penny there. Did she convince the vendors? I'll never know, but she sure could stretch a peso. It thrilled me watch her charades. My mother would never lie like that in front of me.

"No se le va una," Mami said after the phone call. Belén didn't miss a beat. And I had to control myself because she didn't know the half of it.

Belén stayed in touch with Loren and with us. Whenever the prisoners were allowed visitors Loren could count on seeing Belén and his godmother Marita, Mami's closest friend. Belén would drop us a few lines, telling us how she found Loren. Lilo, Papi's Fidelista brother, never visited, so we guessed he was still a hardcore *comunista*. I can only imagine Lilo's elation when, on December 2, 1961 Fidel proclaimed he was a Marxist-

Leninist. Cuba was now officially the first communist country in the hemisphere, an ally of the Soviet Union at the height of the Cold War.

The United States trade embargo had only succeeded in prolonging the left-wing's romantic notion that Fidel was a modern-day David ready to take on Goliath. Herbert Mathews, a New York Times reporter and columnist was (in my opinion) in no small measure responsible for this romance. When he first interviewed Fidel in the Sierra Maestra Mountains in 1957, he compared him to Robin Hood and he hadn't changed his mind since. My father, who was a fan of William Buckley, not solely because he was a right-winger but also because he deemed Buckley's diction and command of the English language "unparalleled," was ecstatic when *The National Review* mocked *The New York Times* left-of-center stance with a picture of Castro over the caption "I got my job through *The New York Times*," the tagline of Times billboard ads. It was practically impossible to take the subway without seeing the poster.

On March 29, 1962 mass trials started for the 1,189 men captured when the invasion floundered. A few members of the brigade faced *el paredón*, supposedly for committing crimes under Batista's regime. The remaining *brigadistas,* or as the government called them *gusanos,* lowly worms, were subjected to a televised trial, a long ritual of humiliation in which they were lectured on their crimes as mercenaries and terrorists. In keeping with their *gusano* status, the prisoners wore brand-new yellow t-shirts. When American newspapers carried photographs of the trials, we scrutinized every news picture hoping to find Loren's face, but they were too inky and smudgy to be of any help. Papi kept saying, "Nothing will happen to them. The eyes of the world are fixed on Cuba."

Still frail, not fully recovered from surgery, my mother said in a voice so weak it was hard to hear, "*No hay peor ciego que el que no quiere ver*". There are none so blind as those who will not see.

"I'm the only realist here," Papi said. In all those years of marriage he never came close to realizing how his persistent glass-half-full attitude irked my mother.

"Someone has got to face the fact that Loren will be tried for treason by *una partida de comunistas,*" by a bunch of communists, my mother said, sounding fatigued by now. She was right. But even Mami didn't expect the thirty-year sentence. When she learned of it her eyes filled with tears and I think I heard her say, "I'll never see him again."

"They won't serve their term," Papi said.

My yearbook senior picture.

With my brother Loren after Easter mass 1963.

Chapter Fifteen

I suspect Latin-American Institute's relative proximity to Port Authority's Bus Terminal played a part in my parents' decision to send me there. I'll never know. Come Fall I started commuting to New York five days a week. Whatever disenchantment I'd felt about not being allowed to go to college vanished in the face of Manhattan's extraordinary vitality.

Monday through Friday I'd walk across 42nd Street, past the sleazy area with the crotch-less panties, always recalling my first embarrassing jaunt here with Mami, past Times Square and its news ticker, past Bryant's Park, right behind the formidable New York City Library. Bryant Park was a sewer back then. Derelicts camped out on the park's cold stone benches, winos drank cheap Thunderbird out of paper bags while junkies with the heebie-jeebies waited for their next fix. Despite my young age I can't recall being offended by New York City's seediness, by its in-your-face rawness. Quite the contrary, each morning when I got off the bus at the terminal I felt liberated. Manhattan always seems to have room for one more outsider, one more accent, one more story, one more dream, and one more drama. In New York City I liked the way I sounded, liked being a Cuban exile with a story to tell. "I'm Cuban," I'd say when asked and then people would want to hear my take on the revolution or something else of consequence. Not once was I asked why my ears were pierced. My business-school classmates were mostly Latin Americans or as we say today, Latinas, with some of them favoring Castro's revolution. Every day I dreaded returning to sleepy-time Ridgefield Park. Often I'd try to stretch my time in the city. I'd stop at Grand Central station and sit on the long dark wooden benches in the waiting room, cigarette in hand, wondering about the lives of the elegant men and women who rushed past me on their way home to Connecticut. Smoking was just one of the things I could flagrantly do in Manhattan but not in New Jersey.

"Sorry, I missed the bus," I'd say when I got home.

The ease with which I made friends astonished me. Practically every day I lunched with two Venezuelan girls, Rebeca and Sally. They lived at the YWCA and were counting the days until they landed a job and got their own apartment in Manhattan. Sally, of Danish ancestry, was tall, long-limbed and freckled. She spoke Spanish with an accent. Rebeca, her petite counterpart, had a delicate beauty, like a porcelain doll. Because of her daintiness and charm I failed to notice how opinionated she was.

Around the time we becoming friends the greatest nuclear confrontation of the twentieth century erupted: the Cuban Missile Crisis. On October 15, 1962 a U-2 spy plane secretly photographed nuclear missile sites being built by the Soviets in Cuba. In a televised address on October 22nd President Kennedy announced the discovery of missiles on Cuban soil and his intention to implement an offensive weapons quarantine against Cuba. It would prevent all ships carrying military arms, from any country from delivering those weapons to Cuba, creating a naval blockade of the island. American military forces were on high alert and they had readied missiles to launch. Twenty SAC bombers were airborne, equipped with nuclear bombs. For thirteen days, the world stood at the brink of nuclear war. All because of Cuba, that little pleasure-loving, pleasure-giving sugarcane island that Americans could not stay away from. Cuba, rapturously intoxicating, home of Bacardí rum, mojitos daiquiris; the birthplace of *el danzón, la rumba, el son, el mambo, el bolero, el cha-cha-cha*. That Cuba. The United States' naval blockade forced the Soviet freighters bound for Cuba to stop on the high seas. The freighters stopped but did not turn around.

The world held its breath. The freighters carried missiles and supplies destined for bases that the Soviet Union had constructed in secrecy following the Bay of Pigs Invasion.

"Cuba is not worth a nuclear war," Rebeca said nonchalantly over lunch at a Madison Avenue coffee shop. Of the three of us she was the only one who read the *New York Times*. I can still recall how insignificant I felt. In my exiled world, Cuba was *"el ombligo del mundo"* the world's belly button, so it shocked me to learn how dismissive others could be. I kept thinking every day, Belén and Loren are still in Cuba. During the first week of the crisis I could hardly sleep. At home, the crisis was a constant topic. As the days passed, we increasingly worried the crisis might trigger a nuclear war.

Before the October Crisis, everything had pointed to the Bay of Pigs prisoners' imminent release. A new committee, laboriously named The Cuban Families Committee for the Liberation of the Bay of Pigs Prisoners of War, hired a highly experienced New York lawyer to represent the prisoners: James B. Donovan. Donovan had succeeded in exchanging Soviet spy Rudolf Abel for the release of U-2 pilot Frances Gary Powers from a Soviet prison. They shot Powers' spy plane down over Russia in May 1960 by Soviet missiles. An able negotiator, Donovan quickly proposed an exchange of prisoners for food and medicine. JFK's brother, Attorney General Bobby Kennedy, joined in the effort, soliciting contributions from the American Pharmaceutical Association.

After twenty months of negotiations Castro released most of the prisoners on December 24, 1962 in exchange for $53 million in food and medicine supplies corporations all over the country had donated.

Loren landed at Florida's Opa Locka Airport on Christmas Eve, Nochebuena. They took him and his fellow brigadistas in buses to the Dinner Key Auditorium in Coconut Grove, Miami, where a rapturous crowd of thousands of Cuban exiles awaited them. Not one of us was there to greet him. A premature, ill-fated trip to Miami had drained all our resources. A few months prior to Loren's release, Donovan's negotiations had been moving along so swiftly that Miami-Cubans were convinced the prisoners would be liberated momentarily. Papi had two brothers in Miami, each with a son in prison, and they also believed the *brigadistas* would be back in Miami in a matter of days. Reassured by his brothers' enthusiasm, my father asked for a few days off.

"My son has been imprisoned since the Bay of Pigs fiasco," Papi told his boss at Railway Express Agency. "He'll be freed any day now and the wife and I want to bring him home."

Who with a heart would have denied him? Without further ado Papi decided we should leave for Miami as soon as possible.

"Puchita, you're doing fine at school, so missing a few days won't hurt you," my mother told me after my father returned from work. I knew there was no way she would leave me home alone. It was a relief to miss school, so it delighted me to tag along. The three of us took off in a used, light-green Rambler sedan that Papi had just bought. It was a grueling trip, and I suspect our individual determination not to mention Loren's arrival (fearing we'd jinx it) considerably lengthened it. The few times we mentioned Loren's release, for it was impossible not to do so, we'd preface it with *"Si con el favor de Dios Loren regresa."* If, God willing, Loren returns.

Miami was still Nostalgia Central, only more so. A surreal *cubanismo* enveloped its southwest quarter. The store windows of *La Calle Ocho*—an area that came to be known as la sagüesera (Cubans pronounced southwest as sagües)—epitomized the past: characteristic Cuban rocking chairs, statues of the bona fide Cuban saints Santa Bárbara and San Lázaro, first-communion and *quinceañera* dresses, *guayaberas, santería* amulets, 22K gold chains you could tie a cow with. You name it, *La Calle Ocho* had it. *Las mismas cosas,* same things, different place I thought as I noticed the sign of a family-owned funeral parlor where I had attended my first wake back in Havana. I had no problems revisiting the past. The way I remembered it, my life in Cuba was paradisiacal. I later learned this is typical of exiles: we all left behind paradise.

"Qué lástima que no nos pudimos quedar aquí." I told my parents. *"Es cómo estar en Cuba."* A pity we couldn't have stayed here. It's like being in Cuba.

Years later, when the opportunity to move to Miami presented itself, I did everything I could to avoid living there.

We ended up renting an efficiency apartment in a modest motel just a few blocks away from *el apartamentico* where we'd lived when we first arrived from Cuba and waited. Then waited some more. Our hasty trip ended up being a waste of time, money, and effort. No one knew when the prisoners would be released. Not one person had any way of knowing the

Castro brothers would demand another $2.9 million at the last minute, leaving everyone scrambling to find more cash. When we ran out of money and Papi ran out of vacation days, we headed back to New Jersey, dispirited and empty-handed. To this day I recall the heartbreaking silence of our return trip; grief sealed our lips. We might as well have driven a hearse on our way back, so charged was the air with unspoken recriminations and undisguised heartaches. I know it doesn't seem like a big deal these many years later, but back then we felt the least we owed Loren was our presence. We knew he'd be looking for us in the crowd, knew how brokenhearted he'd be when we were nowhere to be found.

It was Christmas Day, and my parents and I moved about uneasily amidst the smoky hustle and bustle at La Guardia Airport. We'd been waiting for this moment for so long we still couldn't believe Loren was returning. I'd have given up my winter coat for a cigarette, but I still couldn't smoke in my parents' presence, even though my mother knew I smoked. "Puchita you might as well save all the money you spend on gum," she'd told me one afternoon when I'd returned from school, "I know you smoke." Still, it was a matter of respect back then. I thought hard about going to the ladies' room and having a smoke there, but bore in mind Miami could smell a cigarette lit in another floor. I stayed put.

"Mami," I asked, twisting my hair by the gate, "does Loren know we went to Miami to wait for him?"

"How could he, Puchita?" She wasn't being

insensitive; it had always been her habit to remind me I was quite capable of putting two and two together. Much later in life I'd be that kind of teacher: "How can buffalos live in the forest? Wouldn't they be banging their heads against trees all the time?"

I was getting back my two brothers that day. Good thing too; I didn't like being the only one around, the sole focus of attention. Fello was due to arrive first, so his whole family would greet Loren. On the way to La Guardia we'd speculated on how Loren might look after twenty months in prison. "*Flaco,*" I said. Skinny. Such a limited imagination....

Now I could see him behind the glass partition. It wasn't his being skinny I focused on; it was his pallor. "*Luce amarillo,*" I said the moment I set eyes on him. He looks yellow.

"*Ictericia,*" said the doctor. Jaundice.

Loren's weight loss made his prominent jaw—*la quijada* Nodarse—jut out like an anvil. His smile was different, toothier. But it was his sallowness that got to me. I was used to seeing him deeply tanned or at least olive-skinned. Flashing his piano-keyboard smile, Papi gave his son a big hug and Mami couldn't stop kissing him, "*Ay Lorencito, que felicidad verte, mi cielo.*" My mother liked to call her children *mi cielo,* my heaven. Fello shook Loren's hand and said something like "It's good to see you." None of us knew how to account for his British phlegm.

On the way home Loren just stared out of the window. I

don't remember his saying much although I recall hearing several *"Gracias a Dios"* on the way back to Ridgefield Park. He later told us that on the flight to Florida the prisoners had been briefed about what to say and what not to say when they landed. Specifically, they were told not to mention the US failure to provide air support. I'm sure the directive didn't extend to their communications with their immediate families, but a few prisoners were still in Castro's jails, and those freed didn't want to jeopardize their release.

"We were so worried when your name didn't appear on any list," said Mami.

"I was in hiding," Loren said, and that was pretty much it. I'd hoped to hear more. I'd grown up watching WWII movies and wanted to know where he'd hidden, for how long, how he'd kept himself alive, how close the enemy was, and whether they had caught him or had, God forbid, surrendered. I was left wanting. Years later I learned Loren had sailed from Guatemala on the Houston, a commercial freighter chartered by the CIA to transport the brigade's 2nd and 5th battalions. Aside from being unremittingly attacked by Castro's rockets, the captain of the Houston got his stricken vessel to a sandbar close to shore, giving the men on board a reasonable chance of escape.

We celebrated Nochebuena a day later as if we were in Cuba. We wolfed down white rice, black beans, *yuca con mojito*, *lechón (*pork drenched in garlic), green and ripe plantains. Mami kept asking Loren, *"¿Más? ¿Un poquito más?"* But Loren would just shake his head. I wanted him to pick on me, or pick on Fello, like he always did, but he didn't. He looked sad, and I wondered when he'd be the old Loren again.

"What did they feed you, Loren?" Mami asked.

"When the negotiations started, boiled macaroni. I'll never eat macaroni again."

"And before the negotiations?"

"You don't want to know," Loren said.

"*Loren cuéntame de Belén.*" I said. Tell me about Belén. I couldn't wait any longer.

"She came to see me whenever she could. She was incredible."

"We know that, but how is she?"

"You know Belén, she always looks the same. She doesn't age."

"But I mean, did she ask about me?"

"What do you think?" My mother's son. I wanted to know much more but knew he was tired and I should let him be. I was jealous he got to see Belén. I wasn't about to complain about anything that night. We all felt blessed Loren was home again. Later that evening he asked my mother, "Did you get the money?" And for what seemed like forever, a crushing silence hung in the air.

"We had to use most of it, Loren. I'm sorry."

"*No importa,*" Loren said. I don't care what he said; his face told me how disappointed he was. Then, as if in an afterthought, he added, "That's what it was for. *Para la familia.*" Did my secretarial school money come out of Loren's allowance? Probably. Was it used to help Fello? Certainly. Poor Loren. Later that evening Loren looked me up and down and said, "You back to normal."

"Meaning?" I asked.

"You're not fat anymore."
As good as a compliment.

On December 29, 1962 my parents and I huddled on the brown sofa in front of the TV while Loren sat in one of the sorry Household Finance turquoise chairs. Veterans of the Bay of Pigs Invasion filled the Orange Bowl stadium in Florida.

Before a crowd of roughly forty thousand Cubans, President Kennedy and Jackie honored the members of Brigade 2506. A chic, radiant Jackie, in a stylish two-piece sleeveless outfit, stepped up to the microphone. Leaving behind the whispery, baby-girl voice we all knew so well, she spoke to the crowd in Castilian Spanish: "I feel proud that my son has known these officers." Cuban mothers wept. "It is my wish and my hope that someday my son may be a man at least half as brave as the members of Brigade 2506." Kennedy accepted the brigade's battle flag, smuggled out of Cuba by one of its members, and told the released prisoners, "I can assure you this flag will be returned to this brigade in a free Havana. The strongest wish of the people of this country is that Cuba shall one day be free again."

Loren looked at the TV screen and said, *"Hipócrita."*

We knew Loren and his fellow prisoners had been greeted by a euphoric crowd of thousands of Cuban exiles at the Dinner Key Auditorium on the outskirts of Miami. We didn't know *La Linda* Lilia Maria had been there, spotted him, and shouted his name repeatedly until he'd caught her eye. Shapely, stately, seductive Lilia Maria had dated my brother in Havana, but they'd lost touch after she left Cuba with her family. I don't know whether Lilia Maria was there for Loren's homecoming or for the many former prisoners she and her family knew from Havana. It's amazing she spotted Loren among thousands of people. Loren had kept the encounter to himself, its only evidence being the unfailingly lengthy nocturnal letters he wrote upon his return.

"I want to spend time in Miami before looking for a job," he announced one evening.

"¿Tan pronto?" my mother asked. So soon?

"La brigada is having a reunion."

He wasn't gone long, maybe a week or so. When he returned I saw, standing at the front door next to him a tall, slender, dark-haired guy. "Puchita," Loren said, *"Este es mi amigo Panchito. Él estuvo conmigo en la invasión."* For a fellow *brigadista*, Panchito was none the worse for wear. I shook his hand and said *"Encantada."* We checked each other out.

"So you're visiting?" I asked.

"Visiting Miami. I live in Newark."

It didn't speak well of him that he lived in Newark but for once I kept my mouth shut. He was in his early twenties and like Loren was trying to figure out what to do next with his life. I didn't ask him when he left Cuba, but I knew it had to be early; otherwise he wouldn't have been able to join in the invasion. I found him virile. While my previous boyfriend, for all his intellect and bonhomie, had the physique of a reader, Panchito, over six feet tall, with a bushy chest, panoramic shoulders, and a silo for a neck, exuded testosterone. As we chatted I learned that like most Cuban males he was into sports and politics. Big time. Neither remotely interested me, but I couldn't have cared less, such was the sexual pull.

La Linda Lilia Maria and Loren married on May 23, 1964. The Coral Gables ceremony took me back to weddings I'd attended in Havana. Friends from El Vedado Tennis, aunts, uncles, cousins, and fellow *brigadistas* peopled the church. Ileana and Margarita,, schoolmates both, were there, their friendship warming my heart like the Floridian sun. Living up north, I'd forgotten how much Cuban women love to get all spiffed up, how they dress to the nines and show off their hourglass figures. Such things had continued to matter in Miami as much as they had mattered in Havana. Since I was a kid I kept hearing people say, "*Hay que dar una buena impresión*," meaning you have to make an impression. Paying notice to the women with their coiffed hair, high heels, and stockings, I felt as if I'd never left Havana. The bride herself could have made the cover of *Vanidades* in her formal wedding dress, a trailing white satin gown that cinched her movie-star waist. My parents' fleeting radiance reminded me how the pursuit of happiness had been but a roller coaster ride for them.

I sat at the outdoor wedding reception, checking people out. I was surrounded by Cubans who, having left so much behind, now belonged to Miami's burgeoning middle class. The bride's family was faring better than most. In Cuba, Lilia Maria's father had worked as a chief engineer for a top American oil company, but that's not where the money came from. If I remember correctly both her parents came from old money. Lilia Maria had gone to the best Catholic girls' school in Cuba and had attended *El Country*, a golf country club in the outskirts of Havana. Mami, sitting at the head of the table, was engaged in an animated conversation with Lilia Maria's mother. This was the perfect moment. Good manners would prevent my mother from saying anything. I searched my handbag for a pack of Salems, took out a cigarette, lit it, and inhaled deeply. She shot me a look that said it all. I ignored it and finished my cigarette.

Panchito and I had decided to vacation a few days in Miami. I stayed with Ileana and he got a cheap room at a nearby motel. During our brief trip his *cubanismo* reemerged as speedily as he drove his rented red convertible, top down, stopping here for a *cafecito*, there to see a friend or two. Even a fool could tell he longed to be part of *la comunidad*, part of *Brigada 2506*, part of the *cubaneo*. I couldn't kid myself, this was his turf. My gut told me that one way or another he'd end up living in Miami; that he'd return to his tribe, and it scared me. All around me Cubans kept repeating the exiles' refrain, "next year in Cuba," while digging deeper into Florida's terrain. I couldn't see how this place could ever feel like home; something in me rejected the notion that Miami could replace Havana. Or perhaps something in me realized the past wasn't what it used to be.

Loren's marriage brought our family together again. Conveniently, our landlords decided to spend a year in Portugal. Loren and his bride moved into their upstairs apartment and he found a job at Newark airport. Fello, having recently finished medical school in Mexico, was an intern at Middlesex General Hospital in New Brunswick. He, his wife, and their first baby lived in the hospital's residential quarters, roughly fifty minutes away from us. And most importantly for me—Panchito still lived nearby in Newark, so it worked for everybody. On Sundays we always got together. Holidays, birthdays, and anniversaries were family affairs just like they'd been back in Cuba.

Panchito and I fought like bulldogs. He wanted to control me and I wouldn't let him. I should wear a girdle; I could have no male friends because "There's no such thing as a friendship between a man and a woman." I had to call him during my lunch hour and if I didn't go straight home after work I was to report to him beforehand. He had to know where I was, with whom, and what I was doing at any given time. On my birthday he forbade me to lunch with my boss, but I went anyway and a fight ensued. We had a terrible row when he demanded I call a guy I once had a crush on (when I was fourteen!) and ask him to return the photographs I'd sent him. I remember saying, "Panchito, I didn't even know you then."

"It doesn't matter. I don't want any man carrying your picture around."

Who said he carried them around? He'd probably thrown them away or, at best, they were lying in the bottom of a drawer, all but forgotten. *Cursi,* that's what it was. Tacky. Although humiliated, I asked the guy (who I'd stopped liking ages and ages ago) to return my picture and to this day I can't believe I could have been such a jerk. I felt like I had a dog collar around my neck with Panchito grasping a two-foot leash.

Our incompatibilities aside, I was determined to marry Panchito. Like all well-brought-up Latin-American girls of my generation I'd been programmed to marry and procreate, in that order. Certain that marriage and family would give meaning to my existence, I clung to Panchito for dear life. Forget we wanted different things: I wanted a life in the city, he a life in the suburbs; I worldliness, he domesticity; I independence, he control. Once we got married, we could work it all out.

I got a call from my childhood friend Gema, still in Florida, asking me to be her bridesmaid. I was happy for her but the wedding announcement was like a slap in the face. Panchito and I had been dating forever, and I didn't even have an engagement ring. I hadn't heard about this guy Gema was marrying, so how long could they have been dating? Gema told me she was having her wedding in Queens to make it easy for her grandparents and the rest of the family to attend.

For the wedding I wore a long, light blue gown with satin shoes to match. Gema's first cousin, Angela, another bridesmaid, wore the same color. Gema married at an indistinct Catholic church in Queens and during the ceremony I kept looking at her and Bruce, trying to decide who was prettier, the groom or the bride. My closet friend was marrying a movie-star-handsome American—blond hair, blue eyes, the whole nine yards. Their wedding prompted me to nag Panchito about our wedding. Eventually I got an engagement ring, but no date was set.

As a young lady, every young man who visited me liked nothing better than to watch televised sports with my father. Panchito was no exception. Papi was a living sports encyclopedia: he knew batting averages by heart; could tell you who broke what record and when; was familiar with that entire hall-of-fame memorabilia; had championship dates on the tip of his tongue. Loren and Lilia Maria would spend Sundays with us. Women gathered around the kitchen table and chatted while my mother cooked. Men gathered in the living room and shouted, jumped off their seats, yelled at the TV sportscasters. Was this my future? Weren't there better ways of spending Sunday afternoons? In fairness I must admit that Panchito would, occasionally, take me to some park in New Jersey (I remember his taking me to Palisades Amusement Park) or in New York (Central Park). But as far as I was concerned these outings were too few and far between. As I write this, I wonder whether our frequent quarrels didn't result from boredom. After all, we were going on three years, and still no wedding date.

Mami greatly enjoyed our Sunday gatherings. It gave her an excuse to cook a special dish. In the vein of people who like to cook, she insisted that it was just as much work to cook for four as it was for six. So everyone usually stayed for dinner. During those evenings it felt good to have a family, to break bread together, to eat *ropa vieja* or *arroz con pollo* or *carne mechada* and be transported to a happier time, even if the conversation always centered on Castro, who my father unfailingly referred to as *El Monstruo*. After dinner we would drag some of our kitchen chairs to the living room so we could all sit and watch *The Ed Sullivan Show* on our little black-and-white television. Every Sunday my father felt compelled to criticize Ed Sullivan's appearance.

"Have you ever seen anybody so graceless?" Or, "If he feels so ill at ease in front of the cameras, why not give the job to someone else?" *Criticones.*

One Sunday, on February 9, 1964, we were all gathered in front of the TV when Ed Sullivan introduced The Beatles. It was their first trip to America. My father took one look at them and told my mother, with that disdain that makes words slip out the corner of a down-turned mouth, *"¡Qué partida de peludos!"* What a hairy bunch! My parents couldn't believe anyone would have the nerve (Hemingway would have said *"cojones"*) to show up on the Ed Sullivan Show looking like that. It was a gut reaction; they saw in The Beatles the same affront displayed by the *barbudos* in Cuba.

When Manolo and Berta returned from their year in Portugal, Loren move his family to Newark. It was closer to his job, and he needed a larger space for his growing family, *La Linda* Lilia Maria having given birth to a daughter. They found an apartment they liked at an affordable luxury high-rise complex called the Colonnade Apartments, designed by world-famous architect Mies van der Rohe. My parents thought it looked like a good location, and since Mami was intent on helping Loren and Lilia Maria by caring for their daughter, we all ended up moving to the same complex, although in different buildings. The Colonnade comprised four buildings, all with a curtain wall facade, the technique he used in which glass is hung on a steel frame. The interior of the building where we lived had been sectioned into two separate entities, each with a lobby furnished with four of the architect's signature Barcelona chairs. The complex offered door-to-door service to Manhattan's Port Authority Bus Terminal. Large buses arrived every thirty minutes during the morning and evening rush hour. Papi and I took the bus to work, but at different times. Every morning the same people waited for the bus, people who, like most New Yorkers, weren't overly friendly. One morning, not long after moving in, I noticed a new ruggedly handsome face in the group, and my life was never the same again.

Chapter Sixteen

When I saw him eyeing the seat next to me, my first thought was, do I really want to be next to him?

"May I?" asked the handsome disheveled stranger, pointing to the vacant seat.

"Of course," I replied, after quickly reminding myself to be courteous to all forms of life.

It was 7:30 in the morning, and he reeked of alcohol. As if reading my mind, he said, unapologetically and with unparalleled charm, "Some people have orange juice for breakfast; I prefer sherry." I should have known then he was a smooth-talking rake, but I found his unorthodoxy appealing. "Bernard Cooper," he said, offering his hand. "I usually take the earlier bus, but I guess I got lucky today." He spoke softly, but with certainty, in an inviting, literate fashion.

"Nice meeting you. Maria Nodarse," I said, shaking his

hand. "I take this bus every day."

"Do I detect an accent?" he asked as he draped his trench coat over his arm. It must have been the way I pronounced "Nodarse."

"I'm Cuban," I said, with hauteur.

"You left after Castro?"

"A year and a half later," I replied.

I could tell he was about to ask something else about my leaving Cuba, but stopped himself. I bet he was thinking my family was reactionary, or against the revolution.

He changed the subject instead.

"Which building do you live in?"

I pointed to it. "What about you?"

"I live in the other building."

I looked into his half-lidded green eyes and found a touch of Robert Mitchum in him.

"I'm a photographer. These days I spend my time inside a developing room. It's very lonely. It's just me and my cat."

"They let you keep a cat at work?"

"I wish; I meant at home."

"I love cats, what kind you have?" I asked. And so it went.

I sensed there was something dodgy about him and blurted out, "I'm engaged."

"I never look at rings," he said. His weathered skin and weary eyes contrasted with his lithe and sinewy body. As he talked, he kept sweeping his salt-and-pepper hair away from his eyes. I'd always wanted a mane of hair like his—straight, thick, and copious. Letting my eyes glance over his hands, no rings were evident, but I noticed he bit his nails, cannibalized them.

He was there the following morning and the morning after that and I flirted with the idea of being a smart ass and saying something like "Has your schedule been changed?" but decided against it. He was a welcome diversion.

I looked forward to his company; he livened up my morning commute. I had no intentions of dating him, had not told a soul about his existence, and had not entertained the possibility of his meeting anyone I knew; that would have embarrassed me. He was not the kind of guy you brought home to meet the folks, but I so delighted in his conversation. Besides, I wasn't about to change my schedule to avoid him. Things may not have gone any farther hadn't it been for the crippling transit strike of January '66. On the first day of the strike he asked me, "Where do you work?"

"Rockefeller Center."

"I work off Madison Avenue. Walk with me crosstown."

Twelve days later, when the strike ended, I had it bad. I'd convinced myself a romance was out of the question since I was engaged—although we'd set no wedding date. But the ring hadn't felt right for a while; we spent too much time at each other's throat. Now I'd met someone who enthralled me and I wasn't about to let him slip through my fingers. My traditional upbringing didn't allow me to have dinner with another man while I was engaged so I felt I had no choice but to tell Panchito I wanted to go out with someone else. After what felt like forever he said, "So does that mean you want to break off the engagement. Is that it?"

"I guess so."

"If there's one thing I've been proud of," he said "it was my certainty you were always faithful."

"But, Panchito, I've always been faithful to you. I met someone else but I haven't even gone out with him."

"Then don't."

"I have to. I owe it to myself. All we do is fight Panchito. We don't really belong together."

He wouldn't hear of it. The next morning I found him waiting for me at the bus stop. Bernard was already there, and I wanted to die. There was nowhere to hide. Please, Bernard, don't say hello, don't come over. I hadn't yet realized how slick Bernard was. He climbed up into the bus like he didn't even know me.

Panchito didn't want the ring back, but I insisted. Now I was free to dine with Bernard. We ate at a West Village restaurant with a European flair, bright walls and colorful oil paintings, the waiters' waists draped in white cloth. Bernard helped me with my coat, ordered a dry, straight-up Beefeater martini for himself and a Harvey's Bristol Cream sherry for me. When I was about to light a cigarette, he took it out of my mouth and put it into his, lit it, exhaled slowly and deliberately, and finally returned it. Out of a Bogart movie.

"I recommend the sweetbreads," he said, and I acquiesced without having a clue what sweetbreads were.

"The lady will have the sweetbreads," he told the waiter, "and I will have the rack of lamb." He ordered a bottle of red wine and chose my dessert: "The lady will have the Peach Melba and we'd like two Courvoisier, please." He didn't miss a beat—made sure he got me home early, walked me to the door, thanked me for a delightful evening, and didn't even try to kiss me. When my mother opened the door, I could tell she didn't like what she saw, but that night she didn't say a thing.

It wasn't long before I learned Bernard liked to frequent several West Village restaurants, all with first-rate cuisine, all with a separate bar, all with bartenders who knew what he drank. His favorite watering hole was Ernie's, where he'd go straight to the jukebox and play Billy Holiday's "Yesterday." He repeated the line, "days I knew as happy, sweet sequestered days."

"Who uses words like 'sequestered' now?" he'd ask. He also played Dinah Washington's "What a Difference a Day Makes," and when he heard the line, "find romance on your menu," he'd say, "Poets, that's what they were back then."

I didn't stand a chance. I'd thought these rogues only existed in the movies.

Chapter Seventeen

Loren himself told me the story. He was about to line up for the bus when he realized he'd forgotten my birthday, dashed to the Port Authority bookstore, and grabbed a copy of what he thought was *Madame Curie*, except it was *Madame Bovary*. I doubt I'd have found Madame Curie's scientific endeavors as compelling as Emma's adulterous escapades. *Madame Bovary* made a reader out of me. As a child my poor mother had read to me nightly. She'd always included books among my Christmas presents. She had read aloud passages of *Anna Karenina*, *The Brothers Karamazov*, short stories by Bonin, all while I sat across from her on the porch—all to no avail. Adultery, that's what did it, and I'd have been content to keep on reading about disgraced heroines had it not been for Bernard's reading assignments: Wiley's *Generation of*

Vipers, Ellison's *Invisible Man*, Wells' *1984*, Mailer's *Advertisements for Myself*, London's *Martín Eden*. When it came to movies, Bernard made sure—although I had spent my youthful Sundays in Cuba watching matinees with my mother—that I got an exemplary cinematic education. Actually, according to Bernard, we saw films, not movies. At the time the Village was peppered with art houses showcasing a particular director's work. Bernard introduced me to Bergman, Fellini, Antonioni, Truffaut, and Buñuel. "It's important to think of movies as a continuum," he said, "as part of a director's output." Today I could say, *"Oeuvre*, Bernard, a director's oeuvre."* I enjoyed being introduced to the multitude of things that Bernard knew from experience and he undoubtedly enjoyed showing me these things. In truth, I've always liked learning more than knowing; it's the newness that turns me on.

My parents couldn't grasp my keenness for this boozy scoundrel laboring to remake me. What did I find so attractive about a disheveled man eighteen years my senior? So what if he was tall and had a good body (men had bodies, women had figures) when he looked shabby and reeked of liquor? And while my parents merely opposed him, Loren loathed him. One night when my folks were out, Loren let himself into the apartment with the spare key they had given him, maybe hoping to catch us in *flagrante delicto*. He found us sitting beside each other on the couch watching TV.

For some reason Bernard was still wearing his rumpled trench coat and Loren treat him like a flasher, shouting, "Get out! Get out!"

Loren wanted a fight—ever since he came out of prison he was a breathing Molotov cocktail—but Bernard was too wily to indulge him and headed for the door saying, "Goodnight. See you tomorrow." Such a voice he had.

I yelled at Loren, "Mind your own goddamn business," and followed Bernard. I didn't want to stay under the same roof with Loren and I slammed the door on my way out.

The clues were all there: at times Bernard stood me up or was incredibly late; he would only give me his office number because he claimed his home phone had been disconnected due to billing mistakes; he reeked of alcohol at all hours; he looked like hell warmed over. But the more my family attacked Bernard, the more I loved him. They were wrong about one thing: Bernard hadn't seduced me. While every Saturday night Panchito and I had made out in the back seat of his car at the local drive-in movie, Bernard, sixteen years Panchito's senior, had yet to make a move. I couldn't make sense of it. Was there something wrong with me? With him? A month or so into our courtship I finally seduced him. At the beginning we'd rendezvous at his friend Bob's apartment. I thought if we made love in his apartment, I wouldn't feel quite so tawdry, but Bernard claimed it would be too risky, someone from my family might see us coming and going.

Chapter Eighteen

Despite all efforts, my family failed to acclimate to *El Norte's* short drab days and long dreary winters. Accustomed to being outdoors in the luminous tropical sun—at the country club, walking the old streets of downtown Havana, or lounging on our front porch—being cooped up inside an apartment five months out the year drew out the worst in all of us. Those hermetic winter days turned our dispositions as gray as the sky above us. We sounded like the dispirited characters of a Dostoyevsky novel. Also, because *El Frío* numbed Mami's hands and feet to a debilitating degree, she was forced to rely on my father (the only one who could drive) to get everything she needed from the outside world. Dependency had never suited her and they argued constantly. All too many times my penny-pinching father returned from the grocery with cheaper products than my mother had asked for. "I specifically wrote Hunts," my mother would snap. Then, while cooking, she'd call him to the kitchen and pick up the cheap can of, say, tomato sauce, hold it over the top of the pot and say, *"¿Ésto? Ésto es agua."* This? This is water. All this because of *El Frío*, all this because we lived in *El Norte,* when we should have been living in Havana or Miami, roasting under a flaming sun.

Papi suffered the most during those slate-colored months that wrapped us all in gloom. Before the promise of spring, he would succumb to another nervous breakdown. I wished he'd show more spunk: stand on his feet, be the family breadwinner once more. I knew starting life anew in his late forties in a foreign land was tough, but that didn't prevent me from comparing him to other exiles, successful in their new lives. And it wasn't like I was comparing him to outrageously successful Cubans like the by now proverbial Desi Arnaz or the once-and-future president of Coca-Cola. No, I was comparing him to the average Cuban, able to start a small business, able to get a good job, able to buy a decent house and get ahead. Look at Pepe, his former doubles partner, now tennis pro at some fancy hotel in Hollywood Beach. Papi had taught tennis at a New Jersey country club one summer. But having been honored to play in the Davis Cup tennis championship in 1933 he never entertained the idea of earning his living playing tennis. Maybe getting paid to play a sport he so loved was something akin to prostitution. Didn't bother Pepe though, who besides whatever he got paid for his lessons profited from a sports store he had the sagacity to open on the hotel premises. And look at Gema's grandfather, an old man, writing away for a Spanish-language newspaper in New York. I could go on.

My father was intelligent, handsome, socially adept, charismatic, fluent in English, and a lawyer to boot, so why couldn't he make it in this country of immigrants? I'm not completely heartless, I hated feeling like a cold and an unsympathetic daughter but I couldn't help myself. Every day I heard stories of medicine making great advances; didn't they have a pill that could make Papi whole again? I'm sure that if my father's *enfermedad de los nervios*, his illness of the nerves, had had a physical manifestation, I would have been a kinder judge.

By late winter they had promoted Papi. He no longer had to work at the warehouse; he was now an office clerk at Railway Express Agency's headquarters. The promotion meant the world to him because it made him a white-collar worker once again, which he considered his birthright. Across the street from the building, on the southwest corner of 42nd Street and Third Avenue, there was a Horn & Hardart Automat. Any devotee of old Hollywood movies knows what they looked like. They displayed ready-to-eat foods behind small glass doors with chrome-plated knobs, walls of them. The doors popped open after you deposited the correct number of coins in the slot. You needed exact change, which you could get from the cashier counter in the center of the room. While I was in secretarial school, I made a habit of meeting Papi for lunch at the Automat once a week. I loved that place, loved to stand in front of the glass doors and watch food servings automatically materialize once the cube was empty. Bit by bit I was learning to be a New Yorker. I always got there first, grabbed a table and gazed about, taking in everything and everybody. What better place for people watching than New York City? It was all novel, even the revolving doors.

I spotted Papi coming out of the revolving door and was struck by how handsome he looked in business clothes. He liked to dress professionally even if he was a typist. Papi pulled up a chair and immediately announced, "they have just offered me a job as a sales representative." I can see his smile today. It was like hearing music from an ice cream wagon.

To prepare for his promotion, Papi brought home a thick binder listing REA's shipping rates across the nation. After watching the evening news he'd spread out on the ugly brown couch in our living room with the binder and notepads, reading aloud page after page of rates, to memorize them.

"Lorenzo," Mami would tell him, "no one can expect you to remember all that information; I'm sure you're just supposed to consult it." He'd ignore her and continue fixating on committing pages of rate details to memory. Later, before turning in, he'd test himself. Unable to recall the information, he'd get frustrated and grumbling to himself, rubbing his hands, getting fidgety, his agitation increasing every day until it turned to frenzy. My mother and I knew what came next.

As the only daughter, I'd become my mother's

reluctant confidante and had listened to far too many of her tales of heartbreaks and disappointments. There was nothing unusual about it, especially in Latin families with the assumption that the daughter's life would be similar to her mother's. More than once I'd heard her say my father was more interested in pleasing others than in pleasing her. And there might have been a grain of truth in her remark. I wasn't the only one wishing for a pill that could make Papi's demons go away.

Chapter Nineteen

One raw wintry night Bernard and I missed the last bus to the Colonnades. We'd been having such a good time dining with another couple, the hours had slipped by. Anne and Larry lived in a handsome post Second World War apartment building on West 23rd Street, not far from the Chelsea Hotel. Although a studio, it was a roomy apartment, with a typical American kitchen—counter space, table, chairs, the works. They were an odd couple. Larry, older than Annie, had a forceful personality and that evening he dominated the conversation with anecdotes of notable photo shootings, some of which hung on the wall along with outstanding black-and-white photographs. Had I known him better, I'd have asked for the negative of two portraits and one still life. Annie, originally from the Midwest, didn't like attracting attention. Although much younger than Larry her hair was already thinning, and she wore thick old-lady's glasses. I remember sitting there and dreaming up ways to improve her appearance. When Larry said he wanted to take pictures of me, I finally got around to looking at the clock and panicked.

By the time Bernard and I got to the Port Authority, our bus had gone. The first thought to cross my mind was how my lateness would anger my mother; she so vehemently disapproved of Bernard that it didn't take much to set her off. We waited a while and then hopped onto a bus going to downtown Newark. There was little traffic, so the ride didn't take long, but the subsequent hike to the nearest taxi stand was torture. The sidewalks were slippery, covered with ice. I cowered against a gust that pierced my coat and pricked my skin with icy needles. Even with my back turned to the wind I couldn't stop shivering. I noticed the shoveled snow had turned chewing-gum gray. No wonder I thought Newark was the pits.

"Bernard, don't you hate living in a place this cold and gray?"

"I don't like it any more than you do."

"So why live here?"

"Habit, I guess. Generations of Russian Jews must have prepared me for this."

He seemed immune to the cold—probably all that booze inside of him. I needed to get home. By Cuban standards I was scandalously late. I prayed a taxi would come *pronto*.

"*Cómo se dice* immediately?" Bernard asked.

"*Inmediatamente.*"

"We need a taxi im-me-di-a-ta-men-te. *Si?*"

"*Sí.*"

I saw something move behind some bare bushes. A black-and-white kitten. "Misu, Misu, Misu," I called.

"You calling the kitten 'Missus'? Like in 'Missus, now you stay right there and I'll bring you a cold drink.'"

"I've no idea what you're talking about. I'm calling the kitten Misu because that's how they call cats in Cuba. It's from a children's book. Never heard of Micifuz?"

"Puss'n Boots?"

"Micifuz!"

When Misu began rubbing against my boot, I took it to be an omen. "I'll keep you," I said. The poor thing was wet and didn't even try to run away. I held him inside my coat and heard him purr and purr.

Even though I opened the apartment door with the stealth of a thief, my mother heard me come in. She stood in the small hallway, her eyes tight, her lips pressed. She wasn't even going to kiss me. I put the kitten on the floor gently. I knew she had every reason to be pissed at me but I hadn't expected her to take her anger out on the kitten. "You're not keeping it," she said, sounding like The Great Dictator. "I'm not having any animals in this apartment."

Taken aback, I replied, "I pay half the rent here, and that gives me rights." I didn't know what was happening to me; I wasn't accustomed to contradicting my mother. I wanted out. Whenever I walked into the apartment, I stepped into a world that was passé, full of antiquated traditions, preposterous rules, outdated gender roles; a world of yore, out of sync with my life—the life of a modern woman living in the States in the early '60s—not of a traditional young lady living in Cuba.

"I want to get my own apartment," I said the next day during dinner.

"You do that, you might as well forget we exist because we'll have nothing to do with you," my father said. I wasn't surprised. In his culture—which had, unnoticed, stopped being mine—a woman lived at home until she married and, if she didn't marry, that's where she stayed, caring for her ageing parents. My father hadn't been allowed to marry until his older sister Leila walked down the aisle; otherwise she would have been thought of as a *solterona,* an old maid, and no man would have had her. The way I saw it, I'd lost enough already and didn't need to add my parents to the list. I knew, or thought I knew, they'd banish me forever if I moved out. Cubans are all about dignity and indignation. Getting my own apartment would have constituted an affront—*una ofensa*—to my parents' dignity. I grew up listening to people who'd say with no small amount of pride, "*Yo no le hablo.*" I don't speak to him (or her). My father would say of his older brother Lilo, an unlikely *Fidelista,* "*Yo no le hablo a comunistas.*" I don't speak to communists.

To this day I find myself trying to interpret the meaning of silence, wondering what I did to deserve it, silence being the courier of disappointment, disaffection, disloyalty, dislike. I chatter my life away, finding comfort in the sound of my own voice because the absence of words is the harbinger of doom.

For me getting my own place was an American rite of passage: it's what you do here before you get married. But I was alone on this. Fello had married after finishing his medical studies in Mexico, and Loren had arrived here knowing he'd be joining an invasion in no time and saw living with my parents as something temporary. But they were in their early twenties when they left Cuba. I was fourteen. No one seemed to realize what a difference that made. Had they all forgotten how adolescence makes you porous, turns you into a sponge, sucking up whatever comes your way?

I didn't bring up the subject again. Not with them anyway. It was hard to admit, but I wanted to tell someone about it.

"You know, Sally, the next time I might just ask for permission to get an apartment in our same building," I said over lunch a few days later.

"What good would that do you?" Sally replied very matter-of-factly.

"Well, it's like getting my freedom little by little," I said.

"It makes no sense. Besides the whole thing sounds like a guilt trip." Easy for her to say when she and Rebeca had their families in Venezuela. They could get their own apartment in the Upper East Side without insulting anyone. But Rebeca had a Puerto Rican friend called Millie, and she too had an apartment. Here again her family lived abroad.

"It's not a guilt trip, Sally." I was just getting acquainted with Manhattan's therapist's lingo. "It's tradition. It's not anything any young woman would do in Cuba."

"But you don't live in Cuba," she replied. I looked at her with that tell-me-something-I-don't-know gaze. "And Maria, I've seen plenty of those dutiful daughters in Venezuela grow old in their parental home. They never break free. You just have to do it."

Tell them that, I thought. Like the Cubans in Miami my parents had left Cuba with their traditions intact or as it was commonly referred to, "with all that luggage." In Miami I probably wouldn't have even wanted my own apartment because all my friends would still be living with their parents. But not only didn't I live in Cuba, I didn't live in Miami either. *Dale tiempo al tiempo,* give time, time. And so I did. Things remained the same: my parents' hostility towards Bernard unabated, my resentment towards my parents constant, and the elephant in the room ever present.

I need not have worried. Everything changed without my participation.

"I'm out of a job," I remember Papi telling my mother. "REA has gone bankrupt." My eyes flew instantly to Mami, certain we were wondering the same thing: how long before he has another nervous breakdown?

"We should move to Miami," Papi added. "Agueda, you need to live in a warmer climate and now that those Cubans are doing so well I'm certain I can find a job."

That's not how a depressed man sounds I heard myself thinking. Was it the prospect of moving to Miami? My father had been working for Railway Express for almost twenty-five years but instead of feeling dejected, he'd found reason to be enthusiastic. In Miami he'd be close to friends and family. In Miami people knew him. Optimist that he was, he probably thought one of his many friends would offer him a job. I could tell Mami was trying to make sense of all of this. She may have been thinking she'd have more freedom in Miami. She could go out on her own more frequently, and she too had friends in Miami. I don't think either of them so much as contemplated the thought I wouldn't join them. Why would they? They expected me to follow them everywhere until I married, and for them matrimony didn't encompass Bernard. At once I realized that Papi's unemployment threw living arrangements up in the air. The thought of moving to Miami never crossed my mind. If my parents wanted to move, I'd be making some serious changes to my life.

I needed time to figure things out. Since my earlier "I want-my-own-apartment" announcement I'd been getting the silent treatment, or was it the cold shoulder? Regardless what I might call it, with my Catholic guilt and fear of rejection that proclamation quickly fell to the wayside. Some days I thought I'd stay because I couldn't imagine living without Bernard. But then, after another drunken evening with him, I couldn't picture us with a real future together. Other days I couldn't imagine living that far away from my mother. She must have sensed my inquietude. As the weeks went by and the move grew closer, she became even more vociferous about her contempt for Bernard.

"*Cuando tú ibas, yo venía*," she said, intimating that she was older and wiser than I, an opening that caused me to dread what would follow. "So I'm telling you," she'd gone on, "that when two people get together, one decent and the other a lowlife, the lowlife never rises to the occasion. No, what always happens—and I've seen it over and over again—is that the lowlife drags his partner down to his level." Stop, please. If you go on, I'm going to scream. "If one is an alcoholic, and the other isn't, the two end up being drunks; it's never the other way around. And, Puchi, I cannot stand to watch him drag you down to his level."

"He's not a lowlife!" I cried. "He's just different! He's hip." I stormed out of the apartment in tears. I needed to talk to Bernard. I headed for the lobby, walked over to the next building, found his apartment number in the directory, took the elevator to his floor, and knocked on his door. A Cupid-like, vapid-looking, youthful platinum blonde opened the door.

"Sorry," I said, "I've got the wrong apartment."

"I don't think so. I've been expecting this."

"I'm looking for Bernard. I'm his girlfriend."

"I'm his wife, Nicky."

I froze; I couldn't have heard her correctly. "Say again?"

"Come in." She was pulling back the door.

I tentatively stepped into the living room. It looked liked a two-bedroom apartment, just like ours. Hearing me, Bernard came out of a bedroom, looking scruffy and inebriated.

"At last the farce is over." His words, verbatim, as he

came into the living room.

"Farce! You think this is funny?"

Had he rehearsed this moment? Had he foreseen this happening and calculated a response? Did he have practice with this? I must not have been the first to knock on this door; is that why his wife immediately knew who I was?

"How could you?" I blurted out between sobs as I hurried toward the door. I rushed to the elevator, pushed the button for basement and dashed to the parking lot where I wept unrestrained. Soon enough Bernard stepped through the basement door.

"How could you?" I asked, my vocabulary reduced to those three words. He reached for me, trying to put his arms around me but I tore away from him.

"Stay away from me, you bastard!" He looked like he was about to cry. "Don't you dare upstage me, you son of a bitch."

"Please let me explain," he said in that feathery voice that had done me in. "It's not what you think. It's not a real marriage; hasn't been one for years. We lead separate lives, we have separate bedrooms."

"But you lied!"

"Because I love you more than life itself," Love me more than life itself? Where did he get that shit from? He saw at once that his flair for the dramatic had failed him. "I've dreaded this moment more than you'll ever know," he said, "but I'm glad it's over. I cannot forgive myself for hurting you like this. Can I expect you to forgive me? Of course I can't. But believe me when I say I never intended to hurt you. Why do you think I kept my hands to myself for so long? I'd sooner die than hurt you. The only reason I didn't tell you about Nicky is because I couldn't bear the thought of losing you."

"Well, you have. You've lost me. I'm going to Miami with my parents."

He wiped the tears with his hands and paused. "You know, deep inside, you know I'm your best friend."

"Some friend! Try being something else."

"And as your best friend, I've got to tell you that regardless of me, or if you forgive me or not, you're twenty-one years old and it's high time for you to cut the umbilical cord and live your own life."

"I'll never forgive you," I said and walked away.

I'd been certain I'd left my innocence in the backseat of Panchito's car, but I hadn't. What remained disappeared when I heard Bernard say, "The farce is over." Later my friends would ask, "Didn't you suspect something when he never invited you up to his apartment?" No. I was too naïve to contemplate that level of duplicity. If my friends suspected it all along they weren't about to admit it now. Had it crossed my parents' mind? Hardly. It was ammunition, and they'd have used it. No, no one thought him capable of pulling this off. Besides, he seemed to be always available. Week nights. Weekends. Except he wasn't available at all.

Nicky answering the door; Nicky telling me she was his wife; Bernard saying, "The farce is over." Where did he get that line from? Moliere? Voltaire? I kept replaying the scene, always allowing for a different ending—one that gave me the best line. "Mendacity," that's what I should have said. Bernard would have known; he was always quoting Tennessee Williams: "Deliberate cruelty is not forgivable." I spoke of little else, told the story to anyone who'd listen. And now, when I'd thought it was all over, Bernard had called.

I sat with my friend Sally in her itsy-bitsy studio apartment in New York's Upper Eastside. Sally and Rebeca were the two friends from secretarial school I'd stayed in touch with long after graduation. They'd grown up together in a Venezuelan oil camp. Rebeca, the one I'd originally felt closer to, had moved to Washington, DC and after she'd left, Sally and I had seen more of each other. Rebeca always dressed to the nines, her clothes from renowned Fifth Avenue stores, while Sally managed her budget with an eye toward retirement. Although in her early twenties, Sally already favored sensible shoes.

Sally's boyfriend lived in Connecticut and whenever she visited him, she'd let me have the key to her apartment. Bernard and I spent many weekends there. The studio's furniture came from a store called Castro Convertibles. Everyone knew the brand from a huge billboard in Times Square that showed an adorable little girl opening the sofa bed. That easy. The coffee table was also convertible, opening into a full-size dining room table. Two Danish chairs offered additional seating. You live in Manhattan and you learn the value of floor space.

We both sat on the sofa. A bottle of wine and two wine glasses sat on the convertible coffee table. I remember the wine being an insipid rose but I drank it anyway. A cigarette in hand, I was telling Sally about my romantic misadventures. "Bernard wants us to be friends."

"Why would you give the time of day to a married alkie who conned you like that?" she asked.

Why indeed? I knew Sally thought I was wasting my time with him so I didn't expect her to say anything different. But I also knew I'd never get her to understand me. Because I wasn't ready to lose yet another person from my life. Because I'd convinced myself I couldn't live without him. But I didn't want to admit that to Sally. I wasn't interested in listening to her no-nonsense appraisal of my situation. I played the daughter to her maternal role. "Friends, Sally. What's wrong with being friends?" I asked. I lit a cigarette and took my time inhaling and exhaling as I thought things over. I was almost certain I'd stay in New York. Change petrifies me. Leaving Cuba, leaving behind what defined me—everything and everyone I knew and loved—had become a permanent affliction. Sitting across from Sally in her studio, I thought of my life in New York City. I have friends. I have a job. I know my way around New York. And while I also have friends in Miami, I don't know how to drive. Scariest of all, I don't know my way around Miami. Manhattan is a grid; I can draw it on a cocktail napkin. Miami is a labyrinthine city with poor mass transport. My gut told me it would take a hell of a long time to become as independent in Miami as I am in New York. Bernard's words echoed in my ears. "Strictly as a friend," he'd said in that raspy, alluring voice that never failed to weaken my resolve, "I'd like to help you find an apartment in the city. It's not easy, you know."

"Yeah, I'd like us to be friends," I told Sally. I'd finally come around. Maybe I could make this work. I knew I was giving in, just as I knew by then that finding an adequate apartment in Manhattan is an awesome task. By virtue of my working in the city for so long I was comfortable and confident finding my way around Manhattan. But moving into an apartment, figuring out what I could or could not afford, committing myself to a lease, getting my utilities turned on, was a lot to learn, and I was starting at zero. Could I let Bernard help? Why not? Besides, he owed me something for his deception. Yes Bernard, I'm capable of severing the umbilical cord, thank you very much.

We typically met at a bar and grill near 23rd Street. Bernard frequently worked late and meeting near his office saved us time since I wanted to find an apartment in the Village. Bernard always arrived with a *New York Times* classified section rolled up under his arm. We'd order drinks, open the paper, and start circling ads. Soon we found a desirable sublet in a post-war, six-story, red-brick building on 9th Street, a mere three blocks from Washington Square Park. Unlike other apartments we'd looked at, this was a building with a uniformed twenty-four-seven doorman, with a lobby the width of a block, and a back door that opened onto 8th Street, a thoroughfare packed with all kinds of stores. There was a glitch: the renter wouldn't sublet unless we paid a fortune for his furniture—a small pea-soup green sofa upholstered in silk shantung, a thick, lush carpet the color of French's mustard, a fake marble fireplace, a wall of mirrors better suited for a ballet studio. I wouldn't budge.

"It's not the furniture I like, Bernard," I said, unaware we were being sold the right to sublet.

Bernard whispered into my ear, "After all I've put you through, the least I can do is buy you this sublet."

"I have to think about it."

"You'll lose it, you know," Bernard said.

"I need some time," I told the guy.

"Give us an hour or so," Bernard added.

The apartment was close to the Strand Bookstore, eighteen miles of new, used, and rare books, a New York institution. Bernard had first taken me there during the early days of my tutelage and I enjoyed the feel of the place, its mustiness.

"I want to check out the special editions," Bernard said. "You never know." I headed for the Spanish-language section. I liked to look for Spanish books for my mother but they weren't easy to find. I was leafing through coffee table art books when Bernard found me. He was holding a thin, navy-blue leather edition imprinted in gold. "It's a surprise," he said, and I looked away. He stood at the end of the cashier counter line and wrote this dedication on the cover page of Aesop's Fables:

*For my dear friend Maria de los Angeles,
Kind old men
Who give you furs and sables
Only live in Aesop's Fables.*

How many men could come up with that? No matter how hard I tried, I couldn't resist him, he was inimitable. And yet that day, for the first time I'd seen through him and, much to my surprise, I'd played along when he said, "Let me buy this for you; it's the least I can do." You bet your ass. You owe me.

I alone signed the lease of the coveted Greenwich Village apartment. It was a good deal since the post-war apartment building fell within New York City's Rent Stabilization guidelines, which protects tenants from sharp rent increases while allowing them to renew their leases.

I was enthused to the limit to have my first very own apartment. And in the perfect location: Greenwich Village, The Big Apple. I couldn't wait to get into it. Bernard drafted his friend Bob to help move my bedroom set, clothes, and few boxes of books from my parents' apartment. And Misu. After the move, Jack-of-all-trades Bernard (carpenter, electrician, plumber, handyman) set out to put up shelves, rewire lamps, refinish furniture, all with the ease of a pro. The men in my family were useless outside the office, so the wall of shelves Bernard came up with dazzled me. He mounted half the shelves symmetrically and half asymmetrically, against an orange background. I don't know how many bottles of Taylor

Sherry he consumed in the process, but the shelves ended up level. Stealthily, he brought in a fresh pair of socks and Jockey shorts, and it wasn't long before his spare shirts hung in my. He'd come over with a bottle of sherry and a magnum of white wine and before we knew it, it was too late for him to catch the bus to the Colonnades, and he'd pass out on the pea-soup green couch. I didn't mind; it's not like I wanted him under the same roof with his cherubic wife. After several weeks of this nonsense, Bernard was once again in my bed.

Bernard left Nicki as if he were going on vacation, a suitcase in each hand. But I had rules. Do not answer the phone; it could be my mother. Don't leave your stuff out; the super might let himself in, and so on and so forth. Bernard didn't object to anything. I didn't need to ask him to use the buildings back door; he volunteered. "I'm old guard," he said, "Don't like people opening doors for me." I don't think that's why he avoided coming through the lobby. He enjoyed the surreptitiousness that allowed him to sneak in unnoticed. He was like a cat prowling in the middle of the night.

Mothers are always right: Bernard didn't become an honest man; I became a duplicitous woman. But I was living my life the way I wanted, and I was fairly happy with myself as long as I avoided thinking about my parents. I'd invited my brother and his wife to visit me to show them how well I was doing and, hopefully, we'd have a nice Sunday dinner together somewhere. Before their arrival I'd went through the apartment with a fine-tooth comb, careful there were no telltale signs of cohabitation. I had no time to listen to any of Loren's bull about who I dated.

"I'll call you later on," Bernard said on his way out. I knew he wouldn't. He most likely would stumble in well after I was a sleep.

I wondered whether Loren and Lilia Maria regretted agreeing to come over as much as I lamented having suggested it. Loren's aversion to the city dated back to my uncle's death, when he and Papi had to stay in one of those one-night cheap hotels in what was then called Needle Park. Loren clung to that flop-house image of New York—the city as a cesspool, full of junkies, alkies, thugs, bums.

I knew Lilia Maria was pregnant and due in a matter of weeks but hadn't expected her to be that big—and beautiful. It was a sluggish afternoon when they visited, the air oppressive, sticky as flypaper. The open window didn't cool the room; it invited the city's clatter, that indistinct mix of blaring sirens, blasting boom boxes, and ceaseless honking. Loren will get his chance to ask me how I can live in such a place. But kids have a way of stealing the show and Sofie, my two-year-old niece, went straight to the window and looked out with inquisitiveness. When my niece was born I was delighted to see she'd inherited her mother's peaches-and-cream complexion. She was like the Gerber baby, with her rosy cheeks, golden thin hair, and a dimple in her smile. Loren, who had my father's Mediterranean complexion, and was incapable of resisting a racial joke, was fond of saying *"Como se mejoro la raza"* or "How we've improved the race." I couldn't take my eyes off her; she looked like a porcelain Cupid.

"We're moving to Miami," Loren announced before I could suggest we go to an air-conditioned restaurant. "We haven't felt safe in Newark since the riots. We're not going to stick around and wait for the next one."

"That was a year ago, Loren," I said, referring to the '67 Newark riots which had started at the mostly black Central Ward precinct and had spread all over the city. I realize now I might have sounded dismissive, but the image of whole neighborhoods going up in fire was fresh in my mind. Two dozen people had died.

"You never liked it there, Loren," I said, "and I don't blame you. Newark is New Jersey's armpit, but I seriously doubt there will be more riots."

"I don't want to argue. Besides, we hate the weather here. Miami is a much better place to live. Remember when you didn't want to leave Miami?"

I didn't want to revisit that incurably nostalgic fourteen-year-old girl who longed to reconnect with the only life she knew.

"I want to be close to *los viejos*," Loren said, "and Lilia Maria wants to be close to her parents. Why don't you come with us?"

I remember thinking they were better than me. Then I realized they had nothing to hide.

"Do you have a job?" I asked.

"I've got a lot of friends there; I'll get something. Lilia Maria will get a job in no time. We'll be fine."

"Too bad you're moving. I'll miss you."

"You should come."

"I don't think so. I really love New York. Besides, Loren, I don't have a driver's license, and it's a pain in the neck to get around in Miami without a car."

"But you'll be here all by yourself,"

"I have a job here," I said.

"You can get a job as a bilingual secretary in Miami."

"And how am I going to get there? I'm not here by myself, Loren. I have friends here that are like family. And they're single and we do stuff together; we have the same interests. All my friends in Miami are married, with kids. How would I fit in? No, I'm better off staying here. Like I said, I love New York."

"I don't know what you see in New York."

"Loren, por Dios, Nueva York es el ombligo del mundo." Loren, for God's sake, New York is the navel of the world.

"You'll love Miami if you give it a chance."

"I'm a New Yorker, Loren. I don't want to learn how to be Cuban all over again."

"So now you're not even Cuban?"

"Of course I'm Cuban, but I'm a Cuban living in New York, not a Cuban living in the past. Not a professional Cuban."

"Cubans in Miami don't live in the past," Loren said, raising his voice. "They wouldn't be doing so well if they did. And what's this about 'professional' Cubans?"

"I'm talking about those Cubans whose lives are consumed by anti-Castro politics. Cubans who only talk about how rich they used to be before the Revolution took everything away from them. Cubans who insist everything was better in Cuba. If you are to believe them,

Cuba had to be the size of Canada, every family with a sugar mill."

Lilia Maria suddenly interrupted me before I could really go at Loren. *"Nunca en mi vida,* will I forget the riots," she said. She'd been unusually quiet until then. Lilia Maria didn't want Loren to lose his temper. I realized then the summer race riots had played a pivotal role in their decision to move to Florida. "I didn't think I would see another day," she went on. "They barricaded us in the Colonnades. Under martial law! In the United States! And I had Sofie. I was petrified. Petrified! I'm not exaggerating. I thought we'd die there. I'm never going through that again! *¡Nunca! ¡Jamás!"*

Loren and his family left for Miami shortly after Lilia Maria gave birth to a baby boy. Since Papi and Mami moved Loren, and I hadn't spent time together to speak of, but having him nearby was still reassuring. Fello had settled in Texas after finishing his residency in internal medicine at the University of Texas' MD Anderson Cancer Center. Not having family around made me feel like a donut—the hole defined me. I grabbed my pack of cigarettes, lit up, and let my mind saunter into the past. When did we give up hope? When did we stop waiting for the revolution to fail? Or was it just me?

Chapter Twenty

Just back from work, I took a magnum of Folonari out of the refrigerator, poured myself a glass of white wine, and waited. Bernard had been working a lot of overtime so we seldom ate before eight. He didn't even have time to pour himself a drink before I started complaining about how much I hated my job. Being a secretary was getting me down. Maybe it had to do with working on Wall Street, not understanding finance, and lacking the interest to learn about it.

"They walk around in their three-piece suits, full of themselves, telling me to get them coffee, or find them a phone book, or this or that. Why can't they get their own damned coffee? It makes me feel like I'm their maid."

"Babes, I wouldn't take it personally if I were you."

"How should I take it?"

"You're working for a bunch of greedy capitalists.

How they treat you isn't related to you. It's who they are."

"And who are they?"

"Pigs, capitalist pigs."

"I'll try to remember that next time I'm getting them a cup of coffee. I'm sure it will help."

"I'm sending you to college. I'll find a way. You're too bright for this. You're bored."

"I'm bored all right, but if you can't save enough money for a divorce lawyer, how do you think you're going to send me to college?"

"I have a divorce lawyer," Bernard said.

"And?"

"I have to give him more money, that's all. You can go to Hunter College. Any city college."

"But then we'd have to live on one salary."

"We'll work it out after I get divorced." He took one last drag from the unfiltered cigarette and put it out on the dinner plate.

"I wish you wouldn't do that," I said.

Bernard couldn't sleep through the night; he couldn't go that long without a drink. An eerie sense of emptiness would wake me up, and when I'd find myself alone in the queen-sized bed, I'd get pissed off and go looking for him. There he was, passed out on the green sofa, his left arm dangling near a bottle of sherry, a heaping ashtray and a crumpled empty red pack of Pall Mall close by.

"Wake up, wake up" I'd say. "You need to go back to bed." Led by some primeval instinct I'd walk him to the bedroom, wondering why in the hell I was still by his side. The book dedications? The birthday piñata? The notes scribbled on paper napkins atop my brown-bag lunch? Or the phrases written with toothpaste on the bathroom mirror? How many women have been loved like this?

Except, I no longer found his eccentricities inimitable and irresistible; now I found them alarming. In April, when I went to get help for my taxes I asked, "What about you?"

"I used to claim my cats as dependents," he said with a wry smile.

"And now?"

"Now I don't file."

"Can you go to jail for that?"

"Only if I get caught."

The possibility of getting caught never crossed his mind. I was proof of this certainty; he didn't think I'd find out he was married. And I wondered once more why I was still with him, what was I waiting for?

One evening we were at Sterns, a now defunct New York City department store on East 42nd Street, trying to find a wedding gift for his childhood friend Ernie. Bernard had his mind set on a silver tea set.

"Americans don't drink tea," I said.

"Russian Jews do. I want them to have something beautiful to remind them of their wedding."

Two tea sets caught his eye, one silver-plated and one sterling silver. He picked up the pieces from both sets and showed me the difference in weight. He was torn.

"They're both beautiful, Bernard. Pick the one you can afford."

Right in front of my eyes he loosened the noose on the price tags and exchanged them.

"You can't do that!" I said. Am I supposed to stick around until he gets arrested? I walked away and waited for him in front of the store. He walked out of Sterns carrying a big box inside a shopping bag.

"I can't go on like this,"

"What are you talking about?"

"Don't even try, Bernard."

"Oh, that! Sterns can afford it."

"That's not the point."

"The point being?"

I was done with sermonizing. I couldn't watch him self-destruct any longer. "You can't even sit through a double feature without a drink, Bernard."

"I need to save a couple of grand so I can get into rehab."

"You can go to Alcoholics Anonymous, Bernard. AA is free."

"AA operates at a very low intellectual level. I went to three meetings. They sit there and talk of God. They might not call it God, but it's God all right."

"Do something!"

"I will; get into a rehab clinic." By then I knew the outcome of these sporadic, abortive discussions. Bernard would remove the framed Braque piece he claimed was an unsigned, unnumbered lithograph from the orange wall and have it assessed. He was certain it was worth a few grand. Was he deceiving me again or had he started to believe his own lies? Wasn't he saving to pay off the divorce lawyer? He couldn't afford a divorce, how was he going to swing rehab? Maybe another farce in the works.

"I want to meet your lawyer," I said the day I saw him rip off Sterns.

"If that's what you want."

"It is."

He went through the motions. We both got off work early and took the tube to Newark. "Let's have a drink," he said right after getting off the train. We went inside a dingy bar and he lit a Pall Mall. He asked the bartender for a very dry, straight-up vodka martini with an olive—as if the olive mattered. I wanted nothing. He gulped down the vodka, and with that glibness he could so easily rally, he said, staring at the bottom of his empty martini glass, "There is no lawyer."

I've heard stories of women putting up with chronic infidelity, with physical abuse, with public humiliation, all in the name of love. Whenever my mother listened to such tales she'd wait silently until they ended and then she'd say, "My husband can hit me once, but he better never fall asleep again." What would she think of her daughter now?

With the words, "there is no lawyer," still resounding in my ears, I stood up, looked down on him, and said, "That's it." I walked out of the bar alone, feeling like Bambi after the fire.

Chapter Twenty One

From my desk I could see the Staten Island ferry leaving the southern tip of Manhattan, commuters hurrying to the terminal, tourists strolling in Battery Park, New Yorkers lining up in front of hot dog carts and pretzel stands.

"Maria, I need you to take a letter," Mr. Hellman called.

I picked up my steno pad and a pencil and walked across the long rectangular room, a sizeable expanse of open space that accommodated four brokers and one other secretary. I took a seat in front of Mr. Hellman, my least favorite broker. His urgent letter was all of one paragraph long and so banal I wondered why he'd even bothered. After finishing secretarial school, I'd bounced through a half dozen different jobs before stumbling in the door of this large private equity firm that was looking for a bilingual secretary. Financial jargon, cigar smoke, and hot air filled the office. The pay was okay but the financial world bored me. Of our department's four brokers I liked one: Mr. L., a soft-spoken, gentle man, over six feet tall. His slouching posture, black hair, and bushy eyebrows reminded me of Walter Matthau. He was courteous to all, but even more so to underlings. He never failed to introduce his visitors to everyone in the office. It was late afternoon, and he'd just spotted me staring at the phone on my desk.

"You always think he's not going to call, but he always does," Mr. L. said.

It was getting close to five and the guy I'd been dating still hadn't called.

"That obvious, eh?" I remarked. I didn't mind his butting in; I felt comfortable with Mr. L. "He waits until the very last minute to ring," I added.

I knew what my fella was doing. It was part of the control game many eligible New York bachelors liked to play. We'd frequently meet for cocktails after work and maybe dinner or something. But with him it was always; "I won't know when I'm done until the last minute, I'll call you." I knew this was about not taking him for granted and I, like a sucker, wouldn't make any other plans until I heard from him.

"I doubt he's going to start calling you any earlier." Mr. L. said. "Looks like he's a procrastinator."

And what the hell is a procrastinator? I'd have to look it up.

"So you're telling me I shouldn't expect him to change?"

"I'm saying that's the way he is."

"He thinks I don't know what he's doing," I said.

"And that is?"

"Reminding me who's calling the shots."

The other brokers were already gone, racing to catch their commuter trains, just the two of us in the office. These brief sporadic exchanges usually took place when Mr. L. was on his way out to lunch or heading to Grand Central to go home but now he was pacing about, waiting for his last appointment. And I was eager for the guy to arrive so they'd both leave before my potential date called. I watched him layer up—scarf, coat, hat, gloves, the whole nine yards, each a slightly different shade of black, and I recalled that not so long ago a summer dress and a pair of sandals had gotten me out the door.

"Do you miss Cuba?" he asked. A hell of a question, just like that, out of the blue.

"Every single winter."

"No, seriously."

"I am serious."

Just then, in walked a tall, stout, olive-skinned man wearing an open black cashmere coat and a hat. I guessed maybe early 40s, around Mr. L's age. Under his coat was a dark blue, three-piece pin-striped suit, the Monopoly-game banker sprung to mind. His slicked back, dark hair and complexion reminded me of my father. Or perhaps it was his charisma that brought Papi to mind.

"Maria, do you know Nate?" Mr. L. asked.

"Haven't had the pleasure," Nate said, extending his hand.

The first time the very charming Nate asked me to

lunch, I accepted the invitation with trepidation. There was something intriguing about him that made me want to get to know him better; but I also found that to be a tad intimidating. I'm certain that during those first lunches I smoked more than I ate. Nate was an important player among the Wall Street rich and powerful. It took me a while to feel at ease with a big shot like him. Since meeting him we had gotten together for lunch about twice a month, usually at one his favorite haunts where it seemed everyone in the room knew him. Our lunch conversations revolved around the miserable weather and the Cuban Chronicles but I sensed he was becoming curious of my own plans.

"How come you didn't go to college?" He eventually got around to asking.

"No money. My parents could barely afford to keep my oldest brother in medical school in Mexico," I said.

"Well, I don't know about your culture but in the Jewish culture the person who has received an education feels an obligation to help others in the family get an education."

"He got married, had kids."

"Still... What about your other brother?"

"Wife and kids too. He didn't go to college. He joined the Bay of Pigs invasion and then spent two years in Castro's jails. But now he's getting a degree at night."

"In prison," he said.

"Pardon?"

"In prison. Jail is for criminals. You can go to prison for a number of reasons."

"Oh, I didn't know that." Without realizing it, the

moment I said "Oh, I didn't know that" Nate became my guru.

"So if you don't care for secretarial work, what are you going to do?" he asked.

"I think I'm going to be a stewardess."

"A glorified waitress," he said.

"Yeah, but a waitress who gets to see the world. That's something, no?"

"Why don't you go to school at night, like your brother?"

"I do, but I don't get credit for my courses because I didn't take algebra or any of that stuff. I take classes for the fun of it. I'm taking a course on the movies right now."

"Where?"

"The New School for Social Research; it's close by."

"So what else have you taken?"

"Mostly art classes, art history, drawing the human form, stuff like that."

"Would you like to go to college?"

"Sure, but I'm telling you, I can't because when it comes to math and science I'm really stupid."

"Ignorant."

"No, stupid. In Cuba my parents got me a tutor to help me pass algebra and even with a tutor I barely passed it," I said laughing. "He was from Spain and he'd say, '*No seas estúpida*.'" I mimicked a pure Castilian accent and cracked myself up.

Nate's jaw dropped to his napkin. "That's awful. Nobody should call a student stupid."

"But it's true." I said.

"No wonder," he said.

"No wonder what?"

"No wonder you're afraid to take courses. There are ways around not having the right background. I have a friend who's a tenured professor at Columbia. Maybe he can help you get a job on campus," Nate said. "I think you'll be happier working on campus than here." I made a mental note to look up "tenured."

"That wouldn't take much," I said smiling.

"If you get a job on campus, you get free tuition."

"What about all those courses I didn't take?"

"Your life is hardly over, you can take them now," he said with a smile.

Funny, how something so simple hadn't crossed my mind.

Chapter Twenty Two

I got off the subway at 116th Street—Columbia University—one of the oldest and most beautiful subway stops in the city. The station, a historical landmark dating back to 1904, still retains its original tile workmanship. Showcasing the university's colors, white subway tiles and smaller navy-blue and light-blue tiles display the university's logo and convey a Beaux Arts sensibility to the station's waiting area.

Columbia University is not far from Harlem. It was my first time that far uptown and I felt touristy in my unfamiliarity. A bit uptight as well. The afternoon was mild enough, in the mid-thirties, not bad for February. I went through the iconic gates, walked down College Walk—majestic trees lining both sides of the promenade—and was duly impressed by the commanding campus. A short way up the walk, I came to Low Library, and that's when I first saw the bronze statue of the Alma Mater. The Alma Mater on the steps of Low Library was almost identical to the Alma Mater on the impressive *escalinata*, the steps that cascaded down from the Universidad the La Habana onto a Vedado street. I stared in disbelief and climbed up the steps to take a better look. Columbia's classical statue was fashioned after a Greek goddess whose name escaped me then. I remembered hearing Cuba's Alma Mater was modeled after the beautiful young daughter of a university professor. I leaned against the statue's pedestal, a good spot from which to survey the campus. Butler Library, an imposing neoclassical building, stood directly opposite. Engraved above the library's arcade of ionic columns were the names of great writers, philosophers, thinkers. It pleased me to realize I was familiar with each of them.

I was at Columbia to meet Nate's tenured-professor friend. If I impressed him he'd recommend me for a campus job. A secretarial job at the university would pay less than what I was making at Wall Street but would exempt me from paying tuition for six college courses. After working as a bilingual secretary for several years I knew I was better suited to earning less and getting free tuition than to making more and owing Bloomingdale's. I lit a cigarette and let my mind ponder the possibilities of student life. A middle-aged fellow smoker was heading my way. He was slight of build, bearded and bespectacled. I remember him sporting a tweed jacket, very academic.

"Are you Maria?"

"Yes, I am. Are you Peter?"

"How about some lunch? I know a good Greek restaurant nearby. Do you like Greek food?"

"Love it." I'd never had it. I'd ask him for a recommendation when it was time to order.

He led the way to the Symposium, a small and colorful restaurant a few blocks from the university. Right away I realized how formally I dressed—high heels, stockings, the works. People around me favored afghan coats or fringe jackets and bell-bottom jeans. As soon as we settled into our seats, he asked why I'd left Cuba. My canned response became the preamble to an analysis of the pros and cons of socialism. Is this what going to Columbia will to be like?

At long last he asked, "How can I help?"

"I need a job on campus so I can go to college at night."

"I'll be happy to write you a letter of recommendation," he said. I couldn't thank him enough but intuited my gratitude made him uneasy.

During the long subway ride back to Wall Street I thought about my visit to the campus. It had stirred something in me, had placed me at a crossroads. Can I really do this? Isn't this out of my league? The only way to find out is to apply. After applying for admission for the fall semester I could think of nothing else. Imagine me of all people attending one of the world's greatest universities. Like a fabled castle in the air. Nothing else mattered—not that I couldn't stand my job (I'd be leaving it soon), not that I had no one in my life (I wouldn't have the time to date anyway), not that I'd have to get a roommate (I wouldn't be spending that much time in the apartment). I thought about not having to bring anybody coffee or soda or whatever; not having to wear stockings and heels, not having to say, "May I ask who's calling, please?" I'd be able to dress casually, not sloppily, casually, and when people asked me what I was doing I'd say, "studying and working," making sure studying came first.

That spring, on April 23rd to be precise, I came home from work, switched on the TV and caught the evening news. Columbia University students had taken over the gym under construction at Morningside Park (the boundary between Columbia and Harlem) and were occupying a campus building, Hamilton Hall. The following day I couldn't cover my electric typewriter fast enough; I wanted to be home in time for the news. Students now also occupied Low Library, the awe-inspiring building behind the Alma Mater. The spoiled, thankless brats were still there the following day, and the next day as well. Before the end of the week, the ingrates (did they have a clue how good they had it?) occupied five university buildings. Then, on April 30, 1968, the NYPD stormed onto the campus, swinging nightsticks, clubbing unarmed students, whacking heads. The sight of policemen bludgeoning defenseless demonstrators—even after they had fallen to the ground—reminded me of the 1957 police raids at the University of Havana. I'd seen pictures of the beatings, of bloodied students at the university's *escalinata,* and now as I watched the police thrash Columbia's demonstrators, all I could think of was

Dios mío, como en Cuba.

Here's the thing, with the exception of my all-consuming *Cubanismo*, I'd been indifferent to politics. I didn't read the paper and when I did, I'd read about local news and about the arts. Like most Cuban exiles my father believed in the United States' participation in the Vietnam War. He talked about the domino theory, how if we allowed one country to fall to communism all the neighboring countries would follow. Now, with American university students vehemently demonstrating against the war in Vietnam, I paid more attention to follow the news.

The year 1968 remains the most turbulent year I've lived—more so than 1959, the year Castro and his troops descended upon Havana. The Vietcong Tet offensive had started on January 30th and the next four months witnessed a precipitous escalation of the war. In February, in one week alone, 543 Americans were killed and 2,547 wounded, mostly drafted teenagers, boys who were predominantly poor and or black, and lacking the academic skills to get into some college where they could have taken advantage of the draft-deferment program. Those who could afford to leave the country did, and hundreds of young men fled to Canada to avoid combat. When, at the end of February, Walter Cronkite, the most respected newsman in America, returned from a fact-gathering trip to Vietnam and proclaimed "America cannot win this war," everyone took notice. The Vietnam War split the country in two and on March 31st President Johnson announced he would not be seeking reelection.

On the fourth day of April of that tempestuous year someone murdered Dr. Martín Luther King while he stood on the balcony outside his room at the Lorraine Motel in Memphis, Tennessee. The nation was shaken to its core. Dr. King's assassination, the interminable struggle for civil rights, the constant abuse of blacks by police and civil authorities, and the preponderance of black men being drafted fueled riots in Baltimore, Boston, Chicago, Detroit, Kansas City, Newark, and Washington, D.C. Fire engulfed our major cities, frequently burning out the poverty-ridden neighborhoods that needed the most help.

I remember watching the televised riots with disengaged disbelief. No way, not in the States. I'd grown up on a steady diet of post-war Hollywood movies depicting a nation full of optimism and endless possibilities, a nation engaged in the pursuit of happiness. The plight of American inner cities, the hopelessness of the urban poor, the desperation of American blacks were all foreign to me until I started listening to Dr. Martín Luther King. His assassination and the rioting that followed appalled me. Where I come from people didn't set fire to their own neighborhoods. Where I come from if students engaged in acts of civil disobedience they risked never being seen again. As the riots unhinged the nation, major philanthropies pouring money into universities, charging them to address the plight of American ghettoes. That's what started the urban-studies craze. In New York, the Ford Foundation gave Columbia University millions to fund an urban studies center, directing the university to find ways to rescue neighboring Harlem. I benefitted from one of those grants when I was hired as a secretary at the newly established Urban Center on campus.

I'd never come across such a diverse organization. The director of the Urban Center, an elegant, tall, and slim black lawyer who'd established himself as a defender of civil rights, had just ended his tenure as the first black ambassador to Ghana (and Africa). His deputy director, the man who hired me, was a legal scholar on sabbatical from George Washington University. Both men had been active in the Peace Corps.

At the outset, the center counted less than ten employees, all liberal intellectuals intent on improving the lives of people of color. The center was located in the basement of Lewisohn Hall. The rest of the 1905 building was home to Columbia's School of General Studies, a school specifically created—largely in response to the needs of returning WWII veterans—for students with nontraditional academic backgrounds. Most GS students had either never attended college or could attend only part time. All this fit me like a glove. I wasted no time submitting my application which was quickly accepted, since GS didn't require the traditional college preparation I lacked—physics, chemistry, algebra, geometry. General Studies had its own entrance exam, and I was good at writing essays.

Chapter Twenty Three

My *cubanismo* got a shot in the arm when I enrolled in a literature course called *Martí*. Born in Havana in 1853, José Martí was one of Latin America's greatest literary figures: a journalist, poet, and writer. The son of Spanish immigrants, Martí, a political activist, was thrown in prison by the colonial government and condemned to forced labor when he was only sixteen. He was released in 1871 and deported to Spain. But even in exile his tireless commitment to a free Cuba never faltered. He died during Cuba's War of Independence against Spain, known in the States as the Spanish-American War. Cubans call him *El Apóstol*, The Apostle, for devoting his life to Cuba's independence.

Our professor informed us that the course's textbook, an anthology of Martí's work, could only be purchased at a Spanish-language bookstore, Librería Las Américas, on

East 23rd Street. Bernard used to work at 21st and Lexington so I thought I knew the area well. But in spite of my incursions into several nondescript buildings I couldn't find the bookstore. I was near Third Avenue by the time I found a sign for Las Américas in the small lobby of an old building. The bookstore was on the second floor so I warily proceeded to climb the narrow staircase until I stood in front of a dark, heavy, partly open door. From the doorway I caught sight of what looked like a mountain range of books. Bookcases replete with books threatened an avalanche. Books that didn't block windows or aisles ran amok all over the store. Agog, I tried to scrutinize the room, wondering how and where to find the *Antología*. When I heard an undeniably Cuban voice, I wondered whether it was *el librero*. Suddenly a slight middle-aged man, with a mane of unruly salt-and-pepper hair came out of nowhere. Is he talking to me? No, he's with another customer. From across the room he shot me a smile and said, *"Enseguida te atiendo."* I'll be right with you. Good thing he was slender; otherwise he'd never get past the stacks of books.

A young man with long hair, wearing a t-shirt and jeans, was in the process of thanking profusely the man I assumed owned the store. *"Te lo agradezco de todo corazon,"* he said pointing to the volume he was holding, *"y en cuanto pueda te pago."* I thank you with all my heart and will pay you as soon as I can." As the young man was about to exit, he turned his head around and said, *"Gracias, Pedro."* Pedro nodded. He then walked up to me, extended his hand and said, "Pedro Yanes."

"Maria Nodarse." We shook hands.

"¿La hija de Lorenzo Nodarse, director de deportes?" He wanted to know whether my father was the former sports commissioner.

"Sí. Estoy buscando la Antología de José Martí," I told him.

"¿La de Susana Redondo y Anthony Tudisco? Pedro asked.

"Si, esa."

He turned to his left and went straight to a pile of books at the end of a sagging wooden shelf, picked up the book at the very top, and looking at the cover said with a smile *"Tremenda Martiana."* My jaw hit street level. I was to visit Las Americas regularly for years to come, and during all that time no one was able to find anything in that store other than Pedro.

"¿Cuánto cuesta?" I asked. How much?

"Con esos ojos, nada." With those eyes, nothing.

Pedro knew my father and asked after him. I briefly described my family's life after the revolution and explained how my father's frailness rendered him incapable of adapting to his present situation. *Problemas de los nervios,* I remember saying. Problems of the nerves. The conversation soon turned to the whereabouts of so and so. A frequent exercise back then and still a popular one today among Cubans. He was engaging and easy to talk to. I'd missed having someone to speak Spanish with, now that I no longer had family nearby., There was something about Pedro's comportment, his passion for literature, his live-or-die endeavor to recommend the perfect book, the comfort under his skin, that led me to believe, he'd rather be in this bookstore than anywhere else in the world, except Cuba of course. Pedro, I gathered, had found himself the perfect niche. Our conversation that fall afternoon would change my life once more. I longed to be moored like him and as time went by, he helped anchor me.

Outside, sundown hemmed the city's skyline in a bright orange, evoking the tropical sunsets of my youth. I headed for the Lexington Avenue subway, went down the stairs, and grabbed an empty bench. I skimmed the *Antología*. I looked up *Versos Sencillos,* the poems I'd memorized at Phillips School. It had been a while since I'd read in Spanish. In Cuba I preferred playing to reading but my mother kept buying me books. I thought about the books left behind and felt a knot in my stomach when I remembered, not for the first time, what a fool I'd made of myself when I was eleven or so. This was before my two brothers left, before *abuela* died. The dining table was full when I sat down to eat. My grandmother, my parents, and Fello, all avid readers, liked to discuss the books and authors they were reading. As a rule, my father read biographies, particularly those written by Emil Ludwig or Stephan Zweig, but he also had a fondness for memorizing inspiring quotations. He had this book called *"Frases célebres de hombres célebres,"* which he took from room to room, memorizing quotes. Whenever I could, I'd pick up the book and read the quotations under *"Amor."* On this particular afternoon my parents and Fello were talking about prolific authors. I felt left out and, remembering *Frases célebres,* I said, *"El autor más prolífico es Anónimo*" (anonymous). Abuela was the only one who didn't double up laughing. After what seemed an eternity Mami said *"Basta."* Enough already. Who'd have thought back then that my first college course would be literature?

In class I'd sit up front and take down the bulk of the lecture in shorthand. I already knew what I was studying for: I'd be a professor just like Susana Redondo. Did I say she was Cuban? Like the well-heeled Cuban ladies of my youth, she had aged gracefully, silver strands in a bun. Generally, I didn't raise my hand in class, afraid of revealing I was the only one with no college prep behind me, which of course was a figment of my imagination. That first year at Columbia I tiptoed my way around, mindful of not angering the gods, still wary of where and who I was.

I felt insecure about the nuances of my native language. As a bilingual secretary I'd always relied on my spelling but now I had to do academic writing and was afraid of getting it wrong. I'd go to the Las Americas and ask Pedro how to quote from a text, how to write a footnote, a bibliography. I'd have him read my papers before I turned them in to make sure I hadn't missed any *acentos.* Every time I approached him Pedro acted like he had all the time in the world. I soon realized he was like that with everyone. Some took advantage of his excessive generosity but he wouldn't waste a minute thinking about it. His bookstore was always full, and if a student needed a book and had no money to buy it, Pedro would give him the book saying, *"Págame cuando puedas,"* Pay me when you can. He'd been a journalist in Cuba, and was now working on a PhD in Spanish literature from NYU, which was only a couple of blocks from my apartment. After class sometimes he'd take me to a Cuban Chinese restaurant on West Fourteenth Street. Magdalena, a curvaceous middle-aged woman with bleached blonde hair, had married a Chinese man in Cuba and she ran the restaurant. Magdalena knew what Pedro liked to eat and made sure it was always there for him. One evening as we were leaving Magdalena's Pedro said, *"Un día de estos, te voy a llevar a comer comida casera,"* promising to take me to a restaurant where I would taste homemade Cuban food.

The doorman buzzed and there was Pedro in a two-seater convertible sports car I didn't even know he owned. He drove to Union City, New Jersey, the town where we first stayed when we came up north. So many Cuban refugees had settled there since that they often called it Havana-on-the-Hudson. Pedro walked into a family restaurant like he owned the place. I knew I wanted *ropa vieja* (shredded beef in a tomato sauce). Mami and Belén both made a mean *ropa vieja* I could still taste. This restaurant's version was good enough, but I wouldn't call it "home cooking."

After dinner we walked down the city's main drag, *"Berguenlein"* as the local Cubans call it. Inside a Cuban bodega I found *un palo de trapear,* a Cuban mop, a contraption that looks like a polo mallet with a skirt. I picked up a bottle of *agua de violeta*, the violet cologne my mother sprinkled on my hair before pulling it into a ponytail. On the way out I grabbed a bar of *dulce de guayaba*. How to thank Pedro for this nostalgia shuttle?

Back home I called my mother. *"Mami, ¿adivina lo que encontré?"* Guess what I found? *"Un palo de trapear."*

I didn't even consider buying the Cuban mop, not with Pedro driving a sports car. Besides, I didn't need a mop to clean an apartment with wooden floors in the living room and bedroom; I'd learned that much in New Jersey.

"Mami, do you remember when Manolo came up from the basement about to kill us because the floor leaked?" I was referring to the house where we first lived in New Jersey. Most Cubans live in houses with tile floors that are mopped daily. In Ridgefield Park we mopped the hardwood floor. Manolo had been pressing grapes in the basement when he saw water drip from the ceiling. He rushed upstairs, banged on our door and when he saw us, his face as red as an overripe tomato and his carotid artery about to burst, he said, loudly, "What do you think you're doing?"

"Trapeando el piso," said my mother. Mopping.

"You don't mop these floors; you wax them!" And to think he used to be such a gentleman.

Like two girls remembering a longtime prank, we couldn't stop giggling. I couldn't help thinking if I lived closer to her, she'd laugh more often.

Chapter Twenty Four

The swinging '60s: sex, drugs, and rock'n'roll. While my contemporaries turned on, tuned in, and dropped out, I stuck to booze. With my family tree branching out into clinical depression I wasn't about to mess with psychedelic drugs. That's why I didn't go to Woodstock, didn't want to be in the middle of a drug-crazed crowd. But when the Woodstock documentary hit the movie houses, I couldn't wait to see what I'd missed. I got lucky: my building's doorman announced that Barry, my former roommate's ex-boyfriend, was in the lobby. Barry was a wanderer, so whenever he was in the city, he'd show up unannounced. "Send him up," I said.

"Oh my God, so good to see you," I said after hugging him. "What a surprise! Where have you been hiding?"

"Thailand, I have a friend who lives there. Most beautiful country I've seen so far." Barry's choices always surprised me. Why go to Southeast Asia when he hadn't been in Europe?

"What are you waiting for? Come in, come in. Look at how tanned you are. You look great! Tell me about your trip."

Great storyteller, Barry. He knew how to show you a place. If talking about food, the fish were so fresh they quivered, the vegetables just gathered so that you could smell the soil in your plate.

"Stop. You're making me want to go, and I'm middle class; I want to see Paris first. Hey, *Woodstock* is playing across the street. Want to see it?"

"How's Norma doing?" he asked, referring to his former girlfriend.

"Married, with a kid. In seventh heaven. Married a lawyer. They live in the Upper Westside."

"That's why I ran," Barry said.

"Why's that?" I asked.

"Because I knew she wanted to get married."

"All's well that ends well," I said. "So you want to go to the movies?"

"It's beautiful out there," Barry said pointing out the window He was right. For a change the sky was bright blue, not gray, and a soft wind had blown away most pollutants, so that the sun shone with uncommon bravado. "I don't feel like being cooped up in a theater," Barry said. I knew he had a point, but I didn't want to see *Woodstock* by myself.

"Pretty please. Barry. I really, really want to see it. Tell you what, I'll treat."

"I take it you didn't go to the festival," he said.

"I take two showers a day. Can you picture me rolling in the mud?" I replied.

"I forget. But I don't remember your being into music? Are you?"

"Not really." It was something I hated to admit, that I wasn't into music, being Cuban and all.

"So tell me, why do you want to see the movie?"

"Because it's like this major sociological event. I mean, nothing like this has ever happened before, all those half-naked people thumbing their noses at the establishment, making love, smoking dope in front of TV cameras. I have to see it to believe it."

"I wouldn't call it making love."

"What would you call it?"

"Fucking."

"Barry!"

"You're far more middle class than I realized."

"Without a doubt," I said.

The rockumentary about the 1969 bacchanalia was released in 1970 and played at art house cinemas. There was a small movie theater across the street from my apartment, the Eighth Street Playhouse. Barry acquiesced, and we stood in line briefly before walking into a packed theater. I'd only heard how wild Woodstock had been, watching it was something else. I'd look at Barry from the corner of my eye but I couldn't read him. Flabbergasted, I watched an estimated 300 thousand mud-covered, long-haired, half-naked peaceniks smoke dope, drop acid, get drunk, and get laid. These were supposed to be my peers, my generation. Little as I knew about myself in my twenties I was convinced I'd never be one of them.

The film recorded the end of the Age of Aquarius. Woodstock, the pinnacle of the counter-culture, turned out to be its apocalyptic finale. Perhaps Woodstock was to blame for leading many to believe the '60s was a sewer of a decade. I never saw it that way. Granted Woodstock was a drug-crazed bacchanal, but I don't think it was emblematic of the '60s. When I think of the '60s, I think of political activism: the civil rights movement, antiwar demonstrations, the feminist revolution. I think of a time when we all thought we could make the future more just. I couldn't think of a time when political activism wasn't quashed in Cuba so I was all for it, the more the better.

Where I worked played a huge roll in my support of political action. I paid close attention to current events, and the impact they had on the poor, the colored, and the disenfranchised. My boss at the Urban Center, an organization tasked with empowering the urban poor, took me under his wing. His tutelage was invaluable. I joined him and other coworkers in Washington, DC to participate in the Poor People's March of June 1968. There were roughly 50,000 people in our capital, all protesting our government's meager response to its citizens' needs. I had no doubt I was in the right place. The professionals at the center took a stand against the status quo and I wanted to be just like them. They all lent me their support. No one there doubted I'd graduate from college and succeed.

A year after enrolling in the Martí course, a university scholarship allowed me to become a full-time student. Most of my fellow evening students had full-time jobs and struggled to better themselves. They were mature, straight-laced, goal-oriented people I admired. Now my academic world was turned upside-down. My male classmates were peaceniks, radicalized anti-war Vietnam veterans, or gung ho anticommunist veterans. My female classmates were mostly strident feminists and empty-nesters with long flowing hair, who wore either oversized tunics or tee-shirts without the benefit of a bra. The men looked scruffy, many of them bearded and wearing military boots, a look that didn't conjure pleasant associations. I knew the School of General Studies was fashioned for nontraditional students but still I hadn't expected this motley crew. I'm a baby-boomer and my generation was coming of age in an era of cataclysmic shifts.

As a foreigner I was required to take two semesters of American literature. I soon developed a crush on my professor not unlike the crush I had on Mr. G. back in Ridgefield Park High. My current thirtyish English professor was stylish and dark—but not tall. His charcoal hair was speckled with silver strands and his bushy eyebrows sheltered fierce brown eyes. After a few weeks I noticed he'd fuss with papers on his desk until I left the classroom. Soon after I walked out, he'd leave the building and join me, as if by chance.

"Is this one of your required courses?" he asked.

"Yeah."

"Because you're from?"

"Cuba."

And then he praised the revolution with its free health care, free education, food for all, you name it. I'd given up contradicting this pervasive utopian version of the

Cuban revolution. "Because it was bad then doesn't mean it's good now." I said. When we parted I wondered whether he was interested in my view at all. Obviously not, otherwise he'd have asked something. The following week he casually followed me out of the building again.

"Do you want to have a drink?" he asked.

"I have a class."

"Maybe another time."

"Sure, another time."

Coming from a patriarchal culture I interpreted his invitation as a seal of approval. That's what it took, dating the professor, for me to raise my hand in class. Walking next to him across campus gave me the illusion I was some hot tamale, when what I really was, as they say in Cuba, was *mangos bajitos*—low-hanging fruit. I was so impressed by his scholarship, so spellbound by the way he gently massaged his silver-speckled black beard as he paused before highlighting some obscure allegory, it never occurred to me I was just one of many. I was so intent in being part of the erudite world to which he rightly belonged I was blind to his womanizing. We went out, off and on, until I realized I meant nothing to him. Often I didn't like myself after seeing him. Was this the price of emancipation? I couldn't tell. All I knew was that whenever I attempted to keep one foot in the women's movement and one in my culture, I lost my balance. Maybe they were right—those who said not to trust anyone over thirty.

Katya, my alter ego for years to come, sat a row ahead of me in Casanova's class. Apart from the American literature class, we were both taking Greek, Biblical, and Roman Literature with Albert Goldman. Katya was roughly my age, of average height with long straight dark hair I'd kill for (we all wanted to look like Joan Baez back then). We got friendly in no time, both looking to compare notes and talk about our classes and our professors.

Unlike me, Katya had two years of English literature under her belt, a feat that by my nascent standards made her an outright scholar. Her intellect, her eccentricity, her flair for the dramatic all dazzled me. No degree of distraction, or accidental mismatch, could account for Katya's singular outfits. Her attires required a bravura I wholly lacked and envied at the same time; they were akin to proclamations. She had very strong opinions on every title we read and spoke her mind. Her willfulness was disconcerting to some classmates, but I found it refreshingly honest. I knew she favored early American literature more than I did, but no matter the subject, I always took her remarks as the gospel.

We'd just left a lecture on the classics when she said, "The world's greatest literature and the guy can put you to sleep."

"The world's greatest literature?" I finally dared ask, "You really think so? I prefer the Russians."

"You know why you don't realize how great Greek literature is? Because he's reading it like it's the fucking phonebook, that's why. I'm going to complain."

"I wouldn't. Goldman is a big shot. He's the music critic for *Life* magazine," I said. "You'll have nothing to gain by complaining. But you're right; it's obvious he doesn't give a shit about this course. He's boring me to death. I bet he's been reading those yellow notes for at least a decade. Jesus, they crackle! I'm afraid they will crumble in his hands any day now. But take my word for it, Katya, he's not always like that. I have him for Pop Culture and he's a rock star there. You have no idea how funny he is."

"You're kidding, right?"

"No, his other class is packed. You have to register early, otherwise you can't get in."

"What's the name again?"

"Pop Culture, and don't knock it. It's a great class: *Catch 22, The Story of O, Tropic of Cancer*. Sometimes we watch old TV programs like *Sid Caesar's Show of Shows*. Maybe I appreciate it more because it's all new to me. You should come one day. It's so packed no one will notice."

Balding, white-haired, with wire-rimmed thick round glasses and a round pudgy face, Albert Goldman reminded me of Benjamin Franklin—certainly not someone who, at first glance, looked like he had it in him to be funny. But put him on a stage, watch his stand-up comedy act, note the eccentricity of his intellect, the range of his eclectic associations, and you have a dazzling entertainer. Pop Culture was Goldman's beloved class and his students hero-worshipped him.

Tuesday and Thursday mornings, I'd see him with a long face, stooped over, dragging his feet on his way to his classics' class, but if I happened to catch sight of him later on, when he was heading for Pop, his head was held high and there was a spring in his step. He couldn't wait to get to the hall where he served as master of ceremony once more. One October afternoon he walked into class looking like he'd just heard his dog had been run over by a car. Stooping more than usual, he dropped his beaten up leather briefcase on his desk and stared out the window.

"Jimi Hendrix died from an overdose in September. Twenty-eight years old, that's how old he was. Now Janis Joplin's dead from an overdose. Twenty-seven years old. What the hell's happening to this country?"

I was in the habit of crossing Broadway and going to the Chock Full o'Nuts coffee shop at the corner of 116th Street. With the Christmas decorations gone, I stared at the blunt misery of January. How I loathed the new year, with its steel-gray sky, slushy streets, sooty snow, and short dark days. A visit to Chock Full o'Nuts perked me up. The chain made the best whole-wheat sugar doughnuts in all New York—crispy, freshly fried, and liberally dusted with powdered sugar. I wolfed down one doughnut—my only pleasure thus far that joyless January afternoon—and was contemplating having another. I looked up and saw in the mirrored wall across from me a white mouth and a black coat speckled with confectioner's sugar. Let it go. Try to rub it off and you'll have a gray coat.

My gaze wandered to the pedestrians streaming by the large windows. I'd become a ravenous people watcher.

Katya must have been a hundred yards away when I spotted her coming up the street in another of her inimitable outfits. She was impossible to miss: a short A-line orange coat, orangey tights and, of course, a beret—black at least.

"You're wearing your food again," she said, as she sat down next to me.

"I'll never be a princess."

"Afraid not. Anyway, what I wanted to say is, I'd like you to meet my parents this summer."

"I didn't get you a coffee, I didn't want it get cold, you want some?" I asked.

"Yeah, I'll get it. Did you hear what I said?"

"But they live in California, and I don't have money."

"I know. I'll buy the ticket. It's a present. Don't feel guilty. I really, really want you to meet them," Katya said.

"Can you afford it?"

"Yeah, I have money saved."

"Where in California do they live?"

"In Lompoc. We can take the train from Lompoc up the coast to San Francisco. It's not very far."

"San Francisco? Really? I've been dying to visit San Francisco all my life," I said. Well, maybe not all, but certainly since watching *Vertigo* at one of Havana's fancier movie theaters I'd wanted to stand in front of the Golden Gate Bridge in the same spot where Kim Novak jumped into the bay. "Can we go to the beach in Lompoc?"

"The beach isn't far. But the water is really, really cold. Freezing actually. I don't think you'd enjoy it."

"I will." I said.

Just another Columbia University student.

Chapter Twenty Five

I was way off the mark imagining Lompoc as a picturesque coastal town. First, it's a few miles inland; second, it's a military town roughly twelve miles southeast of the humongous Vandenberg Air Force Base. Cookie-cutter military houses and trees too young to matter—that's what I thought when I got to the neighborhood where Katya's folks lived. I knew a dull week awaited me. I shouldn't have been so quick to presume. Lompoc, home to La Purisima Mission, is in Santa Barbara County and Katya's parents drove us to Mission Santa Barbara, the queen of all California missions. Katya's father took his time showing us around, driving past extraordinary vistas. The Santa Barbara landscape may not be as dramatic as the French Riviera's but it easily comes in second.

We meandered up Pacific Coast Highway all the way

to San Simeon. "Look," Katya said pointing to the top of a hill, "See that building on top? That's Hearst Castle!" She knew I'd seen *Citizen Cane* many times. From the highway I could barely discern the castle. I was more interested in the zebras and antelope grazing on the hillsides.

"What's this about the zebras?" I asked.

"He had a zoo up there. Even with lions and bears." Katya explained.

"Can we go inside?"

"It's too expensive," Katya said.

"It's also closed by now anyway," her father said.

"Well, I got a peek of Xanadu," I said trying to be gracious. "Why do you want to live in Greece?" I asked. "I want to move here."

This was the first time I'd stayed with an American family. Although some of my New York friends were American, most were foreigners. My Latin American Institute pals, Sally and Rebeca, were Venezuelan, and Silvia, my high school buddy, was Cuban. Katya's family took me by surprise. Because of her eccentricity I hadn't expected Katya to come from a typical American family, but she did. Her father had spent his working life in the military, retiring at an early age. Her mother, slender and blonde, looked happy and balanced. I found it odd they didn't watch television; they did crafts instead, but that was about it. After dinner, Katya's mother would dig out boxes of colored beads, wires, and the like. Katya's sister, who lived nearby with her husband and baby would drop by and join us in our jewelry-making endeavors. Were all American families like this? I had no clue, but I'm artsy-fartsy and was enjoying making earrings and bracelets. I wanted to make sure I finished my beaded earrings before going to San Francisco.

I think of myself as a devoted fatalist. Since being forced to leave Cuba at the cusp of my adolescence, I've come to expect the other shoe to drop any moment now. As a Murphy's Law devotee, I believe if anything can go wrong, it will. Furthermore, I believe the chances of something going wrong increase in direct proportion to how well they seem to be going at the time.

My sense of pending doom prevented me from spending more than two nights away from my apartment without leaving a phone number where my parents could reach me. Predictably, as Katya and I readied to go to San Francisco, the dreaded phone call came.

"Your father is hospitalized, and I need you by my side," my mother said straightaway.

"But I'm going to San Francisco!"

"For how many days? Can't you cut your trip short and fly to Miami instead of New York?"

I didn't know how to tell Katya. I was certain she'd used up all her savings to purchase my airline ticket.

"That's so selfish!" Katya said when she heard. No one had ever called my mother selfish. That's the last thing she was. Mami had spent her life taking care of others. "I think that's really shitty," Katya kept going. Had she stopped to look at my eyes she'd have realized how hurtful I found what she was saying. "A guilt trip is what it is. And so unfair!" she went on. "You should call her back and tell her you're not going. Doesn't your brother live in Miami? Why can't she lean on him and let you have a good time?"

"I guess I'm the one she needs now," I said meekly. "We can still go for a couple of days," I added.

"Yeah, a couple of days… That's not exactly what I had in mind."

In the end she accepted my peace offering, and we decided to go ahead with our shortened trip. Katya wasn't happy, but there was nothing else to be done.

"Take the window seat," she said when we boarded the train. Not even the splendorous Pacific Ocean had what it took to cheer me up. Real or imaginary, I felt bad vibes coming my way and I couldn't blame her. If only I could make her see how fragile my family was.

"Where are we staying?" I asked after making myself comfortable. With everything that was going on, I'd forgotten to ask.

"We'll get a bed at the Y," she said.

I had never traveled like this. Before getting on a plane or taking a bus or train, I always knew where I'd be staying, for how long, what I'd be doing, and with whom. But I wanted to be hip and kept to myself how weird I found it not to plan.

After the train pulled into San Francisco, we searched for a phone booth with a readable phonebook. We had no idea where the Y was or, in fact, anything else. Not even a city map in our pocket. Katya had back-packed her way through Europe and had learned to travel super light and now finding myself switching my thirty-pound bag from hand to hand, I wished I'd done the same.

"Hey, need some help?" yelled out a guy with a carroty beard and matching pony tail. He pulled his head back through the window of his VW Bug and maneuvered it into an empty parking space next to us. "Lars," he said by way of introduction. "Where can I take you guys?" With a face as white as a gallon of milk he must have been grateful to have freckles.

"We're looking for a Y or a hostel, a cheap place to stay." Katya said.

"You know what? I live in a student house in Berkeley and the guy who runs it is out of town. You guys can stay in his room if you want to. He won't mind. He's cool."

Katya and I exchanged looks, shrugged our shoulders, and climbed into the Bug. In New York I'd sooner die than get into a stranger's car, but there's travelling for you. On our way to Berkeley, I got my first view of the Golden Gate Bridge. Like in the movies. What a backdrop!

Lars parked in front of what looked like a fraternity house, large, lived-in. The interior of the house revealed how the Beatles' influence had persevered. Bright, ornately embellished Indian fabric camouflaged the living room's ratty furniture. A vibrant batik doubled as a tablecloth. Ashes of burnt incense sticks lined long and narrow wooden burners, the scent of sandalwood and jasmine still in the air. "We're more popular than Jesus" John Lennon had said in a 1966 interview. Two years later the rock band journeyed to India in search of spirituality. I remember this because when the Beatles were into their sitar phase young people discovered yoga, incense, brass bells, long skirts, all things Indian. I shouldn't have been surprised. This was Berkeley after all. Very cool, groovy, man.

Lars worked as a substitute teacher. When he didn't have a long-term assignment, he'd call the office each morning to check in. Between Berkeley and San Francisco he worked every day, he explained.

"I won't sub while you're around. I'll show you the place."

"You sure? I mean, we don't want to be a drag," I said.

Our self-appointed tour guide drove us across the Golden Gate Bridge. People like to say, "It doesn't disappoint," but that's so lame. I decided then and there I'd spend my life traveling.

"You're lucky it's not overcast today," Lars said.

"I know. I mean, it's like the most amazing view ever. I can't believe I'm here. And you live here! I mean, like how neat is that?"

Lars drove us to San Rafael so we could see Frank Lloyd Wright's Marin County Civic Center before taking us to Fisherman's Wharf for a late lunch of clam chowder and crusty sourdough bread, my first. That was my only disappointment, the pier. Everything I'd seen so far was brighter, cleaner, lovelier than in Manhattan, but the wharf was seedy and filthy. I guess all wharfs are. Afterwards we took a streetcar up Telegraph Hill. From the top of Telegraph Hill we watched a flaming orange sun bathe the bridge in buttery yellow light. I turned my head and looked at Lars. His hair, the same orange vermillion as the bridge, reminded me of Van Gogh's self-portraits. Did I say he was Dutch? He took hold of my hand and leaned to kiss me. It would have been magical but I wouldn't let him kiss me in front of Katya.

The night before leaving, Lars and a friend of his, Katya and I sat on the floating deck of the trendy Trident bar in Sausalito. Passing through the restaurant as we headed towards the deck I looked up at its celebrated psychedelic ceiling. Blew me away! To think Janis Joplin used to hang out here. I could see her now with beads and scarfs around her neck, with feathers in her hair, and vests I could have killed for. Spellbound, sipping wine on the floating outside deck, I watched the city lights undulate in the water while a foghorn moaned in the misty distance. The night turned chilly and moved close and wrapped an arm around me. Pinch me.

"Are you sure you can't stay for a few more days?"

"Lars, do you think I want to leave?"

At the airport I cried. Like Ingrid Bergman in Casablanca.

Miami. Two deodorant semicircles stained the shocking-pink shirt I wore for the flight. Humidity had turned my naturally curly hair into a Brillo scouring pad. Perspiration glued my bell-bottom jeans to my thighs. I spotted my ultra-tanned brother. He sported Bermuda shorts and loafers—no socks. In Cuba they called Loren *El Negro* because he didn't bronze; he blackened. In the summer Belén, who loved to kid about race, liked to tease him, "*A ver, Loren, enséname la marca de la trusa.*" Come on, Loren; show me you're white under the swimming trunks.

"What do you have here? A corpse?" Loren asked as he picked up my suitcase and tossed it in the trunk. I envied his short-sleeved cotton shirt and cool shorts. Such hairy legs he had! As we drove away, he said, "Do you want to stop by the house and say hello to Lilia Maria and the kids?"

"Tomorrow, Loren," I said. "Right now all I want to do is get under a shower."

"How's Papi?" I asked.

"Not good."

"And Mami?"

"Hanging in there, as always."

"Where is she?"

"In the apartment, with Fello."

"When will I get to see Papi?"

"Tomorrow. Visiting hours are over."

Back then Miami was not the Latin-American capital it is today. In the 1960s the city didn't have the imposing skyline that served as the backdrop for Miami Vice. Looking out the car window on the way to my folks all I could see was land as flat as a strap, with timid structures on top. "*Como un plato,*" I said. Like a plate.

"I like to see the sky," Loren snapped.

"I wasn't being critical. It's just so different from where I come from." I didn't remember his being so defensive before joining the invasion. "*Huelo café!*" I said to change the topic. We were still on Flagler but further south where the discerning aroma wafted through the streets.

Miami transformed itself plenty since our family began vacationing there in the 1950s. Back then we liked to take a break from bustling Havana and lounge in Miami Beach. Hard to believe after all that followed but at that time you could go up to Cubana or Pan Am's counter at Aeropuerto Rancho Boyeros and buy a ticket to Miami for $25. My parents would rent an apartment in one of the seasoned Art Deco buildings that dotted the waterfront in what is now South Beach. As Loren maneuvered Miami's traffic I had this flashback of summery pastel facades, of lobbies covered with loud pink-flamingo carpets, of hallways wallpapered in tropical flora, parrots and all. Fond memories of Miami Beach resurfaced: swimming in the sea, leaving my footprints in the sand, collecting seashells, taking outdoor showers. Gazing out the car window I noticed the prevalence of Spanish signs advertising Cuban restaurants, Cuban cafes, Cuban bakeries. It smelled like nostalgia. Miami didn't feel American; it felt like *el exilio.*

Exiles lose everything that defines them. For what is identity if not *mi tierra, mi idioma, mi cultura, mi gente?* My land, my language, my culture, my people. Miami-Cubans' exaggerated reluctance to adapt stemmed from their inability to return to their roots. They didn't want to assimilate; they wanted to hold on to their culture and native language so they sought their *compatriotas* and formed a *comunidad.* You see it in every major city. Little Havana was not that different from Chinatown, Little Italy, Koreatown, Little Odessa.

"Mami got lucky," I said. "She won't have to speak

English here."

I couldn't remember a time when my mother wasn't trying to learn English. For years she'd taken classes in one of those binational language centers. With a lousy memory, she never made it past low-intermediate. Up north she was always asking *"¿Qué dice ahí?"* What does it say? Once a bookworm, she now had little to read. Spanish books of her liking weren't easy to find. But not being able to read in English didn't stop her from clipping mouthwatering recipes from women's magazines. Some words just wouldn't stick, words like "pour." What does "poor" mean? she'd ask, probably wondering what poverty *(pobreza)* had to do with cooking. And because she had no way of telling which words mattered and which didn't, in her recipe box I'd find index cards labeled "Fluffy Saffron Rice" or "Heavenly Pound Cake."

"That's why she sent the three of us to American schools," Loren remarked with a melancholy smile. "She says you have to learn languages when you're a kid, otherwise it's practically impossible."

Loren parked in front of a charming garden apartment complex with tasteful, well-manicured grounds. Freshly painted bungalows faced a central garden with benches and chairs. I knocked on the door and when I saw my mother's smile I forgot how sweaty I was and gave her a big hug.

"Mami, I missed you so much!" I said, *de corazón,* from the heart. "You look great, you really do! I like your hair." She had switched to auburn brown, and it brought out the beauty of her eyes.

"Show me the place."

"You're looking at it. This is it. Well, this and a kitchen."

She showed me the kitchen, spacious enough to fit in a dining table and chairs. I found it hard to imagine my parents sharing a room all day. My mother liked to read and my father wouldn't miss a televised sports game. Although larger than our first Miami apartment, I thought of what little progress they'd made over the years. *El exilio cubano* had come to embody entrepreneurship, but you wouldn't know it from my folks, but it wasn't for lack of trying.

"Mami, tell me about Papi."

"Things didn't go as well as we thought. He lost his job. It's happened so many times, he just couldn't handle it. To be his age and know you've become unemployable is devastating. He was really down. And I understood. But he lost interest in everything around him. He stopped eating. He couldn't sleep. And you know what happens when you can't sleep, you get anxious and irritable, and the whole thing becomes a vicious circle.

"What I don't understand is how hospitalization helps." I said.

"Well, he can't just sit all day staring at the wall. In the hospital they make him participate in group stuff. And they medicate him."

"What about you, are you ok?"

"Better now that you're here," she said.

Chapter Twenty Six

There are things best forgotten. I can't recall whether my father was hospitalized in a county or state hospital but I know he was inside a mental institution, not a regular medical facility. The windows were secured as they had been at Bellevue. Before we could enter his ward, my brothers were required to empty their pockets and my mother and I had to empty our handbags. I was reminded of leaving Cuba: *"Su cartera por favor."* I looked at Loren in complicit silence, trying to glean answers to questions I dared not ask. Was this the right place for him? Was my father suicidal? Papi was a fervent Catholic who liked to say only cowards committed suicide.

"Even mental illness is better in Cuba," I said to Loren.

I wished Papi could take another rest cure in San Miguel de los Baños as he had after his first nervous breakdown in Cuba. I'd have given anything to get him out of that American psychiatric prison. Katya was wrong; my mother had been right to call me. She was unwell. Life just kept getting worse. Her husband's frail nerves continued to deteriorate, her heart surgery had been less than successful, her three kids lived far apart from each other and were growing increasingly distant. She must have resented my father for letting her down. I know I often did. Mental illness is a bitch; people like to think that with will power you wouldn't have succumbed to it. No one thought that way about diabetics—if you set your mind to it you can produce insulin. But what did I want, justice? Even acknowledging it was an illness I found it hard to accept his depression.

Entering the room we found Papi leaning against his bed, unshaven, stooped over, anxious. His mouth was dry, and he wanted more water. Loren refilled the water glass as we helped him get back in bed. He didn't say *"Puchita qué felicidad el verte,"* as was his habit. He was so remote, staring off into nothingness. I wondered whether he realized I'd come from across the country to see him. I wanted to tell him about San Francisco but didn't see the point. He seemed too heavily medicated to follow a conversation. What drugs were they giving him? Actually, I didn't really want to know. I just wanted him well and home again. We made small talk, and he rubbed his hands and tried to contribute to the conversation without much success. At last he said, "When am I getting out of here?" No one could answer.

I felt a rush of pity for my father. Like all exiles, he'd been robbed of everything that mattered. So had I. The difference was that I, being young, had found a road to a new self—an independent woman. My father's losses were insurmountable. Not only had he lost his identity, he'd also lost his ability to provide for his family. Deprive a man of the means to make a living and you've emasculated him. My father continued to be locked into the man he was in Cuba, unable to surrender the dream of returning to a homeland that no longer existed.

Loren was struggling in Miami, working all day, taking evening courses, living in a house too small for a family of four. But he was happy. He'd already reconnected with his close friends from El Vedado Tennis. In Cuba he'd been to so many schools his real friends were from the club, whereas I'd only attended one school and missed my classmates most. Not that they would have known it—I didn't as much as pick up the phone when I was in Miami. Why would I? *Hay que poner buena cara*, you have to put on your best face, we liked to say, and I couldn't find it in me. All the crises. Why would I want anyone to know? Besides, it wasn't like I could go wherever I wanted. Like so many Manhattanites, I didn't drive, so once in Miami I had to depend on others, leaving me feeling trapped. And so I spent my time either at the hospital or in Mami's little apartment, all the while feeling it wasn't enough: I needed to move to Miami. But what about my apartment? In Manhattan, if you know what's good for you, you give up everything and everybody before you give up your apartment.

A few days later, when the antidepressants kicked in, I bought a return ticket to New York. Nothing else made sense, and it was my home after all. The way I saw it, I had a lot going in New York: a scholarship to a prestigious university, reliable public transportation, a rent-stabilization apartment in a luxury building, a neat roommate, my alter-ego Pedro, friends dating back to secretarial school, and a fabulous neighbor. "Neighbor" Jerry ran the gallery underneath my apartment, and after attending an opening for an upcoming watercolorist I'd pop in on my way to the grocery store asking him if he needed anything. Weekdays when he wasn't busy, we'd have wine, cheese, and crackers and call it a meal or we'd order Chinese food and I'd go out and get beer because wine doesn't go well with Chinese food.

I called California Lars soon after arriving in New York. He hadn't heard from me since I'd left San Francisco. He promised to visit in December and in the months leading to Christmas the image of Lars with his carroty hair and easygoing charm burned in the back of my mind. I talked about him nonstop. "Wait until you meet my Dutchman from Berkeley" I'd tell anyone who'd listen. But–and I know this is a spoiler–I'll jump ahead and acknowledge than when Lars came to visit I didn't want anyone to meet him. The ponytail I'd found so cool in Berkeley looked like unraveled Halloween yarn in New York. He wasn't slight of build but short and skinny or at least that's how he looked buried under the weight of a borrowed, oversized winter coat. And those cheerful lotus-land shirts that looked so groovy in sunny California looked ludicrous under a sweater in black-clad steely Gotham. Whatever was I thinking?

Good thing it was Christmas; nothing beats Christmas in New York. The humongous Christmas tree at Rockefeller Center, the ice rink just below, Saks Fifth Avenue's uber-famous Christmas windows, Radio City Music Hall's show of shows, the Empire State Building's red and green lights beaming festivity into the night. I showed Lars all these sights with genuine New Yorker pride. I'd like to think I was as gracious and welcoming to him in New York as he'd been in San Francisco.

Soon after arriving, Lars called friends of his parents and they invited us over for dinner. I could tell this was one of the highlights of his trip. He was keen on having them meet me. When I met them, I could tell they were a traditional well-off Dutch couple around my parents' age. They lived in a deluxe building on Park Avenue and were very European, very old-world, as was their abode, with its period furniture, long drapes, dark woods, and somber colors. I couldn't help but wonder what they made of Lars and his ponytail. I mean, this couple was stuck-up. Had he wanted to impress me or them? Couldn't he see that the upper-crust disapproved of men with long hair? Was he clueless? I couldn't understand what I'd seen in him. This was the fab guy I'd spent all my time in Miami thinking about. Sad to say despite the places we visited, the dining and the wining, despite all the sightseeing of a city I adored, I couldn't wait for him to leave. Hours stretched like bubble gum. Never-ending days, interminable nights, that's how I remember Lars' visit. I was determined to show him I thoroughly enjoyed his visit after his being so nice to me in California. Then he'd be gone and distance would play its trick. Wrong again. Lars called me the moment he got home, trying to pin down a date for me to visit him. Even on the phone I couldn't get myself to say, "Lars it's over," and I hated myself for being such a wimp. An eternity, that's what it took him to get the message.

All these years later, Bernard was still in the picture. He'd hit bottom with breakneck speed, and I kept seeing him mostly because I felt partially to blame for his horrific descent. Maybe if I hadn't kicked him out of my apartment which, after all, I owed to him, he'd still be just another high-functioning alcoholic. Bernard would drop by out of the blue—the doorman would buzz and announce, "Mr. Cooper is here. Should I send him up?" Sometimes I'd say, "Please tell him I'm sorry but I have company," and sometimes I'd say, "Send him up, please." The sight of him broke my heart, particularly because he used to be so handsome. Now he didn't even make an effort to look presentable. With his bloated face, puffy eyes, broken blood vessels, and pasty complexion he looked like he'd spent the night on skid row. As he walked into the apartment, I noticed him struggling to walk steadily. "I'm taking these horse pills for high-blood pressure," he explained, "and they affect my balance."

How did he manage to survive? He'd been unemployed for months and months and I suspected he was no longer employable. Maybe he was on disability.

"Where are you living?" I had to ask.

"With Annie."

I'd always suspected Annie carried a torch for Bernard. She found everything that came out of his mouth fascinating, would laugh whenever he'd deliver a punch-line before telling the joke, unfailingly agreed with his point of view, no matter how off the bat. And she wasn't twenty years old.

"And Larry?" I asked.

"Larry walked out on her," Bernard said barely audibly.

"And he left her the apartment?" I asked. Shame on me. Bernard talking about heartbreak and me hearing "apartment."

"He split," Bernard said. "Nobody knows where the hell Larry is."

"I've always loved that place. How's Annie doing?"

"Not well, she's lost a lot of hair. I guess that's one of the reasons Larry left her. She wears a wig. But she still has her job, so that's something."

"Some kind of assistant?"

"Office manager. And they really appreciate her efficiency."

"Good."

The last time I saw Bernard was the night he insisted on trying out a new restaurant a few blocks from my apartment. It was the first Greek restaurant in the neighborhood and he was always keen to try new things. I walked; he zigzagged. As luck would have it, when I walked into the small restaurant the first person I saw was a lawyer I'd once dated, with his new girlfriend. My instinct was to turn around and leave but I didn't see how I could gracefully do it. Bernard and I sat down and after reading the menu he ordered "for the lady" as he had since our first date, but now it bothered me. Now I wanted to tell him, "I can order my own food, thank you very much." Midway through dinner he fell off his chair. Literally. I can't remember a time when I was so ashamed to be in public. He straightened himself up. "It's those goddamned pills. I'm going to have to stop taking them."

"Do you want to leave or do you want to finish your meal?" I asked.

"I guess we better leave in case it happens again."

"Let's," I said and got up. Bernard asked for the bill.

A few months had gone by since that ill-fated dinner and the few times I wondered about Bernard. I attributed his silence to that humiliating episode. Actually, I didn't think of him all that often anymore, which is why Bob's call threw me back. Bob lived in the apartment where Bernard and I would rendezvous when we had both lived at the Colonnade in Newark.

"Bernard died," Bob said. My heart sank. I had expected him to always be around.

"Oh, my God, when?"

"Yesterday. Heart attack. Right after leaving his

doctor's office. Can you believe it?"

Bob filled me in with the details of the funeral, to be held the following day. I repeated the information line by line, like an echo, but wasn't taking notes. I had no intention of going to Bernard's funeral.

All at once the blazing rage I'd felt years earlier when I heard him say, "the farce is over," fired up again. The balls! I was young, vulnerable, and malleable. When I warned him I was engaged he had replied, "I don't pay attention to rings." That alone should have been a giveaway. He'd asked me to marry him while he was still married. He'd deceived me in every imaginable way: he was single; he was getting a divorce; he was sending me to college; he was going into rehab. No wonder his wife Nicky was almost half his age; anyone older would have seen through his bullshit. What a sucker I'd been! I was beyond indignant when I thought about his friends, about Bob, Larry, Annie, and everybody else "in the know." At least mild-mannered Midwestern Annie should have been forthright. She could have walked a mile in my shoes but, no, her allegiance was to Bernard. So much for sisterhood. When I met Bernard, my life couldn't have been more sheltered. I only socialized with people my parents approved of, and in Cuba I was always chaperoned. Not by my mother, mind you, but by one of her friends. The realization I'd been conned by someone who professed to love me had left an unsightly scar. I'm not implying I sat at home licking my wounds. But I started to question people's motives and wonder whether they, too, were duplicitous. Yes, it's even possible I was a tad paranoid. All I'm saying is I was damaged goods.

What prospect did a regular guy have after I'd been wined, dined, seduced and, yes, conned—in that order—by a rogue eighteen years my senior? I found most men my age boring. One evening, during that odd interval when Bernard wanted us to be friends he said, "I was your father, your brother, your lover, your best friend. You expected me to fulfill all your needs." Later, in therapy, I realized I had assigned him a paternal role, but I was also reminded he could have refused it. He didn't, my therapist explained, because he profited from my dependency. I agreed. Outside of booze and cigarettes, Bernard was hardly a powerless man.

Years later, in a consciousness-raising group, I uncovered something even more significant. Bernard had met an undefined, lost girl waiting for a white knight to come and rescue her.

Chapter Twenty Seven

When I answered the phone I was surprised to hear Loren's voice, being the middle of a workday. That is, until he said, right off the bat, "I'm on my lunch break so I don't have long to talk. Papi has colon cancer. You need to move to Miami. Mami needs you here."

I was speechless, my God, now what?

"How bad is it Loren?"

"They won't know until they open him up," he said. "But Mami needs you here anyway."

"I can't move to Miami," I snapped. "I've got a scholarship at Columbia and I'm only halfway through." My heart raced. I immediately realized I was expected to behave as if we were still in Cuba. I was the unmarried daughter, *la solterona* or old maid, and as such I was expected to care for my parents until they died.

"The University of Miami is as good as Columbia," Loren retorted. Of course the University of Miami wasn't as good as Columbia, and I wasn't about to give up my scholarship. Would they ever take my life seriously?

"What have they told you about his cancer? What did Fello say about it? Do they have a prognosis? When is the operation?

"No one's told me about surgery yet. They don't think it's spread too much. One of his doctors is talking to Fello about it. I have to get back to work. Call me when you know what you're going to do," Loren said.

What I remember most after hanging up the phone was feeling powerless. Under siege. Not only did my father have cancer, but I was expected to reorganize my life as a result. I was so used to being ordered around that the thought of saying "no" to moving to Miami didn't so much as cross my mind. How can I say no? Papi has cancer. Loren still treated me as his kid sister, and I seemed unable to rebel against him. Once again feeling the victim, I opted for a glass of wine. My heart was still racing, so I poured myself another while staring aimlessly about what passes for a kitchen in a Manhattan apartment. I was mad. I didn't want to think about the dilemma I now faced. I let my mind wander over the various shortcomings of what I saw before me, unconsciously searching out areas I could find objectionable in my home. Looking for some kind of justification to cause me to jettison the life I'd been building. Certain complaints came easy. That joke of a kitchen, the deafening, never-ending city noise that pounded my building night and day, day and night. Still, I didn't want to give up my apartment, or my hard-fought-for Columbia scholarship, or my New York life. Noisy as hell, I admit, but my apartment was charming in a bohemian, eclectic way. It retained Bernard's inimitable imprint: the unsigned (and suspect) Braque lithograph, the orange wall, the shelves and shelves of books, and the playful paper lantern above the Queen Anne desk he'd so lovingly (and drunkenly) stripped. It didn't bother me Bernard had decorated it. I loved that apartment and subsequently I never thought: "That goddamned Bernard; it's his fault I have to live here." Quite the contrary, the apartment helped me understand why I'd found Bernard so appealing.

With a cigarette in one hand and a glass of wine in the other I sat on my Bentwood rocker swaying back and forth, first softly and then furiously, ignoring the damage to the shiny hardwood flooring. My mind was racing a mile a minute. How am I going to get rid of this stuff now? Jeee-sus Puchita, calm down.

When I heard Katya let herself in the front door, I stopped rocking and finished my wine. "There's no good way to say this. You're going to have to find another place to live because I'm moving to Miami," I said.

"Say again?"

"My brother called. My father has colon cancer and Loren says I need to move to Miami. I told him about my scholarship but he said the University of Miami's just as good as Columbia and that my mother needs me."

"Bullshit, and you know it. You're not going to ruin your life because your father has colon cancer," said

Katya. "How's that going to help anybody?" She looked like a bull ready to charge. "What a guilt trip!" she snarled. "Just because they think single women don't have a life doesn't mean you have to buy into it. You know what this is? It's emotional blackmail. You should see a shrink. I'm going to find out if you can see someone at the student clinic." And she did.

The smiling "May-I-help-you?" receptionist behind the short Formica-topped counter asked me to sign in. Even without reading the sign on the door I'd recognized the place as the student clinic. Like in a thousand other clinics, plastic institutional chairs with chrome arms and legs lined the walls. A scratched glass-top cocktail table covered with dated, well-thumbed *Time* and *Life* magazines anchored the room. Some tiles were missing from the gray linoleum floor; cigarette butts had burned others. Everything in the room showed heavy wear. And despondency. Trying to ignore the background Muzak, I forced myself to stay until they called my name.

"Are you always like this?" asked the youthful psychiatrist. What did he mean? I waited for a clarification but none came.

"This what?" I asked.

"This hyper?"

"Guess so," I said. What is he, thirty? Too young to know what he's doing, that's for sure. And where is he from anyway? Colombia? I'm not coming back.

"I have a suggestion," he said after listening to my tale of woe. "Instead of quitting school, why don't you take a leave of absence? Go see your parents and come back."

"What do I tell my professors?"

"I'll take care of that. Just give me a list of your courses."

"What are you going to say?"

"The truth. You have a family emergency and need to leave New York. By the time you get back, I'll have someone lined up for you to see on a regular basis. In the meantime, you have to try to let go of all this guilt. There's no reason why you should give up all you have going for you here because of a sick parent. The fact that you're single doesn't mean you don't have a life."

"That's what my family thinks."

"Then it's up to you to correct their view."

"Nobody talks about anything that matters. It's not like they say it out loud, you know. In Cuba if you don't get married you're supposed to live with your parents and take care of them until they die. I disappointed everyone when I got my own apartment. When my brother called he told me, *'Tú debes venir a vivir aquí.'* You should… but you speak Spanish, right?"

"Yes, and it's the same in Colombia. (I knew it!) That doesn't mean you have to fulfill their unrealistic expectations. Like I said, it's up to you."

"And unspoken," I added.

"Sorry?"

"Unspoken expectations. They don't say, 'Puchita,' (that's my nickname), 'you should be married by now.' I broke an engagement with a guy because he was always telling me what I could and couldn't do. What I could and couldn't wear. I wouldn't put up with his crap. But when it comes from my family I feel if I don't do whatever they expect of me I'm the world's lousiest daughter."

"And why do you think that is?"

And so it went.

Papi never knew he had colon cancer, just like my grandmother never knew she had lung cancer. I guess it's a Cuban thing. My father went into surgery at Mt. Sinai Hospital thinking he was having a polyp extracted. The cancer was caught in its early stage. The outcome pointed to a long, healthy life. Since he didn't require chemo or radiation, no one saw any reason to disclose that it was cancer. In his later years, when a doctor asked him if he'd ever had cancer he'd shake his head convincingly and say, "Never, thank God."

I don't know what I'd have done had the cancer spread. Would I have moved to Miami to assist my mother? There's no point in speculating. This much I know: it was a good thing I'd followed professional advice and not my brother's. I returned to Columbia and picked up where I'd left off.

"You're really putting it away," Katya told me as I poured myself another glass of wine. "You should stop."

"I can't sleep. It helps. I'll stop when I sort things out."

But I knew she was right.

Shortly afterwards I forced myself to call the clinic's psychiatrist. He'd kept his promise and referred me to a psychoanalyst, a Columbia University alumnus who'd see me on a sliding-scale basis. Her office was in the Fifties, off Madison Avenue, in a fancy building with a doorman. It all looked way out of my league but I went ahead anyway. I took the elevator, found her "suite" and took a seat in a spacious off-white waiting room decorated with all the warmth of an iceberg. No plastic chairs here. In fact, there was no one, no patients, no receptionist. Abstract modern paintings, but nothing to read. It spooked me out. It was just me in this frigid waiting room with a door at each end. I couldn't decide whether to knock on the closed door or go back out though the one I came in by. How will she know I'm here? What the hell, I'll knock. Just as I stood up, the door opened, and a young woman walked by me and exited through the front door without even making eye contact. That's Manhattan for you. From the inner doorway, an expensively suited middle-aged woman with jet-black dyed hair styled like a helmet asked me to come in. My first steps into shrinkdom. She offered the couch, and I declined. I sat across from her and once more compulsively recited my crisis of conscience.

At the next session, after minutes of unbearable silence, I blurted out, "I'm really fucked up."

"We need to explore this negative self-image. Why do you think that? Why do think you're 'fucked up?'"

And so it went.

By the end, I saw her longer than I should have. She relied heavily on medications and prescribed me an anti-psychotic drug. I said I was fucked up, but did I say I was a psycho?

"Don't drink with the meds," she said when she gave

me the prescription. Right.

My final appraisal of her is that she was a hair short of being lethal but I really didn't give her a chance. I fought most of her interpretations of my behavior and when she tried to deconstruct my mother, I contradicted her with vehemence. Once, when I felt she was putting my mother down, I said, "You're so wrong."

"You're too guilty to succeed," she said.

And I was.

I still clung to that passive, fatalistic attitude about life I had adopted, a choice that prevented me from taking advantage of real opportunities.

When Katya took off for Greece, I felt like Chaplin without his cane.

No hay mal que por bien no venga. Every cloud has a silver lining. Katya's departure forced me to work on my own act, never a bad thing. I couldn't afford the rent, so I interviewed for roommates. I placed an ad on the *Village Voice* and when people called, I'd ask a lot of questions and if I felt good about the conversation I'd meet them in neutral territory.

I decided on Norma because she was Cuban. Tall, with a good figure and a round, attractive face, Norma's skin was as white as a marshmallow. She'd recently finished college and when I met her she worked as an executive assistant in midtown Manhattan. What I liked best about Norma was despite her European-Jewish ancestry, her sense of humor was as Cuban as Bacardí rum. Cubans like to kid around in a distinctive manner called *"choteo,"* a kind of humor that allows us to survive whatever life throws our way. To *chotear* is to make irreverent remarks lampooning "*el destino*" or fate, authority, convention, solemnity and of course mortality and religiosity. Cubans find life too short to be taken seriously. Superstitious as hell, Cubans see no problem in holding on to contradictory belief systems like Catholicism and *Santeria*. I remember a radio healer called Clavelito whose program started with a trademark *décima* instructing his listeners to place a glass of water on top of the radio to magnetize it. That Norma knew about Clavelito meant the world.

"So when did you leave Cuba?" Norma asked.

"September 1960. And you?" I replied.

"Did you live in Miami?" And so it went.

When Norma moved in I was a full-time student in my junior year and a part-time worker. I still worked at the Urban Center but it was no longer the place I'd been so fond of. My immediate boss had returned to Washington, D.C. The former ambassador now headed a prestigious foundation. A research assistant who'd been a Peace Corps volunteer moved to Tanzania, and I missed them all. I got a lucky break when a bright and charismatic black woman in her early thirties was hired. She was returning to college after a divorce and planned to go to law school. We hit it off in no time. I remember Serena as one of those women who had everything going for her: beauty, intelligence, sophistication, and wit. We lunched together several times a week. Serena had lived in Italy—that's the reason she gave for treating lunch as if it were dinner. She'd always have a Cinzano before lunch and I'd have a Cutty Sark. Sometimes we'd meet for drinks after class. Her insight and common sense led me to seek her advice. She enjoyed dishing it out. I can see her now, square shouldered, sitting across the table from me at the West End. Almost always a turban covered her hair and, with her face framed, her African features were all the more striking. Serena had given up smoking and busied her hands folding and unfolding a paper napkin. She put the napkin down, patting it softly with perfectly manicured hands and picked up her Cinzano. She sipped it slowly and savored it. We were so different; everything she did was deliberate and elegant.

"What are you doing afterwards?" she asked.

"Going to Brentano's."

She laughed. "No, I mean after you get your BA. What are you doing after you graduate? Because unless you get a master's in something, it's back to the typing pool."

"I'm thinking of getting a PhD in Comparative Literature," I said.

"So you can drive a taxi?"

She had a point. A lot of taxi drivers in New York were graduate students (Vietnam War draft deferments) which I took to mean there was no shortage of PhD's.

She locked eyes with me and asked, "Have you thought of applying to the School of Journalism? You can write, you love words, you're a reader."

"Not a newspaper reader. Not even a magazine reader. Actually, not even a short-story reader. Novels, that's my thing."

"So? This is the Latino decade, you'll get a scholarship. You can decide what to do afterwards, but you need a master's."

"Maybe you're right," I said.

Instead of making an appointment with the General Studies counselor, I waited until my young English literature professor had office hours and when she was available, I asked her if she had a few minutes to spare. "I want to go to graduate school," I said. "I want to get a PhD in Comparative Literature, but I need a scholarship. What do you think my chances are?"

What I really wanted to say was, "Linda, I want to be just like you." Embarrassed, I smiled. "Help me."

"You'll get in all right," Linda said.

"But I can't go unless I get a scholarship."

"I don't think it will be easy to get a scholarship, not for literature," she said. "The field is saturated. But it won't kill you to try."

"But are there jobs?"

"If you don't mind teaching English Composition 101 in some Midwestern town, or some god-forsaken place, I'm sure you could land a job at a community college, except I don't see you doing that."

"Doing what?"

"Living in the boondocks teaching introductory courses."

"That bad, eh?"

"Afraid so. But if you apply for graduate school, I'll be happy to write you a letter of recommendation."

I thanked her.

I followed Serena's advice and applied to Columbia

Graduate School of Journalism. Did Title VII get me in? Or was I accepted because I graduated with Honors in English and Comparative Literature? Could it have been my personal essay? I'll never know and it shouldn't matter, except it does. I still hope it wasn't because of Title VII.

That summer I found in my mailbox a large envelope from the Journalism School. It contained, among other things, a little black book, the 1973-1974 School of Journalism "HANDBOOK." The 4" x 6" binder carried pictures and bios of my fellow students. So that's why I had to submit a passport photo. My insecurities flared up as I skimmed though the pages. My future classmates were mostly experienced writers; some had jobs I would have never given up. I hadn't even written for the high school newspaper. Unlike Fello I didn't have it in me to decide what I wanted to be when I grew up.

For my first Reporting & Writing assignment I had to interview the owner of a restaurant that had been closed by the Board of Health. The *New York Times* listed the restaurants that hadn't passed inspection. I wanted to interview the owner of a Chinese restaurant that was on the list. It was on Broadway, near the university. El cheapo.

"Hi," I said as I walked in, "I'm a student at Columbia University's Graduate School of Journalism and I'd like to know how you feel about the Board of Health closing your restaurant."

What did he say exactly? Enough for me to rush out the door.

A major blunder, a monumental mistake, a misjudgment. What had I been thinking when I applied to Journalism School? I must have known, deep inside, I didn't have what it took to be a reporter. I wasn't interested in delving into people's pain. Granted, I liked to write but, unlike other students, I wrote at a glacial pace. When practically every bar in the city with a TV was tuned to the Watergate hearings, and when most of my fellow students dreamed of being the next Bernstein, the next Woodward, I would have been happy joining the Peace Corps.

Even now, as I sat in the West End bar, I couldn't escape the televised Watergate circus. As I pondered the depths of my wineglass, wondering whether or not to drop out of school, in walked lanky, disheveled Tim, a classmate who'd become my friend and drinking buddy. We'd enrolled in the same magazine-writing class and liked to hang out together at village bars near where we both lived. We often warmed the stools of the now defunct Cedar Tavern, a writers' watering hole of some renown.

"What did you do, take a sabbatical?" asked Tim as he plopped down on the stool next to me.

"I'm thinking of dropping out," I said. "I don't know a thing about politics. I'm fed up with Watergate, with Vietnam, I feel like a fish out of water, like such a jerk. I'm not going to make it. You saw me fuck up." Tim had been with me when Mayor Lindsay gave students the opportunity to interview him, and I forgot to turn the tape recorder on.

"You're taking this way too seriously," Tim said. "Everybody screws up. It's no big deal."

"Easy for you to say, Tim. You're a writer. You don't even have to try. You've got talent."

"You don't have to understand politics," Tim said, ignoring the praise. "You can write about what interests you. You're interested in a lot of stuff, write about that."

Maybe he was right. All my life I'd been told I blew everything out of proportion, that I made a mountain out of a molehill, that I took everything to heart. Maria, the Drama Queen.

The day Tim and I graduated, my family wasn't there. Tim's parents took pity on me and invited me to their family's celebratory lunch. A witty and sophisticated pair, they reminded me of Nora and Charles in *The Thin Man*. As we went to the restaurant Tim's father walked with me while Tim walked ahead with his mother. "You know," Tim's father said, "nowadays everybody is boob crazy. Me, I'm a leg man, and you have the most beautiful legs." I looked at him and didn't know what to say but I saw that picaresque smile in his face and realized what a charming man he was. Tim's mother was equally delightful and I could see the debonair couple having the New York life I'd always wanted: Broadway plays, Sardi dinners, actors and writers for friends, the lot. By the time we'd finished lunch I wanted them to adopt me. This is how cool they were: they gave Tim a trench coat as a graduation present.

I'd thought with a degree from Columbia Journalism

School I'd easily get a job, but newspapers and magazines wanted experienced reporters. Every rejection letter chipped away what miniscule confidence I had. I didn't see what the point was. Like all depressed people I didn't think things would get better tomorrow, or next week, or next month. I coiled deep into my shell. I knew about melancholy. I knew about defeat, hopelessness, and paralysis. I called my analyst and asked her to hospitalize me. It was a weekend, but she gave me an appointment.

Bedraggled, I headed uptown. It wasn't like me to leave the village looking like a slob. I walked two blocks to the Astor Place subway station and took the Lexington Avenue line. I'd never seen so many homeless people in that station. I was looking at my future.

My analyst didn't think hospitalization was a good idea. "You know, checking yourself into a psychiatric hospital is something many people come to regret. It can come back to haunt you."

"You mean like Senator Eagleton? Not a chance I'll get that far." I couldn't even imagine applying for a job where psychiatric hospitalization would present a problem. Me?

Still she couldn't put aside the possibility I might harm myself.

"It's not that I want to kill myself. I just don't want to go on," I'd told her over the phone. My doctor err on the side of caution and reserved a bed at St. Luke's Hospital. At first the psychiatric ward looked no different from the rest of the hospital: no bars, no secured windows, not a thing to get freaked out about. The admission process had gone smoothly, and I stood in front of a bulletin board that displayed the schedules of an array of activities: group therapy, art therapy, the usual fare. It was when I walked into some kind of lounge that it hit me. I was in a psychiatric ward. The sight of all those young women with slashed wrists, with self-inflicted wounds, with anorexia, with vacant eyes scared the living shit out of me. When my analyst came to see me the following Sunday, I begged her to discharge me. "I'm not that sick."

"It's learned behavior," she said.

"What is?

"Not coping."

The next day when I left the hospital I wondered what Papi did when he saw all his demons waiting for him at the gate.

Chapter Twenty Eight

What do you think of Castro? Don't you think Cuba is better off now than before?

I was often compelled to lie, to say I was an American, but I didn't want to hear some wise-ass New Yorker retorting, "Really? Because you don't sound American."

By November 1971, I'd been in the United States eleven years. I'd just turned twenty-six, and for way too long when I told people I was Cuban it was Castro they asked about.

I hereby declare an oath that I absolutely and entirely renounce and abjure all allegiance and fidelity to any foreign prince, potentate, state or sovereignty of whom or which I have heretofore been a subject or citizen. Or, in plain English, I renounced being a Cuban citizen.

A week after my birthday, on November 15, 1971, I stood in a lower Manhattan Federal courthouse surrounded by hundreds of other immigrants, all holding small American flags on short wooden sticks, reciting the oath of allegiance to the United States of America.

Decades later whenever I watched an episode of *Law and Order* I'd recall that belly-of-a-whale room packed with young and old men and women, skin tones ranging from chalky white to licorice black, all repeating the oath in dissonance, a chorus of undecipherable accents. Some cried; some hugged their neighbor. I waited for an epiphany. *Nada.* After the ceremony ended, my consciousness still unchanged, I asked myself *¿Y ahora soy americana?* And now I'm an American? Didn't think so. I wasn't a snake; I couldn't shed my skin and slither into a new life. Always impatient, I realized that probably I was being precipitous. Maybe feeling you're a citizen of a country you weren't born to requires a period of gestation. Give it time, Maria.

Five years later, with millions of Americans watching *Roots,* a TV miniseries inspired by Alex Haley's Pulitzer-prize-winning book, the nation's ethnic consciousness skyrocketed like Fourth-of-July fireworks. There were then, at least in New York City, more hyphenated Americans than plain Americans. Afro-American, Irish-American, Italian-American, Native-American, Mexican-American. Not one to be left behind I quickly jumped aboard. *Si, Si,* Cuban-American. I conveniently ignored the fact that most Cubans living in the States never considered themselves to be anything other than Cuban exiles, taking pride in resisting assimilation. As evident in Miami, Cuban exiles worked hard at recreating the communities they'd been forced to leave behind. A life of inclusion by way of exclusion. But why them and not me? Why didn't I find living in a Cuban facsimile as compelling as my Havana classmates did?

The reason, I now suspect, is that the intolerable loss triggered by my uprooting had led me to supplant myself. I'd become someone different: a woman of independent views standing outside the exiles' enclave, but with one eye looking back in, fixed on the remnants of a life that could have been. And now that woman wanted to go home, to the real Cuba, to reconnect with the girl she'd stood in for, the girl who was left behind. In time I'd refer to my return to Cuba as my "Roots" trip, but that was only partly true. This burning desire to go back to the country of my birth was manifold. If I were to rank the motives compelling me to return to my native soil, seeing Belén again would top the list. I needed forgiveness for my seeming ingratitude.

In my dreams I flew to Cuba. Unlike a bird, I did not flap my wings. Instead, I stretched out my arms like rubber bands and plummeted freestyle out of the clouds, the sky a bright turquoise that mirrored the bottom of *la piscina chiquita* where I'd learned to swim. The dream recurred with frightening regularity and ended predictably: I never got there. I'd wake up crushed and spent. If being exiled is longing to return to your country but being unable to, then citizen or no citizen, I was still an exile.

Since 1961, when President Eisenhower severed diplomatic ties with Cuba, American citizens couldn't legally travel to Cuba. As Jimmy Carter campaigned for the 1976 presidential election, he drummed up support for a more liberal US policy towards Cuba, including bringing to an end the crippling economic sanctions and lifting the travel ban. The day of his inauguration I believe for the first time since leaving my homeland in the possibility of a return. And I was right: in March President Carter issued an executive order that lifted travel restrictions to Cuba, a directive that caused my life to change.

A prominent Cuban banker named Bernardo Benes had been traveling to Havana (with the support of high officials in the Carter administration) to meet clandestinely with senior Cuban government officials. In the fall of '78 these secret meetings spearheaded a process Benes called *El Diálogo*. Benes pulled together a group of open-minded Cuban Americans dubbed the Committee of 75 to engage the Cuban government over prisoner releases and the right of exiles to visit family in Cuba. The group's first session with Castro took place on November 22, 1978, and after additional meetings, over 3,000 political prisoners were released and exiles were allowed to return for week-long visits. But the Committee of 75, supposedly representative of the Cuban American community, was too ideologically diverse to speak with one voice and the group quickly dissolved.

In Miami's notoriously confrontational exile community, the members of the Committee of 75 were vilified as traitors. The vociferous Miami-Cubans viewed the existence of the Committee—and the concessions obtained—as a direct affront to their isolationist stance. In Miami, the Committee of 75 members, derisively called "*los dialógueros*," were dismissed as Castro's agents. Miami's virulent Cuban radio stations and sensationalist *periodiquitos* (yellow tabloids) venomously attacked the *comunistas, traidores, agentes de Fidel* who traveled to Cuba. Two Committee of 75 participants, Carlos Muñiz Varela and Eulalio Negrín, were murdered by anti-Castro terrorists. The October 1978 bombing of *El Diario-La Prensa* in New York was connected to an editorial the paper had run in favor of *el diálogo*. As leader of *el diálogo*, Benes received threats and was ostracized by much of *la comunidad*. From my perch in New York I had viewed the beginning of *el diálogo* as a step forward, a process of renewal and reunification, but Miami was a different country.

In Cuba we had learned to live with terrorism. Anti-Batista groups' homemade bombs were regularly hidden in restrooms of movie theaters, nightclubs, restaurants, and department stores. The horrors would be splashed across all of our newspapers. The devices served as intimidating reminders that people had no business amusing themselves while their countrymen were being killed and tortured by Batista's henchmen. And yet the bombs failed to instill terror. At home I heard about a young woman who had lost an arm at the world-famous Tropicana nightclub, renowned for *las mulatas de fuego*, but I don't recall sabotage stopping Cubans from going to nightclubs. Ditto for movie theaters, where bombs were hidden in the bathrooms. I'd be lying if I denied that my family took certain precautions, but our lifestyle didn't change that much. I was told to go to the bathroom before leaving the house—no matter what, public restrooms were not to be used. Sometimes we'd save water in as many containers as we could find because it was rumored the aqueducts were about to be bombed. We made sure we had enough candles for an *apagón* or blackout. Papi called the terrorists *cobardes* even though they stood against Batista.

"Papi," I asked him after Eulalio Negrín was killed in Union City, "what do you think of Cubans killing Cubans here?"

"Terrorists are cowards, no matter what. But I find it indefensible to have a dialogue with a monster like Castro. You don't negotiate with the enemy. You bring them to their knees."

They're Cubans. When did we forget that?

It was never said but nonetheless expected that every Sunday, come hell or high water, I call home. "Home" being, my parents' house. And so I did, with rare exceptions, for as long as they lived. If for any reason I failed to call, my parents, but particularly my father, would conjure such a doomsday scenario (a scenario I could have spared them with a single call), that guilt ate me up for days to come.

This particular Sunday I wanted to let Mami know when I was arriving. I also needed her to ask Loren to pick me up at the airport. I'd visit my folks during Thanksgiving, Christmas, and summer vacations. After the first couple of trips I came to think Miami was a good place for them. So many friends lived nearby and Papi's two brothers had settled there, as had his nephews. In Miami it didn't matter that my mother couldn't speak English. Due to the influx of Cubans, I was certain that local stores would replace the "*Se habla Español*" signs with "English Spoken Here" signs. The novelty of Miami's Cuban *timbiriches*, where I could buy *pastelitos, guarapos, sándwiches cubanos, medianoches, capuchinos, brazos gitanos*, had worn off, along with watching local interviews of old *exilados* playing dominos in *El Sagües*. Whenever anything having to do with Cuba hit the news, TV crews popped up to get the views of the players, clad in their Americanized polyester short-sleeved *guayaberas*. Similarly, if it was election season presidential candidates didn't fail to show up at Little Havana's Versailles restaurant for the prerequisite photo ops with local Cuban leaders. The restaurant more often than not functioned as an impromptu meeting place for Miami's exile community.

At the onset of the Cuban diaspora, it was nearly impossible to find a job in Miami. Families like mine wandered far and wide searching for ways to survive, always telling themselves it was only for the time being. Next year, they were sure, they'd be back in Cuba. *El próximo año en Cuba.* I know of one marriage that dissolved because the husband refused to buy furniture here in the States because they'd be returning to Cuba any day now.

The failure of the Bay of Pigs invasion squashed any illusions of a return. After President Kennedy's betrayal by withdrawing air support during the invasion and the US administration's promise not to invade Cuba if the Soviets dismantled their missiles, Cuban exiles were finally convinced. Americans would not be risking their lives and treasure to overthrow Castro's dictatorship in Cuba. Knowing the American government would take no further actions to free their homeland, many Cuban exiles opted to relocate; especially those who'd been forced to find work in inhospitable climates. Pulled by the magnetism of the Cuban *comunidad*, they moved to Miami by the droves. Miami might not be home, but it was as close to home as they would get. The few Cuban families we knew from New Jersey were already back in Miami. They'd missed *la familia, las visitas* (the casual stop at a friend's house). They missed the sound of their language and the beat of their music. But just as significantly, they'd had it with *el frio*. Better to melt in the familiar heat than to freeze in the alien cold.

Havana had been a cosmopolitan city. It was a densely populated city of arts and culture, built in an eclectic mix of Cuban Baroque, Neoclassical and Moorish architectural styles, and with a long memory of its history. Singers, musicians, all kinds of artists came to Havana to perform in our famous cabarets and nightclubs. Nat King Cole didn't need to use a separate entrance to sing at

Tropicana; there are pictures of him enjoying cocktails at the nightclub's bar. Havana attracted people like Hemingway, Graham Greene, Frank Sinatra, Ava Gardner, Errol Flynn, and Marlon Brando. Like fly-paper, our capital was hard to leave behind. And now in Miami, Cubans huddled together over their espressos and resuscitated the past. Miami allowed Cubans to live and thrive in the United States while having little to do with it. They preferred a small world of familial shorthand. I understood seeking the familiar; it decreases the sense of alienation. In self-defense, Miami-Cubans sought and found their tribe, and this brought them comfort and security. Others had found their past and weren't about to let it go. For them that was the whole point of living in Miami.

For me, a mass-transit urbanite, being in Miami without wheels was like being stranded on a desert island. Not that I had a license; I missed being mobile. Back then Miami's mass transport system was a joke, that much I knew. Some evenings Loren or Lilia Maria would pick me up and I'd visit them. Sometimes Loren would stay with the kids so Lilia Maria and I could go out on a girls' night. Either Saturday or Sunday Loren and Lilia Maria would take me to the beach, and it was heavenly to swim in warm water. But I mainly spent most days sitting in my folks' small apartment, talking, or watching Spanish soaps on TV, which is what Mami and I were doing when Teresa, a close friend from "the old neighborhood," stopped by.

"Igualita," Teresa said the moment she set eyes on me, pointing to the striking resemblance to my mother. I

could see my mother's face glow as she offered Teresa *"una tacita de café."* Even with an almost fifteen-year difference in ages between the two, Teresa and Mami had been close for as long as I can remember. She and her husband—a lawyer so multi-talented he's best described as a Renaissance man—lived with his parents in an expansive and elegant colonial house a block away. In Cuba, Teresa frequently dropped by unexpectedly, and now she'd extended that habit to Miami. At a glance, I was reminded how much those two enjoyed each other's company.

It's safe to say most Miami-Cubans would do almost anything to stay together. Deeply inculcated in both the exile and the immigrant's psyche is the notion you cannot trust anyone outside your family. You trust others at your peril. And so the Cuban family in Miami didn't evolve with the rest of American society.

America in the 60's was a tumultuous place. As with most generations, it's the youth that drives societal and cultural changes, but the scope, the speed, and the magnitude of the transformations that took place during that decade were all but incomprehensible. We dealt with wars, the feminist revolution, men landing on the moon, the pill and the ensuing sexual revolution, the civil rights movement, free speech, hippies, environmentalism, and so much more.

Miami was one of the few large cities bypassed by the antiwar demonstrations of the sixties. Cubans had no beef with Americans fighting communism in Vietnam. They wished Americans had fought communism earlier and closer to home. And while relationships between sisters and brothers, parents and offspring were changing and evolving at a pace society struggled to keep up with, the Cuban Miamian family by and large remained untouched. Back in New Jersey when my parents told me that if I got my own apartment they'd disown me, they weren't emotionally blackmailing me; they were behaving like typical Latin immigrants or exiles. In Miami my generation didn't leave home until it was time to marry. Decades later when I visited friends in Miami, one of my former schoolmates told me that in Miami the parental dream was that your son or daughter marry what they called the three c's: *cubano, católico y conocido* (Cuban, Catholic, and known). Problem was, we Nodarses hadn't lived in Miami long enough to become clannish. My favorite uncle's death in a New Jersey hospital affected the lives of every member of my family in ways we could never have imagined. I can draw a straight line from that event to the liberated woman who lived in my Manhattan apartment. The Cuban diaspora was alive and well in my family: Fello in Texas, Loren in Miami, I in New York. My oldest brother had married a Mexican woman and after my breakup with Panchito I dated only Americans.

That said, I can't remember one hospitalization, and there were several, when the three of us weren't by our parents' side, although the way Loren and I saw it, it was Fello's presence that really mattered. Not just because he was a doctor; that would have been easier to accept. What was hard to swallow was the way both Mami and Papi always deferred to Fello about everything, something that made Loren and me feel we didn't count as much.

I can't say what month or year it was, or whether the sun shone brightly through the window or rain pounded heavily against it. What I remember about the day is Fello saying, "I can't keep leaving my patients and my family behind to come here every time there's a problem. I'll be happy to take care of you in Texas, but I can't keep doing this."

I don't remember ever being as pissed off as when I heard him say that. I couldn't believe my ears, but that's how things were back then. To be a man! My mother hadn't asked for my opinion before telling the counselor, "She's going to secretarial school." She would have never done that to Fello, never in a million years. Women of my mother's generation took it as a given that men had professions and women had babies. Men called the shots, period. It didn't seem to bothered traditional women very much, but it infuriated me. Fello wasn't acting any differently than other men of that era. But what woman who had a profession, thanks to her parents would have said, "If you need me, you better pack and move nearby?" I couldn't think of a single girlfriend who'd say that to her parents. Women, they moved where they were needed and if they didn't, if they said to themselves, to the world, as I had finally learned to do, it's my life, then that millstone burdened them for life. "You're too guilty to succeed," my psychoanalyst had once said—and meant it.

Texas City, Texas is another small Gulf Coast refinery town you can smell from miles away, like Goliath's armpits. Fello rented my parents a downstairs one-bedroom apartment near his house. My mother decorated it with her usual pride. The apartment wasn't far from the clinic where Fello worked—but then, everything in Texas City is close by. An elderly Cuban couple lived a few doors down, and Mami and Carmen hit it off. Carmen had a married daughter who lived nearby and this state of affairs would more than once, prompt my mother to say, "*Nada de esto hubiera pasado en Cuba.* None of this would have happened in Cuba. *Aquí la familia no importa.*" Here family doesn't matter. Hardly a fair comment, especially since Fello dropped in on them twice a day and Loren had recently moved his wife and two young children to a Houston suburb only 20 miles away. Loren visited every other weekend. I continued to be the outlier. All that their move changed for me was which airline ticket I purchased.

Fello continued to be a man of habits and rituals. As just a girl in Cuba, I'd watch him empty his pockets and stack the coins by denomination in a shallow catch-all plate in his bedroom. Here in Texas City he was just as predictable. Each weekday he'd show up at my parents at lunchtime, a stethoscope around his neck, blood pressure cuff in hand. First, he'd kiss them on the cheek, then he'd walk to the kitchen, take out the mini espresso coffeemaker—the one that now has a mustached man's finger pointing up—and make himself and my mother a *cafecito.* Next he took my parents' blood pressure, listened to my mother's heart, and sat in the armchair for no less than five but no more than fifteen minutes. Ditto after work. I knew of no other son who showed such devotion.

Such was the Cuban diaspora that even Texas City had a small exile community of its own. A partner in the clinic that hired my brother was Cuban and several Cuban engineers worked at the nearby Monsanto plant. With an immigrant's nose, they'd found each other and celebrated the holidays together. Fulfilling my filial duties, every Christmas I'd make the pilgrimage from New York City to Houston. At first Loren would pick me up at the airport and drive me to Texas City, but I guess he must have resented that Fello never offered to do it, and eventually he stopped. Afterwards Fello insisted on paying for an airport limousine to drive me to my folks' apartment.

Every Christmas visit was the same, a remembrance of things past. The Texas City Cubans would eat *lechón,* black beans and rice, yucca and plantains, just as Mami, Papi and I had done that first Thanksgiving in Ridgefield Park, New Jersey. It seemed like a lifetime ago when I was a different kind of outsider. Now I lived 1600 miles away in that den of inequity called New York City, single and childless to boot. Christmases left me feeling as much of an outcast as I had in that high school homeroom in New Jersey. Instead of "Do you have refrigerators in Cuba?" or "Did you wear shoes in Cuba?" it was: *"Tienes novio?"* Do you have a boyfriend? *"¿Y no te da miedo vivir en Nueva York sola?"* Doesn't it scare you to live alone in New York? I'd try not to mention any romance on my menu to avoid questions about a forthcoming engagement or worse yet, a wedding. I'd learned that trying to explain my life and how I plodded my way through it was like taking a blind man to the movies.

This particular Christmas I recall standing in the spacious kitchen of Fello's new house watching my mother listen to a lively Cuban school teacher talk about her students. I was glad to see her with Cuban friends, being able to converse in her own tongue. Her eyes sparkled. Her arched eyebrows went up a bit higher. She'd stopped coloring her hair, and silver strands framed her round face. Still a good-looking woman, with a smile that could warm a swimming pool. I could hear my father in the family room telling his captive audience his *Palacio de los Deportes* story, the one about the night he went to the Sports Palace to confront Fidel, put him in his place, and tell him he might have worked for Batista but he was no crook. His impulsive attempt to set the record straight had nearly put his life in peril. "I was almost sent to *el paredón*," Papi was saying.

Fello moved next to me and, chuckling, whispered, "Next time he tells the story, they'll execute him."

Chapter Twenty Nine

I was working at home in my favorite robe. "It will follow you to the subway one day," Tim had said of my long lavender chenille robe, and he wasn't off the mark. I was in the middle of a translation, typing away on my portable electric Smith Corona, coffee and a pack of Parliaments by my side, when the phone rang. I left the dining room table and walked to the kitchen, "Hello."

"Hi, this is David from J. School. Remember me?"

I said something like, "Sure! Hi, how're you doing?" What the hell? He'd been at Journalism School with me but never in the same class. I'd barely known him.

With the prerequisite icebreakers out of the way, David said, "My brother is having a reading of one of his plays at a small theater on the West Side and I wonder whether you'd like to come. Tim's probably coming,"

I knew Tim and David's parents had been friends. Tim

always referred to David and himself as red-diaper babies. Their parents had been members of the communist party and had later worked under the auspices of the WPA (Works Progress Administration) that was part of Roosevelt's New Deal; one as a writer, the other as a theater set designer. It occurred to me David probably thought Tim and I were an item. I wasn't too sure how close Tim and David were. I wondered if Tim knew David was intending to ask me out, if this was indeed what David was doing. However, it didn't really matter. Tim and I were *uña y carne,* as they say in Cuba—as inseparable as nail and skin—but not in the way others might have assumed. We were both mercurial; we knew better than to screw up a great friendship by jumping in the sack.

"Sure, why not," I said and wrote down the details.

For the reading, Tim, over six feet tall, showed up in the tan trench coat his parents had given him for his graduation, well rumpled now. He had a Brit-looking striped scarf around his neck and a rolled-up copy of the *New York Times* tucked under his arm—very *Foreign Correspondent.* That evening I found David as handsome as I had at J-School, but I still felt something was lacking; couldn't put my finger on it. Looking at his well-proportioned body—tall, erect, long-limbed, and broad-shouldered—I wanted to dress him. And, okay, undress him.

"You look great," David said by way of greeting. "You've lost quite a bit of weight."

"Gave up drinking," I said smiling flirtatiously.

"I didn't know you drank that much."

"Nor did I."

I inferred from the familiar faces that David had invited most of the Journalism class to the reading to help fill the room, so, still not entirely sure if this counted as a date or not, I was surprised when he asked Tim and me to go out for a drink afterwards.

"I liked it," I said after the three of us had been ushered to a booth in the small restaurant.

Tim and David started talking about the clearly biographical play, about how both their parents had been practically ruined by the anti-communist witch-hunt of the McCarthy era, a period during the 1950s that had rendered them unable to find work. It was a topic Tim had told me a lot about when we first began hanging out together. A few beers later Tim turned to me and said, "My sister landed a great job at CUNY (the City University of New York) and is looking for editors."

"Oh, my God, that's great."

"Don't get too excited. It's technical work, manuals I think. I'm not interested," he said.

As an editor and writer for one of Hearst's magazines, Tim had no reason to change jobs. He liked what he was doing and was getting invaluable experience—and very little pay. David had outdone Tim, landing a job as editor-in-chief of a trade magazine. Although initially lacking in experience he'd really stepped up to the plate. Working day and night, he'd vastly improved both the look and the content of the magazine. As for me, I'd been offered a good opportunity as a copy editor at a national magazine but, unlike David, I'd squandered it away. Next came a short-lived job as a public relations writer at a Wall Street bank, a kiss-ass job I was unsuited for. As if reading my thoughts David asked, "What are you doing now, Maria?"

"Freelancing. Mostly translations, editorial work in Spanish, stuff like that. A friend of mine bought a Spanish publishing house and I get a lot work from him. I like working there. I have a lot of freedom, but it's hard to pay the rent freelancing." I paused to light a cigarette. "So, Tim," I said, "if your sister is looking for technical editors, I'm game."

"I'll give her a call tomorrow."

Susan hired me on the spot. "See you tomorrow morning," she said. "But remember, we'll be here for maybe two weeks. We're moving to our new offices at One Times Square when they're ready."

"That's great," I said, excited by the idea of working in the same building from where the New Year's Eve ball dropped. As forewarned, the job was mind-numbing, but I worked with such quick-witted, well-read, charismatic people I didn't mind the sleep-inducing manuscripts. After the move I ended up working in a huge office space with an industrial gray carpet and metallic desks, saved by a large window overlooking Broadway. Four of us worked in that room—two male editors (Michael and Richard), one assistant (Gloria, a good-looking black woman with cropped hair), and myself. Michael was a young, handsome poet who spoke fluent Spanish. He'd just returned from Cuba and I was dying to know his impressions of my homeland. I couldn't imagine him in Cuba, not with that fiery orange curly hair and blazing beard. I knew from Susan that Michael had had a long-standing relationship with a Cuban woman and that she and their children had stayed behind. One day, between editing tasks, Michael showed me some poems he had written for an anthology he was working on. What I remember most about those poems was how much he loved my country.

"So, Michael," I finally said one day, "you must have really stood out in Cuba. The only guy I knew with hair like yours was a neighbor we nicknamed *Zanahoria* (carrot)."

Michael looked up and smiled. "It's different now." Oh shit, I thought, here comes the propaganda. "A lot of Russians live there now."

"Of course."

"Where did you live?"

"Labana," I said instead of La Habana and got him to smile again.

"Where in Havana?"

"Elvedao," I said, instead of El Vedado. Not so much as a smile from him.

"Lots of mansions there."

"Not where I lived. Nice houses, but no one would call them mansions. Old neighborhood, mostly middle-class. That's why people started moving to El Nuevo Vedado. You must have seen El Nuevo Vedado."

"When did you leave?"

"September 1960," I said.

The conversation was turning into an interrogation and I gathered Michael was trying to pigeonhole my family, trying to decide whether we were *gusanos,* the lowly worms who left after the revolution, or Batistianos.. Actually his questions were not unlike those most Cubans asked each other when they first met here. Cuban exiles immediately want to know what year you left in order to compartmentalize you. Being compartmentalized helps avoid possible misunderstandings should the discussion turn political. And with Cuban exiles, conversations always turn political. If you left before the Revolution you weren't an exile but an immigrant. If you left immediately after the Revolution you were a *Batistiano;* If you left in '60, '61, or '62 it was probably because your family could no longer make a living and that was kosher. But if you left in the late 60s that meant you most likely had been a *Fidelista,* and now perhaps you had seen the light, or now perhaps you were a Castro spy.

"What did your father do in Cuba?" Michael asked.

"He was a lawyer but didn't practice. He worked for Railway Express Agency, you know, REA, across El Capitolio.*"*

"El Capitolio," Michael said with a sad smile.

"How did you manage to get to Cuba?" I asked.

"With the Venceremos Brigade. You should go." "Venceremos" was the Spanish version of "we shall overcome," a revolutionary motto in Cuba as well as here.

In college I'd heard how the Venceremos Brigade recruited politicized university students, mostly SDS (Students for a Democratic Society) who sympathized with the revolution. The brigade made yearly trips to Cuba where, in a show of solidarity with the revolution, its members worked *mano a mano* with the *campesinos*, cutting sugarcane, building houses and roads, doing their part for the revolution.

"Michael, *mírame."* Look at me, Michael. I tended to

dress fashionably, and I always wore make-up. *"Ahora imagínate que estoy cortando caña."* Now picture me cutting sugarcane.

Rather than answer, Michael smiled again, I'm sure he was thinking *gusana* (worm, as Fidel liked to call us).

"You should go. You don't have to cut cane." Michael said.

"I can't go, Michael. Either my family will kill me or my going will kill them."

"Es tu vida." Michael replied. It's your life.

Why didn't I feel that way? Why did I still need my family's approval? I could go to Cuba and not tell them. But what if something happened to my mother and no one could reach me? Besides, although I wouldn't admit this to Michael, I didn't have the guts to tell my family. I told Gloria the whole story. I'd been training her to become a copy editor, and we had gotten close.

"What's the big deal?" Gloria said. "Go, do your thing."

That room screamed fusion. Richard was Michael's opposite in every way—as tall as Clint Eastwood and just as good looking. Richard had mastered the art of the studied-casual look: offhandedly stylish. A good thing since he was about to marry a fashion model about his own height. Gloria and I liked to muse on how perfectly gorgeous their children would be. Richard's nose was always buried in a manuscript or a book and none of us really got to know him. Between editing jobs Michael, Gloria, and I kicked back and shot the breeze until the next manuscript arrived.

On a morning while we waited for the manuscripts to arrive Richard read while Gloria, Michael, and I complained about Susan's moodiness.

"Man trouble," Gloria said.

"Gloria," I said, "can you do a French braid?"

"I can try," she said. She got up, removed a small rubber band from her desk drawer and with her Afro comb divided my thick mane into three sections. Michael watched with a frown, the scene apparently offensive to his socialist sensitivities. He thought I was demeaning Gloria and said something to the effect that Gloria wasn't my maid.

"You know, Michael, that's your bag," Gloria said. "I don't feel like Aunt Jemima braiding Maria's hair. I'm enjoying it. I don't have girls at home, so cool it."

Michael grunted and left the room.

"Communists are humorless fucks," Richard said and went back to his book.

I was seeing a lot of David, except it felt less like dating, more like joining a bloc. I'd wait for him at a designated place and he'd arrive with one or two friends in tow, chums either from his college days in California, from his salmon-fishing days in Alaska, or from the old neighborhood in Los Angeles. Seeing he wasn't alone, I'd hide my disappointment and feign a smile.

As a girl I had liked groups. In Cuba I belonged to one clique in school and another at the club. But from the moment I stepped into Ridgefield Park High I'd felt like the other one, like the only person in the room who hadn't been offered a seat at the table. If not by my appearance alone, my accent immediately informed others I was different. I was obsessed by what they thought of me. No matter what I wore or how I behaved I couldn't stop feeling inadequate. I didn't fit in. As a transplanted teenager, how else could I feel? I was too insecure to take part in clubs or sports. Uncomfortable inside my skin, with no sense of self-worth, I often wondered whether I'd still be the outgoing, self-confident girl I'd been at Phillips School if I were in a Miami high school. I desperately needed—although I didn't know it at the time—to regain that sense of validation I'd always had in Cuba, that sense of belonging I'd had at school, at the club, in the neighborhood where I'd always lived. In shrinkdom, I'd complain about my increasing sense of alienation, only to be advised to take action: join a church, a team, take some classes. What would be the price for belonging? Fake being a Catholic? Join a team when experience told me my name would be the last one called, and rightly so.

"It's a defense mechanism," the shrink du jour would say. "You've suffered a major trauma and only feel safe in situations whose outcome you think you can control. That's not the case with strangers. You'd rather be alone than risk more losses." She was right. My desire to belong was paled by my fear of rejection. I knew assimilation required compromises, but I'd lost so much of myself already, I was afraid I'd lose whatever was left.

Yet, here I was, caring more and more for a communal guy. Oh well, one of us would change, no big deal.

Coming from a macho culture, my major concern was—and I know how sick this sounds—that David wasn't sufficiently forceful. That he, in my father's parlance, was pusillanimous. Politics had wrought havoc in both our parents' lives but we had drawn opposite lessons from our experiences, lessons which had nothing to do with the fact that David's parents were communists and mine anti-communists. Because of his parents' blacklisting, David was overly cautious and suspicious while I, who had a rug pulled from under my feet, turned reckless. In my gut I knew it was unlikely I could transform David into an intrepid, plucky, devil-may-care guy.

Back then my favorite movie was *Jules and Jim*. David took me to see it again, just the two of us for a change, at the Carnegie Hall Cinema. Afterwards, we went for a drink at a quiet pub across the street.

"I could see that movie over and over again. I've seen it twice before," I said. "That song, I can't get it out of mind. I wish they wouldn't all die at the end."

"How would you have ended it?"

"Oh, I don't know, but I wouldn't have killed them. And you, David, how would you have ended it?"

"Haven't thought about it. But I think you're suffering from the Hollywood happy-ending syndrome."

"You're probably right. Do your parents live near Hollywood?" I asked.

"In Fairfax."

"Where's that?"

"It's a Jewish neighborhood near Wilshire."

"You might as well be talking about China. I don't know LA."

"I'm worried about my mother," he said. "She's had surgery and is not recovering as well as expected."

"I'm sorry," I said, taken aback. Getting anything about his family out of him was like pulling teeth. I often wondered if he'd ever tell me anything personal.

"When she got sick, we realized she did everything. My father doesn't even know how to drive."

"In LA? Really? So who does the grocery shopping and stuff like that?"

"Well, she used to do it but now a woman comes by to help, and my sister, my brother, and I take turns visiting. And they have friends who help. Good friends."

"I didn't know you had a sister. Where is she?"

"In Canada."

"My mother's very sick too," I said. "She's had two heart surgeries. Mitral stenosis, it's called, a narrowing of the mitral valve. I guess in a sense I'm lucky because my oldest brother is a doctor, and he looks after them. He lives nearby and stops by to check on them twice a day."

"That's great. Sorry, didn't mean it that way."

"I know."

I had no way of knowing how this seemingly innocuous exchange of information would impact our relationship.

Weeks went by, and I was yet to be asked to come up to his 16th Street apartment. Did he have to be one-hundred-percent certain I was crazy about him before inviting me? Maybe he needed to be sure I knew what made him tick, so I wouldn't expect anything fancy. When the happy occasion finally came, I briskly walked roughly ten blocks to get there. He lived in a converted townhouse, home to palm-reading gypsies on the ground floor. I wasn't expecting much, yet it astonished me to find a double mattress on the floor, a desk, a table, a couple of chairs, and little else. A Spartan lifestyle indeed. That was as it should be since David intended to take time off work so he could start his first novel. Truth is, he could have been camping out in a subway station and I'd have found a way to romanticize it.

"Want something to drink. Tea? A beer?"

"Not now, thanks. Maybe later."

"You play?" I said, pointing to the guitar leaning against a wall.

"Nothing fancy."

"Would you play for me?"

David picked up his guitar, sat on the mattress, and motioned me to sit next to him. He handed me a yellowish, gently used copy of Pete Seeger's songbook.

"Choose a song," he said.

"I don't know any of these songs. Besides, I can't sing," I said. "I'm tone deaf. In school, when the music teacher auditioned for the chorus I never got past '*re.*' It was '*do*', '*re*', and then "Next!""

"Nonsense, everybody can sing," David said, leftists being all-inclusive and all that.

I didn't want to sing. My family had never been into music. In Cuba, our radio mostly blasted political tirades, whether by Pardo Llada or Chivas, who shot himself on the air—talk about drama. Here in the States it shamed me to be a Cuban with no ear for music, which also meant I was a lousy dancer. "A Cuban who can't dance?" people would ask. In college I'd leave the required music appreciation course with psychosomatic headaches. Two semesters later I couldn't tell the difference between a major and a minor key. Of course, folk music wasn't part of the syllabus so I had no clue who Pete Seeger was, or Arlo Guthrie. I'd never heard of "Frank or of Johnny," of "Swing Low" or of the chariot. David wasted no time explaining his favorite age-old protest songs before strumming his guitar and again I found myself being educated by a man. But this was progress: David was young, single, and sober. Eventually he talked me into attempting to sing "Kumbaya," "Five Hundred Miles," "We Shall Overcome," "Where Have all the Flowers Gone," "Turn! Turn! Turn!," and a few less memorable ones. While singing along with him (a stretch), a new version of America emerge: the America of people of color, of union workers, of the disenfranchised, the America of the have-nots. All the while I was falling in love with him. Thanksgiving week David took a bunch of us to hear Pete Seeger at Carnegie Hall and by then I had the courage to sing along with the crowd, "If I had a hammer, I'd hammer in..."

We spent our first Thanksgiving with a mutual friend from Journalism School. He and his wife had helped David get his second-floor studio in the same building. The basement where the couple lived was the building's *piece de resistance*. Roomy, with a sit-down kitchen anchored by a long dining table and an assortment of chairs, the apartment felt like a home. The moment I saw the large print that hung on the kitchen's main wall I coveted it. It depicted a band of swarthy working men marching down a street.

"I love it! Who painted it? I want a copy!"

"Can't remember," our host said. "Bought it someplace in Italy."

Thirty-six years later I found in Rome a refrigerator magnet with the same image: *The Fourth Estate* by Giuseppe Pelluza da Volpedo. He's believed to have been strongly influenced by progressive and socialist causes in Italy at the turn of 20th century.

Everybody was there that night: Tim and his girlfriend, David's brother, friends from California, a couple of the hostess' friends. Pat carved the bird, raised his glass, and toasted, "Here's confusion to the French." After the boozy dinner we moved to the large living room. David went upstairs to pick up his guitar and, sloshed, we all sang "Goodnight Irene," Pete Seeger's greatest hits, and folk songs I'd never heard before. Much to my surprise I enjoyed the comradery.

Plenty of potluck meals followed. David's friends from California missed Mexican food and David took to hosting taco night. He'd line the table with ground meat, chilies, guacamole, salsa, the works. One of David's California friends talked about making chili rellenos for our next potluck.

"I don't like hot food," I said.

"They're not hot," David said. "You'll like them." Right again.

That first year with David, my proletariat year, I don't remember needing anything but him. Decent weather and we'd stroll to Chinatown where one of his college friends, a painter and horoscope reader had a loft, or we'd wander to Little Italy, get a cappuccino and cannoli at Ferrara's, or just walk two blocks to Washington Square Park for a breath of air and watch the nuts and squirrels. On Sundays, a shirtless, scrawny-looking, bearded, long-haired guy used a huge chain to tow a wheeled upright piano from the East Village to the Washington Arch where he'd bang the hell out of it, and how people loved to watch him! Pianofsky, that's what David called him. Then on our first anniversary we had that where-do-we-go-from–here chat that's never done anybody any good.

"Let's live together for a year or so and see where it takes us," prudent David said.

"Ok," I said.

Since I had the larger apartment, and a lot more furniture, he moved in with me. Ironically, we ended up sleeping on his mattress on the floor because by then I had changed to owning two single beds to accommodate my past roommates. I knew in a perfect world we should have moved into neutral territory, thus avoiding the predictable "it's-your-apartment" quarrels but this was New York City and my place, noisy as it was, was as good as it got. I was determined to make him feel it was also his apartment.

Like Bernard, David preferred coming in through the backdoor, the 8th Street entrance, for which he had a key. I suppose he found it politically awkward to live in a building with a twenty-four-seven uniformed doorman and an Art Nouveau lobby the size of a ballroom.

Not long after moving in, David was on his way out the front door when he stopped at the foyer's mirrored wall to adjust his shirt collar. He had his favorite shirt on, burgundy gingham with long sleeves. "That mirror is way too much," he said referring to the floor-to-ceiling mirror. The mirror, part and parcel of the so-called sublet, was ostentatious like everything else Bernard had purchased to get the apartment.

I had my own reasons not to like it. The wall-to-ceiling mirror took me back to the dance studio at Havana's *El Liceo* where I took after-school and summer ballet classes. "You're wasting your money," the teacher had told my mother. "She has no aptitude." I couldn't have been nine. She broke my heart. Now standing next to David I took a long hard look at it and said, "I hate that mirror. It came with the apartment."

"I was thinking of making this area my office, but this mirror will need to go," he said, still standing in the foyer.

"Sounds like a good idea. Let's try it."

David stepped into the living room, pushed his old desk into the foyer, and we were both amazed by how well it fit.

"I'll put up some shelves here. Sure you don't mind getting rid of the mirror?"

"Trust me, I hate that mirror."

The foyer became his office. David put up three perfectly straight shelves with metal brackets. He was proud of them; first thing he'd ever built. He kept his thesaurus and dictionary there, along with a book of short stories by Shalom Aleichem, *The Water is Wide* by Pat Conroy, Pete Seeger's songbook, and his diary.

While I liked David's friends, I enjoyed going out with

Tim and Rochelle the most. They had moved into David's old apartment building and sometimes joined the California posse gatherings. I had to admit that going to concerts, to Shakespeare in the Park, to Chinatown with a group was more fun than going as a couple. Tim and Rochelle liked to go with us to Jazz at the West End and listen to *The Countsmen*, former sidemen for Count Basie. Unlike contemporary pop musicians, *The Countsmen* sported jackets, dress slacks, lace-up shoes. The band was introduced by Phil Schaap, a kid with a shock of red hair who was so eager to impart his knowledge of jazz he had to be dragged off the stage. His erudition blew me away. Once we asked Gloria to join us. She took one look at Schaap and said, "Looks like that kid should be home having cookies and milk." Phil could have fooled anyone.

"He saved their lives," David said in earnest. I looked at him and knew what would follow. "These are guys who played with Count Basie," he told Gloria when the set ended, "and you know what they were doing? Working as Wall Street messengers. Shining shoes. Driving taxis. Wiping tables. Forgotten. Same with the guys who played with Duke Ellington, The Ellingtonians. Phil found them, got them a gig here. They love him." I was again reminded how badly David wanted life to imitate a Frank Capra movie.

During that year there had been so many times like this, times when I found myself falling in love with something I'd previously known nothing about. What had I known about jazz? About folk music? About politics? Now that we lived together mundane revelations peppered our lives. The first time we went to the grocery store it surprised me to see David reading food labels. Smokers don't read food labels; smokers know something's gotta kill ya. David disapproved of my choice of detergent, the phosphates being bad for the environment and all that, so we bought a bicarbonate of soda detergent, Arm & Hammer. I had no intention of changing brands, so I saved my quarters to buy the single-load Tide boxes from the laundry room's vending machine. Even in Cuba we knew bicarbonate of soda isn't soap.

Chapter Thirty

According to the flyer, Casa de las Américas was on 14th street, off Sixth. Standing in front of the building's stairway, I finished my cigarette and started up the stairs to the club. A riot of conflicting thoughts raced through my mind: Can I really do this? Will I be excommunicated from my family? Why do I need their approval anyway? It's my life after all. My steps slowed as I peered at an open door at the entrance of the hallway. Charge ahead or retreat? Determined to leave my prejudices at the door, I ventured in.

The vast loft reminded me of an old dance hall. A petite, voluptuous woman with cinnamon-colored skin stood inside door and greeted me warmly, her amber almond-shaped eyes smiling at me. *"Hola, me llamo Electra,"* she said, extending her hand. In a New-York-minute I decided to like her and shook her hand with vigor. "Let me introduce you to some people," she said.

Casa de las Américas was a social and political organization founded by Castro's government in the early days of the revolution. I was there to attend a recruitment meeting of Brigada Antonio Maceo, an outfit named after Cuba's liberator in the War of Independence against Spain. The original brigade consisted of fifty-five young Cubans who'd left their homeland as children. On December 1977 the group had visited Cuba at the invitation of a communist government eager to publicize the young exiles' awakened interest in their homeland. Aptly impressed with what they discovered (or, more aptly, what was shown to them) upon their return to the States the fledgling *brigadistas* encouraged other young Cubans to return to their birthplace, and survey the wonders of the revolution. This second trip, the one I was interested in joining, would be more expansive, comprising a hundred or more fellow exiles from all over the United States.

Maybe two dozen people sat in make-do chairs, roughly oriented towards a small metal table stacked with papers and pamphlets. Electra opened a folding chair for me and acquainted me with some people already settled. I surveyed the group: almost everyone was younger than me. A handsome woman in her early thirties stood beside the table preparing to address the group. Silky brown shoulder-length hair framed her fair face. She was in good shape and had a casual self-assured air about her, a kind of Gap look. She spoke with the conviction of a true believer.

"When we got to Cuba what surprised me most was the Cuban-Cubans acceptance of us," she said. I liked that, the Cuban-Cubans. She talked of working with fellow Cubans, of bonding with them, of realizing how much in common she had with the people she'd left behind. "While we had all the advantages of growing up in an affluent country," she added, "they had to make do without so much as toilet paper. And yet they treated us as though we'd never left.

"Our trip was life-changing. We want others to experience what we did. So we're offering this opportunity to exiles from Spain, Mexico, Puerto Rico and all over the United States as long as they meet three requirements, which are listed in our application."

It was required that you left Cuba by family decision; that you had not participated in counterrevolutionary activities; that you opposed the blockade and favored the normalization of relations between the United States and Cuba.

Aside from a desperate longing to see Belén again, I wished to return to my country because I wanted to write about the experience. I was finding it increasingly difficult to reconcile the paradisiacal memories shared by Cuban exiles and the reality of Cuba. I'd read as much about Cuba as I could and what I knew and learned didn't jive with what I'd heard. I knew about the corruption and greed of the old Cuba and about the torture and assassinations that took place under Batista's regime. I knew the state schools and hospitals were pitiful; that's why people who could afford it sent their kids to private schools. I knew most people in the countryside lived in misery and poverty. All this led me to believe I could put together the story of a conflicted exile's return home and then peddle it to some magazine or newspaper.

I had no political affiliations. I made and remade myself repeatedly and knew my life was still a draft. I was yet to arrive at the final version. All those years living in New York City had estranged me from *el exilio*. Surrounded by liberal friends, I felt Miami Cubans had moved too far to the right for my liking just as I had moved too far to the left for their liking. I instinctively rejected all manner of political zealotry regardless of cause. Was I using the exiles' political intransigence as an excuse not to commit myself or was it that I really don't trust doctrinaires, period? Ultimately, it made no difference. I've always had to see things with my own eyes.

One way or another, I was going to Cuba. For maybe $1000, I could have gone with one of the Cuban charter trips that popped up after President Carter lifted the travel ban, but aside from the cost, I would only have one week on the ground. Going with the brigade gave me the opportunity to write about a significant event: a large group of young Cuban exiles returning to their motherland. I'd be able to stay in Cuba for a month, room and board included, while paying a minimal amount for my airline ticket.

That night, during the short walk from my apartment to

the meeting, I thought more about Belén than I had in months. Climbing the stairs to enter the meetinghouse I felt like *Judacita*. I knew in the eyes of my family and the people I'd grown up with I might as well have been standing in front of the Kremlin, lighting Fidel's cigar. How to explain this forthcoming trip to Cuba to my parents, who had suffered so much because of Fidel Castro and his dastardly revolution?

By then I'd concluded the embargo or *el bloqueo* was a joke. It victimized the Cuban people who suffered severe shortages of the most basic necessities, while affording Fidel a perfect excuse for every fiasco in his governance. But the Cuban exile community in Miami was convinced Castro's government would eventually collapse in utter failure, and consequently only supported politicians who bought into their hardline stance. So, no, I didn't have a problem with the trip's requirements. I regained my focus.

"We'll be sleeping at camps and in school dorms," the speaker continued. "We'll be helping workers at a housing project outside Havana. I'm sure you know there's a housing shortage in Cuba. University students and members of ICAP (Cuban Institute of Friendship among Peoples) will be our guides. They're super nice; they were our guides on our first trip. You'll have time to visit family and friends but we have a tight schedule."

"Will we be able to go Varadero?" a member of the group asked. It was unthinkable to go to Cuba and not go to Varadero, our paradisiacal beach.

"I don't know. Like I said, we have a very tight

schedule."

I met more people like me, people who didn't favor the revolution but who'd stopped believing in the American Dream for the same reasons I had. Our doubts about our adopted country united us. We were the newcomers. Our hosts, the ones who'd organized the original trip, were true believers. For them the revolution was the answer although they made it known they didn't expect us to become converts overnight. I guess they expected the trip to win us over.

I went back to Las Americas a few times to meet with the old guard and iron out trip details. The brigade's leaders coached us on what we could take (very little) and what to leave behind—gifts of all kinds. We were advised to dress modestly and show respect. I knew what they were talking about. An unexpected result of *el diálogo* was the sight of returning exiles wearing fine clothes and looking remarkably prosperous, particularly in contrast to the Cubans who'd stayed behind. Wherever we went, we would be representing the brigade and were expected to behave accordingly.

It wasn't long before most of us began feeling somewhat comfortable around each other. A couple of brigade members threw parties at their homes. I still wasn't crazy about the women who were really gung ho about the revolution, with the single exception of Electra. Trust wasn't coming easily with most of this group. I was able to feel comfortable with a young guy called José; we shared the same reservations and similar backgrounds although his was considerably more privileged than mine.

Weeks went by and I still couldn't find the courage to tell my parents. I knew what to expect: words like betrayal, disloyalty, treachery. They would think what the revolution had done to them didn't mean shit, that I'd completely forgotten the vicissitudes we endured trying to survive in this country. Worse still, my actions would sanction the horrors that befell them and I'd be adding to their grief. I routinely called them every Sunday, and every Saturday night I went to bed thinking I should start the conversation saying, "Hi, this is Judacita."

After hanging up the phone David would ask, "Did you tell them?"

"Not yet."

"Get it over with," David would say. Easy for him, his ideology was undistinguishable from that of his parents.

Two days before leaving I called my mother.

"Mami, I'm going to Cuba. I'm going to write an article about my trip and sell it to a magazine."

"Me preocupa que vayas a Cuba," I could understand her concern about going to Cuba and I accepted it without becoming defensive.

It was my father, the man who didn't so much as raise his voice, who made me feel I lived to disappoint him. *"Yo no entiendo cómo puedes ir a Cuba con ese monstruo en el poder."* I cannot understand how you can return to Cuba with that monster in power.

"Papi, para mí esto no es una cuestión política." I took a deep breath. Except I knew everything about Cuba is political. *"Yo quiero ver a Belén. Yo tengo que ver lo que dejé atrás. Además voy a escribir un artículo."* And it

was true: I needed to find out what had happened to Belén. I needed to lay claim to my disinheritance, write it down. I couldn't say it, it was a ridiculous notion, but I wanted to find my identity. Was I Cuban? American? Cuban-American? A hopeless hybrid?

"What if they don't let you leave?" Papi asked. "There were three Nodarses in the invasion and you know what happened to me at El Palacio de los Deportes. Have you thought about that?"

"Papi, I'm going with a group of more than a hundred people. Believe me, they'll let us out. They don't want to feed us."

I was too yellow to tell Loren. His internment in Castro's jails had left him with an extremely shortened fuse, and I was afraid he'd explode. He'd either shout at me or never talk to me again. As for Alfredo, well, I felt he'd always been critical of my life; it was in his DNA, but so was his imperturbability. My mother had been right: we'd stopped being a close-knit family. But how else could it be? My life was unlike theirs in so many ways.

The fear of telling my parents had so obsessed me that I'd given little thought to the trip itself, enveloped in secrecy as it was.

The late '70s witnessed an escalation of terrorist acts carried out by radical right-wing militant Cuban groups. Hardly a time for heretical Cuban exile groups to recruit fellow exiles to visit the land of their birth. Roughly ten weeks before we were due to leave Carlos Muniz Varela, one of the organizers of the original Antonio Maceo Brigade, was gunned down in Puerto Rico. For security reasons only the brigade's leaders were allowed to know the details or our departure date.

On Friday July 13th around 11 pm I received a call telling me to be at JFK airport at eight the next morning. Thirty of us gathered there, boarded a chartered plane and flew directly to Miami International Airport where we waited to join up with fellow voyagers from California, Massachusetts, Puerto Rico, and Mexico.

We loitered about the airport lobby in small groups, cigarettes in just about every mouth. With each new traveler's arrival the smoke clouds grew, as did our level of apprehension. Furtively we scrutinized our surroundings. Our eyes darted towards any stranger that came our way. After several tedious hours, and many empty cigarette packages, we were finally ushered to the plane that would take us the last 90 miles to home. Altogether, 170 of us would make the month-long trip to Cuba. I was terrified.

"Ave Maria Purísima," that's what Belén will say when she lays eyes on me.

Pedro Yanes at Las Americas, Union Square, New York City.

Pedro took this picture of me at Las Americas.

Chapter Thirty One

A cayman in a turquoise sea, that's Cuba from the clouds.
"¡Mira Cuba!" hollered the woman seating behind me. I jumped up from my seat and pressed my nose against the airplane's small window. Colossal royal palm trees jutted out of the lush, verdant countryside. I felt tears running down my cheeks. *Al fin Cuba*! My true identity waited for me in my native ground. A nineteen-year struggle resolved in forty-five minutes, or so I thought then. The plane was descending towards the landing strip too quickly. I wished, like in my dreams, I could swim freestyle through the sky, soaking in Cuba's tropical beauty. Havana's Aeropuerto Rancho Boyeros was now called Aeropuerto José Martí. It saddened me to see Martí's name appropriated once again by a Cuban tyrant, as if patriotism were a matter of nomenclature.

As the plane rolled up to the terminal's gate my eyes were drawn to the second-story terrace where nineteen years earlier Belén and Loren had waved goodbye to my mother and me. News crews waited for us at the foot of the staircase. Peering through the window I saw the old-guard *brigadistas* unfold a large Cuban flag, the cameramen and photographers shooting away. A cluster of official-looking men stood waiting to greet us, taking advantage of the photo op. I felt used; I hadn't agreed to be part of this farce. A knot in my stomach told me I should have known better, should have foreseen this shady alliance. What, after all, was so surprising about the Cuban government milking the return of a group of young Cuban exiles? How opportune to live my life so immersed in the present as to be blinded to what lay ahead.

As I stepped on Cuban soil, I looked up at the bluest of skies and the realization I was in my country again brought me to tears. The crushing humidity and heat redolent of an equatorial jungle took me by surprise. I didn't remember Cuba feeling this clammy. Inside the airport terminal the air-conditioner grumbled and did little else. The staleness in the air made the room muggy, musty, and stifling. The sight of olive-green uniformed *Fidelistas* transported me to that life-changing afternoon years earlier, when I stood there watching one of them rummage through my mother's handbag. I looked around trying to find something extrinsic to rein in the emotional chaos that was overtaking me. I wanted to press the pause button for a few minutes. I needed to sort out my feelings, create categories, itemize whatever was happening inside me to find order. My passions were on a collision course and I needed to step aside. Except I couldn't.

"*Su pasaporte por favor.*" The voice belonged to a young, gruff miliciano. I reminded myself that people in Cuba had no reason to like us. I had two passports, my American passport and my so-called Cuban passport, granted by the Czechoslovakian Cuban Interest Section in Washington, DC. I gave him both and he inspected them. Nothing in his humorless face betrayed there being a problem, but he didn't return them.

"*¿Y mis pasaportes?*" I asked.

"*Nosotros nos quédamos con ellos hasta que te vayas.*" I hadn't anticipated the government keeping my passports. It alarmed me to be devoid of identification. I had nothing to identify me, not even a driver's license. What if my mother got worse and I couldn't leave Cuba? I hadn't been in Cuba for an hour and I already missed America's freedom. Settle down. You're overreacting. You need a reality check. Look around. See anyone else panic stricken? Relax!

Outside the airport I saw a woman who'd flown with us interlocked with her father in a snug *abrazo*. It was Carmen, the tall, slender, dark-haired young woman from Boston. Eighteen years earlier Carmen had left without her father. He was one of countless dissidents incarcerated in Cuba's prisons. Now they clung to one another as if their skintight greeting would eradicate their long separation.

Relatives looked like withered sunflowers after having spent the scalding afternoon waiting outside the airport for the plane's arrival. Carmen wasn't the only one reuniting with a loved one, but family reunification would not impede the brigade's gung ho leadership from whisking us away and herding us towards a string of waiting buses.

No one was expecting me, so like a kid I hurried to the first bus and grabbed a window seat near the back. I knew the road to the city well. Palm and banana trees etched the orangey sky, clouds outlined in pink. I wanted to see the flame-colored flamboyances of my youth. I knew we'd pass the sports coliseum, Ciudad Deportiva, the site of Papi's much recited Castro tale. That's the first thing my father's successor (Batista's brother-in-law) built. It was alleged huge kickbacks from sporting events filled many politicians' pockets.

Passing our bus were the same rounded Chevys and Fords of my adolescence. I couldn't recall the last time I'd seen the early '50s pug-nosed Chevys or the two-toned tail-finned sedans that followed. Now they were classics in America. Just as I had remembered, a large four-tiered fountain adorned a traffic center opposite Ciudad Deportiva and when I yelled, "*Mira, el Bidet de Paulina,*" everyone laughed. I was maybe seven or eight years older than most of my fellow travelers, so I remembered more. The fountain was baptized "Paulina's Bidet" after the widow of President Grau's brother, who had filled in as Cuba's first lady during his tenure.

How long had we been riding this bus? After passing el Bidet de Paulina, the bus turned on to an old narrow rural highway, and I could swear I saw the trees of my youth, royal palms, ceibas, magnolias, and jacarandas. How far was the camp, anyway? I should have used the restroom before leaving the airport. We would be close to the camp by now. When it got dark, I outlined my visit in my head. My aspirations were limited: I wanted to see Belén; I wanted to return to the old neighborhood and see who was still there; I wanted to visit El Vedado Tennis Club and The Phillips School; I wanted to walk down El Malecón, the evocative seawall that stretches five miles along the bay in Havana and in so many ways defines the city. Papi had made me promise I'd visit his sister Leila, who according to him was the only family left in Cuba, as his communist niece didn't count. He'd also asked me to pay my respect at my grandparents' grave. And, as if it had happened the previous week, I recalled our Sunday visits to the famous Cementerio Colón. Week after week, year after year, Papi buying flowers at one of the many flower stands across the cemetery, meeting his two brothers by the family grave, heading for the faucet, filling the marble container, sticking the flowers in. Now the three of them were ready to cross themselves, pay their respects to their father, Colonel Alfredo Nodarse, and talk about politics, baseball or the last boxing match.

The pungent scent of the tropics told me Havana was far behind us. We finally came to a stop and piled out of the buses. In front of us stood the spartan Campamento Julio Mella. "The men this way, the women this way," yelled our escorts, pointing at two long narrow buildings at one side of the compound. We scrambled through the luggage mound, grabbing our bags and heading towards our new lodgings. The women's dorm had two rows of bunk beds pushed against each long wall. Mosquito nets covered the beds, bringing back memories of summer nights of yore. Dog-tired from the day-long trip, I was tempted to jump into bed fully dressed but decided against it in favor of something lighter. I forced myself to open my oversized and overstuffed suitcase. Too late to regret bringing all these clothes. I clawed my way through the suitcase searching for something cool.

Afro-Cuban music filtered in through the dorm's open windows, warming me like a straight shot of rum, beckoning me to join a conga. There, in a central patio, I found los *cubanos americanos* dancing with los *cubanos cubanos*, or as we'd later refer to the group: *los cubanos de aquí*, the Cubans from here, and *los cubanos de allá* (us). But my elation was cut short when the *congoleros* began chanting revolutionary slogans: *Viva Fidel, Viva La Revolución, and Viva Cuba Libre*. Who'd started it? I scavenged my suitcase again looking for my notebook. I had to write this down before forgetting how fast the merriment had turned into propaganda. Also, I had to record the reporters' presence at the airport, their eagerness to portray all of us as Fidelistas. While I searched, revolutionary mottos vibrated in my ears, reverberated in my psyche. Forget about it? Really? Forget I was being watched? Forget there were four communist university students and one member of ICAP for every fifteen of us. One of them per three of us. Us and them, as it was before, as it continued to be.

At six o'clock in the morning loudspeakers blaring out the Cuban song *Emiliano* woke us. I lifted the mosquito net, rolled out of bed, and splashed my face with as much cold water as I could brave. Our job was to help build an apartment complex to house the workers of the nearby Ariguanabo textile factory, an ongoing project started years before by another brigade. They bused us to the site, a wide open field, where we were assigned a task and partnered with one or more local Cuban workers. I was to assist Luis, *el concretero*, the guy mixing concrete, no doubt because I was wearing white shorts and a white top. Tennis, anyone? The hot tropical sun scorched my arms and thighs in no time. Luis, I was sure, must have taken one look at me in that white outfit and decided I was hopeless. Would he joke about me when the day was over?

"All you have to do is fill up the wheelbarrow with concrete and take it over there," Luis said, pointing to a nearby group of neophyte bricklayers. In his early forties, Luis had tanned leathery skin, aquamarine eyes, salt and pepper hair. He was neither tall nor short, a bit on the thin side except for the beer belly. Luis and all the *compañeros* we came into contact with praised the revolution. They were convinced (or acted like) the working classes had benefitted from communism. Their enthusiasm surprised me, but then none of them would have ever said anything to the contrary to any of us.

Sunbaked as I was by the Cuban sun, the following morning I decided to cover up and opted for a pair of navy-blue denim overalls. Although my legs were now sheltered from the sun, the overalls stored heat with perverse efficiency and my covered thighs broiled under the heavy cloth. I knew I wouldn't last the day. I looked around for someone to talk to, and that's when I saw a Cuban-Cuban take off his straw hat, fill it with water, and put it back on his head. I followed his example and, oh, the relief! From that moment on whenever I felt like a well-done steak I headed to the faucet to refill my hat. Looking back, I see a group of young, naive professionals—bilingual teachers, urban planners, social workers, aspiring writers—who despite aching backs and stinging sunburns managed to remain a team. José, the young Cuban New Yorker who was becoming a friend, liked to tease me. "Trust me," he'd say, "one of these days Luis will show up at your apartment door."

I still hadn't talked to Belén. In between meetings there was always a line at the camp's single phone. Who would have guessed communists were so fond of meetings? Finally, I held the phone. I called Belén's number and let it ring and ring but no one answered. I hung up and tried again. "Hurry up," grumbled those behind me. No matter, I let it ring as long as I could. *Nada.* Maybe I had the wrong number! Maybe that's why we hadn't been able to reach Belén for years. I asked around for a phone book but there weren't any. An ICAP guide explained a paper shortage was to blame. "I'll find you one," she said. Later I learned people used the yellow pages for toilet paper.

Chapter Thirty Two

During our first week in Cuba we were not allowed to leave the camp. Every night after our communal dinner they regaled us with speakers who lauded the revolution. Tonight members from *La Unión de Jóvenes Comunistas* (Youth Communist Union) were scheduled to address us. A good number of us resented the rigorous itinerary since, contrary to the planners' assumptions, the most of our group wasn't there to learn about the New Cuba. A lot of us were there to recapture the past, to see friends and relatives we were once certain we'd never see again, to revisit homes and schools we had hastily abandoned, and to recapture a culture that defined us. What's more, after eighteen years Carmen didn't want to wait a week to see her father again. A young woman from San Diego said until she was reunited with her mother who she hadn't seen in ten years, "I'll be here physically but not spiritually." A young man from Boston was desperate to see his uncle, and I wouldn't rest until I found Belén.

Before the meeting started, the ICAP representative had presented me with a battered old yellow phone book, *la guía*. "Make sure to return it," she told me. *La guía*'s wobbly spine couldn't hold its grip on the tattered pages. I quickly looked for Sanchez, Belén. Pages and pages and pages of Sanchez, then out of nowhere I remembered Omoa. Omoa 357, her address.

A woman from the Grupo Atención came to tell me the meeting was about to start so I held onto *la guía* and followed her into the cafeteria. Here we go, with all the horrors of before and all the wonders of after, that's how our *compañeros* spoke, "*Antes de la revolución*," a living hell; "*Después de la revolución*," a workers' paradise. The speakers that night all followed the same formula and then the unthinkable happened. In his naiveté the young speaker asked if there were any questions. Octavio, a twenty-nine-year-old political writer and gay activist from Washington D.C. stood up and, identifying himself as a homosexual, asked, "Why aren't homosexuals allowed in the Communist Party?"

"*Fortunately,*" replied the UJC representative, "I don't think there are too many."

"I do, I do," answered Octavio getting angry.

"I mean in Cuba."

"Here, too," shouted Octavio.

"Fortunately," the young speaker repeated, "there aren't many. We do not persecute homosexuals, we do not try to eliminate homosexuality, but that's not the kind of man our society wants to develop. We promote the normal and logical development of the family, made up of *un macho y una hembra* who use their genital organs as nature intended them to."

The lines were instantly drawn and everybody was watching to see who applauded who. Then Octavio spoke up: "That's a pity," he said, referring to the ongoing discrimination, "because it forces many to live a lie."

The raucous exchange allowed me to sneak out of the cafeteria and try calling Belén again. I picked up the flimsy *guía* and with my thumb pressed against the tattered page where I had found Belén's phone number I said aloud, *"Dios mío ayúdame, Qué esté viva por favor."* God, please let her be alive.

"Oigo," said a female voice.

"Belén?" I asked, knowing it wasn't her voice.

"¿Quién habla?"

"Puchita."

"Belén murió," she said flatly. Belén died. I had refused to entertain this possibility. In New Jersey, when Fello had casually said, *"Lo más probable es que Belén se murió."* (Belén is probably dead), I fought back every consonant and vowel in his statement.

"¿Cuándo?" I asked.

"Hace como un año." A year, I'd missed her by a year.

"¿Y Manolo?"

"También murió," she said. So Manolo had also died.

"¿Cuándo?"

"Hace poco." Recently.

I didn't know Manolo all that well, but with him dead, how was I to find out how Belén died? Where she was buried?

He probably couldn't live without her. "*Gracias,*" I said.

I don't recall hanging up the phone. All I remember is that on my way to the dorm I felt my legs go numb. Fearful I might not make it to the dormitory, I sat on the floor and rested my back against the wall. That's when her death clawed my gut, that's when I was disemboweled. I buried my head between my legs and wailed. I missed you by a year, Belén. Last year I could have told you, "Belén, I love you as much today as I did back then. I just went boy-crazy for a while and then I couldn't find you." And then you would have seen in my eyes how much I love you.

The day after my phone call and the incident with Octavio, or "*lo que pasó con Octavio,*" a member of the leadership committee addressed a group of us. "The applause for Octavio was completely out of line," she said. "We're guests of the Cuban government and it's not our place to tell people here how to run their lives." I wasn't the only one thinking it was not her place to tell us who we could and could not applaud.

When the time came to say goodbye to the workers at the building site, I realized I'd grown fond of Luis. It hadn't taken him long to mock my incompetence, to tell me I always did things the hardest way possible—*la manera más difícil de hacer las cosas*—or to make fun of my outfits. That day he said, "I'm going to miss all this food." Everybody knew food in Cuba was scarce, that people lived on meager ration-card allotments, but you wouldn't know it in our midst. We had a mid-morning snack (*bocaditos* and juice) then lunch, followed by a mid-afternoon snack or *merienda*, then dinner back at the camp.

"Want to go for a walk?" Luis asked.

"Sure, it's our break."

"Where you two going?" one of the workers asked.

"Someplace where we can make out." I said in jest and kept on walking.

When we were out of earshot, Luis said, "Everybody working here was carefully chosen. They don't miss a thing. At home it's the same; neighbors spend their lives spying on neighbors. Believe me, if I could get my hands on a boat, I'd be out of here tomorrow. You said you live in New York?"

"You have a pencil or something to write down my address?"

He wrote down my phone number, and I told him to call me when he got to the States, but I never heard from him again. Maybe he didn't try to leave, maybe he went to Miami. I hope he's not at the bottom of the Gulf of Mexico. His comments, particularly about people spying on their neighbors, his desire to leave his native soil, the brigade's attempt to quash minor dissent, complete with instructions on what to say and what not to say made me realize the wisdom of my parents' decision. I've always had a big mouth, and I thought just as they had camps to "re-educate" homosexuals, they had also places for people like me.

Mixing cement with Luis, dressed like a tennis player.

Mixing cement, more knowledgeable now.

Chapter Thirty Three

Slippery Havana, still out of reach. Saturday, they told us. After nearly two decades of longing, I was all set to snatch it from the past, transport it to the present, make it all mine again.

The day started with a visit to El Hospital Psiquiátrico, one of the revolution's major achievements. The psychiatric hospital, on the outskirts of Havana, formerly called Mazorra, was infamous for its mistreatment of the mentally ill. As the buses pulled up to the asylum there he was, sitting in a rocker with his white hair and his cape: El Caballero de Paris. Everyone who'd ever lived in Havana remembers hearing dozens of anecdotes about the peaceful madman, the Gentleman from Paris, who strolled about the city in a decrepit black cape, pencils and notebooks in hand, sporting a somewhat intellectual aura, an effect dispelled by long and frizzy white matted hair and matted goatee. Well-spoken, he was fond of talking to passersby about books, poetry, his take on life. He never asked for money (although he'd accept it) but would give you a card he'd made, a poem he'd written. As a kid, I'd guessed neither his hair nor his beard had been washed for years. Today, with a cape that matched his suit, and his white hair now clean, he still seemed as much a part of Havana's landscape as El Morro Castle.

A woman in the group approached him and in a reverent tone said, "I still have a poem you gave me sixteen years ago." Now in his eighties, El Caballero replied nostalgically, *"Ah, sí,* I used to write poems in those days." I could imagine her having to decide which of her many belongings to take into exile and choosing that rumpled piece of paper with a poem by Cuba's foremost nut. For about thirty minutes El Caballero stood smiling amidst 170 Cubans who snapped photographs of him to remind their parents of happier days before they pulled their roots from their native soil.

The hospital's patients put on an impressive stage show, the women in long gowns, the men in balloon-sleeved *rumbero* shirts knotted at the waist. The romantic songs of yesteryear and the rhythmic dances I grew up with added to the sentimentality aroused by our encounter with El Caballero de Paris. Our time at the Hospital Psiquiátrico moved the most skeptical of us. As the bus left the hospital I could hear flattering remarks, praise for the revolution. Of course I was impressed by the hospital but my mind was elsewhere. I couldn't stop thinking about the woman who told El Caballero de Paris she'd taken his poem into exile. I imagined myself telling

Belén, "You know that miniature *Imitation of Christ* you gave me at the airport? I keep in my nightstand."

Mementos. When I'd least expect it I'd long for something left behind, like the amazing illustrations of the Grimm's Brothers fairytale book I found one morning under the Christmas tree, the ink drawings so lavish glassine shielded them; or like the seafoam green music box on my night table that Mami rewound after reading to me. It wasn't unusual for her to walk out of my room to the sound of Strauss' "Los Patinadores" or "Skaters Waltz." "*Qué sueñes con los angelitos,*" she'd say on her way out. Dream with the angels.

After leaving El Hospital Psiquiátrico a young woman from ICAP reminded us it was carnival night in Havana.
"In July?" I asked.
"What better time to celebrate *el 26 de Julio?*"
In its shrewdness the government rescheduled carnivals so they would coincide with the anniversary of the revolution. The fact that July was one of our hottest months paled in comparison with the opportunities the date presented. Time was when the carnivals preceded Lent, so that people could squeeze in as much music, dance, and celebrations before forty days of renunciation. In pre-revolutionary Cuba carnivals offered *los pobres* the opportunity to outdo *los ricos,* they were like a collective resistance against the pull of the privileged. Residents of Havana's *repartos* or suburbs and slum dwellers alike

paraded down the Malecón in *comparsas* or congas in a riot of color, choreography, and music. I remember a *comparsa* called "Los Dandys," the men wearing top hats and the women blue satin dresses. The *comparseros* from the infamous barrio Atarás called themselves *los* Marqueses de Atarás, their choreography so distinct they were admired across the island, the men wearing white top hats and white tails. The *comparsas* were led by *faroleros*, men carrying lanterns on five-foot poles. Grand, festooned *carrozas* (floats) advertised businesses and social groups while bathing beauties in swimsuits or sexy evening gowns smiled and danced for the crowds. Sandwiched between the *carrozas* were the latest convertible cars packed with white kids and teenagers wearing costumes, throwing confetti, and waving to the crowds. Those were the carnivals of my youth.

Tonight was something else. The evening belonged to Fellini. *Los congoleros* swayed shovels and other proletariat tools to the pulse of conga drums while scantily dressed, voluptuous *cubanas* swung their wide hips, strutted their stuff, mounted atop gussied-up tractors and trucks that replaced the allegorical floats of the past. Their steaminess was reminiscent of the debauchery of the '50s. There was something so life-affirming in these variations that I wasn't disappointed. Quite the contrary, I marveled. I've always savored our propensity to improvise.

Street stands sold warm rum and hot beer and though the night was as steamy as the tractor-riding mulatas I drank both. Several Cuba Libres later I didn't give a damn about being a lousy dancer and I joined the crowds frolicking towards the Malecón. By three in the morning, my shoulders, hips, and feet ached from hours of dancing. I sat on the seawall and let the crashing waves spray my feet. The harbor's balmy breeze blew my hair and caressed my face and shoulders with the sultriness of the tropics.

Not all had changed—young couples still kissed and embraced along the seawall. For a brief moment, past and present fused, and I was again fooled into believing this was still my country. Nancy, one of my *compañeras,* must have been similarly transported. She was reduced to tears and told a nearby clutch of Cubans, "You don't know what you have. Don't let anybody take it away from you."

I understood her perfectly; I had not expected the clash of two worlds, of the old Cuba and the new Cuba. The tension between the two pulled me apart. I longed for a resolution but knew if I forced myself to choose, my pick would color the remainder of my stay. Like Nancy I wanted to embrace my own Cubanness, *mi cubanismo.* I'd sort things out later.

Chapter Thirty Four

At last we were on our own. I quickly grabbed a window seat on the first bus heading for Havana. The two-hour trip felt like an eternity. Everyone was excited, quizzing each other as to what they would do first upon arrival.

During the years I'd been gone, the passage of time had consumed Havana. The city I had loved, the city that had remained intact in my memory, was gone. Wherever I looked all I saw was peeling paint, missing windows, broken-down walls, cracked asphalt, decaying buildings––overwhelming evidence of long-lasting neglect. An odd calm had descended upon the bus's passengers. As if real-world trepidations were pushing out our collective enthusiasm for the journey ahead of us. I got off at a bus stop only a short distance from home. As the bus pulled away, I just stood in place, hastily digging out a cigarette and taking a couple of quick puffs. An otherworldly hand squeezed my stomach, and I tried to ground myself. I'd been dreaming of this moment for what felt like a lifetime. I wasn't going to let my anxieties screw up this chance to reconnect with the girl I'd left behind. The old neighborhood had also deteriorated—but nothing compared to what I'd seen in Old Havana. I scanned the familiar buildings and wondered if my schoolmate Luisito still lived in the apartment building I briefly stood in front of.

A lump grew in my throat as I walked past my house. No tears yet, but I knew they would surface. I pictured my mother sitting on the porch's bamboo rocker, saying something to my grandmother who, pencil in hand, was working on a word puzzle. My home looked the same. "This house was built like a small fortress," my mother liked to say during hurricane season. All the tropical storms ever did to that stone house was to swell the massive mahogany front door so it wouldn't close. We'd secure the windows with wood planks, bring in the porch furniture, and wait the storm out.

I slowly walked past my house and dithered at the street corner trying to decide how to proceed. A man in his late thirties came out of the garage beneath my old home and closed the Spanish wrought-iron gate that secured the driveway. I felt conspicuous standing there by myself. What if the CDR (Committee for the Defense of the Revolution) was watching? Better get it over with. I walked up to the small gate in front of the pathway leading to the front door. "*Señor*," I said, "I lived here before the Revolution and I wonder if you'd be kind enough to let me see my house again?" Shit, I shouldn't have said my house.

"*Claro que sí,*" he said. He took me up the red-tiled steps I used to skip over as a kid and invited me in. "*Entre,*" he said.

I shouldn't have gone in. Outwardly the house looked just as we'd left it, but nothing inside it attested to our ever having lived there. *Mi casa* had shrunk. It was really spacious back then, especially the living and dining room. The longer I lived in my Manhattan apartment, the larger the house where I grew up seemed to get. The way I remembered it, the hallway, showing diplomas and family memorabilia, was endless, long enough for me to say one Our Father on my way to the bathroom, praying there'd be no cockroaches. The sight of a single cockroach would send me scurrying back to bed. Our furniture—the sofa, the side tables, the armchairs, the elaborate dining room set—gone. A portrait of Che hung on top of an ugly sofa. At the end of the hallway now, I looked into my grandmother's bedroom.

"*Aquí falleció mi abuela,*" My grandmother died here, I said thoughtlessly. Not what a Cuban wants to hear, that someone died where his son sleeps. He didn't reply. Instead, he walked into the bedroom, opened the closet and pulled out my father's "Slazenger" tennis racquet.

"My son still plays with it," he said with pride.

"*¡Qué bueno!*" I said, wondering how my father would react to this piece of news. Would he be happy his racquet was being put to good use or would it vex him that a young communist was playing tennis with it?

I walked through the pantry and headed to the

backyard. "That's where my dog is buried," I said, pointing to the soil around a cemented square.

I remembered being very little and Mami letting me go into the backyard in my panties during an *aguacero*, a rainstorm, and watch me get drenched. *"Señora, a Puchita la va a partir un rayo."* Belén never failed to warn my mother I'd be struck by lightning. *"No le va a pasar nada, Belén,"* my mother would reply. And she was right, nothing happened to me

On the way out, I gave the kitchen one last look and imagined her there, her massive body leaning against the wall as though she were propping it up. She and Papi had this routine. When Papi came home from lunch in a sweaty *guayabera*, Belén waited until he finished eating and then asked him, *"Caballero,* you going out like that?"

Papi, sitting at the head of the table, would lower his head and look for a spot in his *guayabera*. Finding nothing, he'd ask Belén, "What's wrong with it?"

"Don't ask me, I'm just the maid."

I'd laugh to myself knowing Belén had made Papi feel shabby. He would put on a fresh shirt.

I thanked my host and left. To hold back my tears I concentrated on what little remained unchanged: the black-and-white tiles, the elaborate wrought-iron railings shaped like arrows, the narrow passageway running from the backyard to the front of the house where the three of us kids, either roller skating or riding a bike, frequently had our heads speared by arrows. We all have the scars to prove it. My mother was in the habit of saying *"tu cabeza tiene más marcas que un mapa"* (your head had more marks than a map) but I never understood the connection.

Chapter Thirty Five

I turned right and slowly wandered up my old street, trying to remember which houses might still have people I knew. I could recall who'd left. The Valdivias, of course, had drawn us to Ridgefield Park. Our family doctor and friend, Dr. Cespedes, who lived two houses down, was now in Miami. Felix B. Caignet, author of the famous, drawn-out telenovela, *El Derecho de Nacer,* whose house was across from the Valdivias had died in 1976. But was Isabel, the neighborhood's bookie, still here? Isabel ran *la bolita,* named after the little numbered balls chosen at random in lotteries. *La bolita* was an illegal offshoot of the national lottery. It was said to conceal their gambling activities, the *boliteros* used a code word for every number. One stood for horse; two for butterfly; three for sailor and so on. I know that whenever Mami remembered one of her dreams, she'd cross the street (when I didn't have school I went along) and tell Isabel what she'd dreamed. Isabel would help Mami decide what number to place her money on. One morning she told Isabel she dreamed she'd died.

"Ocho, muerto," said Isabel.

What! Eight, the day of my birthday, stood for death? Holy shit!

I now stood on the small porch where I'd been introduced to the mysterious world of illegal gambling. The door was closed. "Isabel," I yelled, "Isabel, *es* Puchita."

"¡Puchita!" Isabel screamed. "¡Puchona! (big Puchi, not little Puchi) she said as she pulled me to her and hugged me. "Marta, come see who's here." Marta burst into tears the moment she laid eyes on me and stepped back. *"No lo puedo creer; es qué no lo puedo creer."* She couldn't believe it. Trying to help her get a grip on herself, Isabel told her, "This is no time for tears; we should rejoice. Puchi, how the world turns!" She took a long breath and with watery eyes solemnly said, "Puchita, I'm so sorry about Lorenzo."

"He's still having a tough time," I replied.

"You mean, he's alive?" Isabel asked.

"Yeah. He's not well, but he's alive."

Isabel looked at Marta. Marta raised her eyebrows and shrugged her shoulders.

"Puchita, everybody on this block thinks your father died when he fell out of a fourth-floor window."

"Where did that come from? No, he's very much alive. He's had a hell of a time with *los nervios* but he's still alive."

The three of us started giggling like schoolgirls.

I found them both so old, perhaps not Isabel so much, who was my mother's age, but certainly her daughter. Marta brewed coffee for me. Coffee, rationed at the time, was more precious to Cubans than gold. But that's a Cuban for you, generous to the limit.

"Your mother's lucky number was 22," Isabel said. "No matter what else she bet on, she'd always bet on 22."

"And she won a couple of times?" I asked.

"Yes, a couple of times, playing 22." She grew sad after mentioning it. "*Ésto está horrible,*" she said. "Every block has a CDR. They watch everything that happens on their block and then report it to the local police. *El CDR no se pierde una.*" The CDR doesn't miss a beat. The CDR, or Committee for the Defense of the Revolution is a nationwide network of informants monitoring Cubans from every window, porch, and stoop.

"Right now," Isabel added, "someone is jotting down that you're here, and after you leave she's going to come over and ask me who you are and why you came. You can't be careful enough; you can't trust anybody."

"You know, Isabel, I shouldn't have gone into my house. If I hadn't, I would have kept thinking of it as home. Now I can't, not with Che's portrait hanging in the living room. If I'd stayed across the street, the house would have remained the way I remembered it."

"*¿Un retrato del Che donde estaban las medallas?*" asked Isabel. For as long as I can remember my father's tennis medals had been displayed where Che's portrait now hung. The medals had been professionally mounted against a black velvet background and they were the first thing that caught your eye as you walked into the house. Now Che caught your eye.

"Are they going to lift the blockade?" interrupted Marta. "It's only hurting us." Isabel nodded and said, *"Todo el mundo sabe que Fidel y su pandilla no carecen de nada?"* Everybody knows Fidel and his gang lack for nothing. *"El que sufre es el pueblo."* It's the people who suffer.

It all felt so cozy and familiar, rocking back and forth on that small porch, looking at my house across the street, holding *una tacita de café,* getting a whiff of the jasmine creeping up the trellis, I said, "Loren came in the invasion. And when he was in prison Belén visited him and brought him food. Did you ever see Belén after we left?"

"Belén es una santa," Isabel said. "Right after you left Loren stayed in the house for a while and Belén would come and cook for him. I saw her mopping the porch a few times, right Marta? But after Loren left and your cousin and his wife moved in, she never came back. Have you seen her?"

"Belén died."

"Oh my God, I can't believe it," said Isabel. "I'm so sorry, Puchita. When did she die?"

"About a year ago."

"You can't imagine how sorry I am. I bet you came to see her."

"As I sit here part of me is waiting for *Me Voy.* Do you remember him? Does he still come?"

"Puchita, *ya no hay pregones,*" Isabel said, referring to the musical expression born of street vendors. *Pregones,*

Cuban street music. Each *pregonero* or vendor had a particular chant, catchy rhymes sung in public squares, in parks, in the street, advertising with wordplay and puns what he sold. The *pregonero* I waited for as a kid was a tall, black man who wore a baker's uniform (apron and all) that matched his white hair, which was as spongy as a cloud. On top of his head, beneath the huge basket that carried his mouth-watering delights, sat a small round pillow, also white, to cushion his load. He sold the sweet sugar-sprinkled, syrupy egg bread Cubans called Pan de Gloria. Whenever I heard his deep-throated voice chant *"Me Voy,"* (I'm leaving), I ran inside the house. "Belén, I need a nickel for *Me Voy*." Everyone called him *Me Voy*. Hard to imagine Havana without *pregoneros*, especially since *El Manisero* (*The Peanut Vendor*) was practically our national anthem. Papi liked to tell the story that at the opening ceremony of one Pan-American tennis championship in Central America, the hosts couldn't find the recording of the Cuban anthem and played *The Peanut Vendor* instead.

"There were *pregones* when we left." I said.

"Marta, do you remember when they did away with *pregones?"* Isabel asked.

"I think it was 1968 or thereabouts. *Ofensiva Revolucionaria,* or something like that it was called. It was the end of private business, no matter how small. *Pobres pregoneros* couldn't sell anything anymore. People with hole-in-the-wall stores, they had to close too."

I wanted to spend the afternoon with Isabel and Marta, asking them what else had changed, what else was gone.

It piqued me I had to leave. "Isabel, Marta, I told Papi I'd see his sister, so I've got to go. If it was up to me I'd stay here all afternoon."

"Where does she live?" Marta asked.

"La Víbora." I replied.

"I'll call someone I know who drives a taxi," Isabel offered. Tearful kisses, messages, promises, and hugs later I climbed into an old two-toned Buick taxi and told the driver we'd be making two stops. "First, we'll go El Vedado Tennis and then to La Víbora. I'll pay you for the afternoon." I should have asked the driver to go down Calle 26 so I could see the *farmacia* one more time; assuming it was still standing. Wonderfully rich Cuban mahogany cabinets lined the store. The storefront was wide, with fancy tile floors and glass-encased medicine cabinets. The pharmacist looked like a doctor in his long, white jacket. Most medicines were mixed in the pharmacy, giving the store a mystifying odor. A tiny room behind a curtain enhanced the enigmatic aura. That's where you went in if you needed an injection. Like most people I could have skipped the shot but I admit to loving medicines. My favorite prescription was called *elixir paregórico*, which I was prescribed whenever I had colitis. The elixir, the word itself makes me dreamy, was bright green and was dispensed in very small dark bottles, like a forbidden potion. Blindfold me and I can still recognize its exotic scent. The pharmacist filled the tiny bottle and wrote down how many drops to take, always too few for me.

Chapter Thirty Six

El Vedado once was one of Havana's oldest upper-crust neighborhoods. The original houses were built like fortresses, many with wrought iron fences and spacious front porches shaded by mature luxuriant trees. With the revolution, its population had expanded to include all social classes. Looking out the taxi's windows, I didn't find El Vedado as dilapidated as the other sections of Havana I'd seen on my way to revolutionary museums. The driver stopped at the driveway of a white, classical, three-story mansion where I had spent the bulk of my childhood. Sure, the edifice, built in 1902, would have welcomed a fresh coat of paint, but it was by no means decrepit.

I walked past the two heavy, slightly chipped columns that supported the terrace above the driveway and into the lobby where I'd sit for what felt like hours waiting for my father to pick me up. I'd while away the time watching the switchboard operator who, cool as a summer breeze, would plug and unplug phone cables with astonishing dexterity. "*Un minuto por favor, mientras lo conecto.*" Just a minute while I connect you. She didn't seem to mind my presence. When I got tired of standing I'd walk to the other end of the lobby where I'd continue my wait in the comfort of a supple brown leather sofa. Now the lobby was empty and bare, not even a telephone in sight. Although the regal marble staircase showed signs of wear, it still cascaded with decorum. I walked past the staircase as if I owned the place, and into the next room, formerly the trophy room, where the various awards and trophies won by the club's teams were once proudly displayed. Back then I had very affluent friends, and that is perhaps why I never thought of myself as having a privileged life. In Cuba my family was strictly middle class. It wasn't until we came to the States and had to rebuild our lives from near nothing that I realized the advantages I had enjoyed. In this trip I had been labeled affluent. If I happened to mention we had a cook and a housecleaner or if I let it slip that I went to El Vedado Tennis or had attended the progressive Phillips School, I got bad vibes.

I was stunned to find the club where I grew up vacant, now that it belonged to *el pueblo. ¿Y la gente, dónde esta?* Where were the blacks, the mulattos, the blue-collar workers, and the disenfranchised? *La piscina grande,* the big pool, was empty. I had spent countless afternoons in that pool, first as a tomboy, playing with Maggie, her cousin, and a girl we called Grillo (cricket) and later on as a coquette. This was the deepest and the coldest of the club's three pools and on this particular July afternoon, an afternoon hot enough to melt a rock, the pool was dry as a bone. I remembered my last summer at this pool. All the girls my age wore white starched long-sleeved linen shirts as a cover-up when walking around the pool or going to buy a Coke and a *pastelito*. That summer somebody came up with the idea that the way to get the perfect tan was to coat yourself with a mixture of coconut oil and iodine. It's a miracle we didn't end up with skin looking like red hides. I was orbiting the past when I saw a man heading my way. He looked familiar, and now that he moved closer, I remembered him. He was a former employee. What is he doing here?

"You used to work in the men's locker room?" I asked him before even saying "hello."

"You're Lorenzo's daughter, aren't you? Didn't expect to see you here," he said without volunteering what his present job was. "How's your father?"

"He's had his ups and downs. It hasn't been easy for him. He's doing okay now."

"Your brother still looks like him?"

"That's what everybody says."

I kept quiet about Loren being in the invasion. Like Isabel reminded me, you never know. "Is it all right if I walk around?"

"Claro que sí." Of course.

I headed for *la piscina chiquita*, the kids' pool where I'd learned to swim. The water reflected the same vibrant aquamarine blue that was the bottom of the pool. I remembered, when I was five or six, starting at the shallow end of the pool and inching my way to the deeper, opposite end, holding onto the edge, taking a deep breath, ducking underwater, coming up and doing it again. I had fallen in love with water *en la piscina chiquita*; I'd never known such freedom as I experienced there. This is where I belong, I thought as a child.

"Swimming is like flying, Belén."

"How would you know?" she asked.

"I just know."

At least the pool was clean and full. That meant it was being used. I wandered towards the girls' changing room, memories of my young life cascading through my head. I was wearing a halter-top dress that day, and the sun scalded my shoulders. Pinned to my New York apartment's cork bulletin board was a small black-and-white photograph that came to life as I stood in front of the pool. Papi, Mami, and I were standing by *la piscina chiquita* (the small pool). It must have been Mother's Day because we wore the same plaid halter dress. I was four or five at the time. I wondered how our bare shoulders fared that day. I looked around me. Everything I saw now was as it should be. The crystalline water was enticing so why wasn't a single kid in sight?

The different swimming pools were like rites of passage. Like Goldilocks I went from *la piscina chiquita* to *la piscina mediana* and finally to *la piscina grande*. I remembered how in Cuba you had to wait at least two hours after you ate before getting in the water. If you didn't, you could have an *embolia* (a stroke). Kids and teenagers alike would say, "I can't go in yet because I ate an hour ago." In Cuba you were never too young for a stroke.

Around the time I graduated to *la piscina grande,* `I gained access to the previously forbidden women's locker room: *la taquilla de las mujeres,* and what a crowning glory that was, to be a woman. Attendants in starchy uniforms handed me a fresh white towel imprinted with the royal blue Vedado Tennis Club logo. After a shower I'd take a seat under one of the spaceship-helmet hair dryers. I'd watch the women apply makeup and fix their hair, trying to remember a trick or two. I wasn't allowed to wear makeup yet.

I would train every summer morning so I could take part in the Big-Five swimming matches. I always made the team, and I always got third place in freestyle and breaststroke, a major disappointment to my father, *el campeón.* When I swam I was more concerned with style than speed. I breathed after every stroke because not to have done so would have been inelegant and my determination to swim like a siren slowed me down considerably.

Mami and I had spent quite a few Sunday afternoons watching Esther Williams's movies like *Million Dollar Mermaid* and *Jupiter's Darling.* These aqua musicals with water ballets and synchronized swimming inspired me to swim like her, with fluidity and grace, not speed. Later on in life as my personality dictated my abrupt, hurried, erratic movements, friends were astonished to see how smoothly and sinuously I swam.

Chapter Thirty Seven

On the way to the Spanish colonial neighborhood of La Víbora, where Tía Leila lived, I couldn't help but stare at the state of decay around me. The houses in La Vibora sagged like octogenarian skin. Much of Havana looked like an ageing whore with yesterday's make-up and flaking fingernail polish. But here's the thing: my heart was broken not by the decrepitude I found wherever I looked, but by what I didn't find. Gone were all the street vendors with their fruit and ice cream carts, the *piruleros* or candy men, the *billeteros* with national lottery tickets plastered all over the signboard hanging from their shoulders, front and back. They were hard to ignore. In Habana Vieja they used to work nearly every street corner, and I wished they still did. How shattering to realize our national folklore had been replaced with decaying revolutionary slogans.

I asked the driver to wait for me once more. "I'll pay you for the whole day," I reminded him. I got out of the car intending to finish my cigarette before stepping up to Tía Leila's door (cigarettes gave me courage) but the sun was too intense on my sunburned shoulders. I dropped it on the boiling pavement and stepped on it instead. I wiped the sweat from my forehead, removed my sunglasses, and walked through the wide-open door. A woman I didn't recognize looked at me calmly yet quizzically. *"Yo soy Puchita, la sobrina de Leila,"* I'm her niece. Tía Leila was sitting in a rocking chair in an anteroom of sorts. It shocked me to see how brittle and ancient she'd become. The stranger helped her get up from the rocker, handed her a black wooden cane, and said, "Leila, I'll come back later."

Tía Leila's hair, black when I'd last seen her, was now white as milk and she seemed to have aged forty years instead of nineteen. She had shriveled and was considerably thinner. I could tell she was trying to figure out who I was.

"Tía Leila, *es* Puchita." I said.

"¡Puchita!" It was my voice she recognized. I wondered if she was having trouble seeing me. We held each other; there was so little of her. She wore a black and white dress; the kind Latin women would wear after they come out of mourning. I'd been gone for nineteen years and yet I could see nothing new in the house, nothing fresh. A look around the living room left me feeling I'd stepped into a time warp. It was all the same as I remembered, and at the same time it was so much worse. I was reminded of thrift shops in Manhattan's marginal neighborhoods, of battered furniture left on New York sidewalks in the secrecy of night, their owners too ashamed to give it to the Salvation Army. Everything that surrounded Tía Leila was tattered, done for, the worse for wear. A cracked cane rocker in urgent need of caning rested upside down atop the faded, frayed sofa; the rest of the furniture was impossible to recognize. Paint peeling from the walls and ceiling, chunks of plaster unaccounted for. "I'm so sorry I didn't recognize you," she said, "but they haven't replaced my glasses. It's been over four months now." My eighty-three-year-old aunt who used to give me a peso when we visited her on Sundays had lost her husband, Tío Isidoro, two months earlier. I didn't know; no one had told my father. I couldn't bear the thought of her staying here, in this wreckage, alone.

"I have nobody left," she said.

Tío Isidoro had decided not to go with Nenita, their only daughter, when she and her husband packed up their two kids and left in 1960. He and Leila hadn't wanted to burden them while they tried to start a new life in America. "Who could have said this would last this long? I haven't seen my daughter for nineteen years." She kept repeating "*diecinueve años*" as if I didn't know.

"You know, Tía Leila," I said, "the new American president has started a family reunification program and I'm sure you'll qualify. I'm sure you can live with Nenita in Miami now that Tío Isidoro is gone. *Aprovecha esta oportunidad.*" Take advantage of this opportunity.

She wouldn't hear of it.

"We spent fifty-two years together, and I want to rest next to him. You know, Puchita, I have all these *cartas de pésames*, (condolence letters) I can't read because the government won't replace my glasses."

"I'll read them for you,"

I removed the useless wicker rocker and helped her sit down at one end of the ragged sofa. When I sat next to her she curled against me like a kitten, fidgeting with a white cotton handkerchief in her right hand. As I read the letters, she'd discretely dab her tears with her handkerchief. My own eyes watered as I went along and then I started to cry in earnest. Just being there broke my heart. To see her looking that frail, that old, that lonely, and to have to leave her living by herself in that dilapidated house she wouldn't leave was more than I could accept, and I tried very hard not to sob. When I finished reading the letters I needed to blow my nose, so I went to get a tissue out of my handbag and realized I didn't have any. In the bathroom the only paper I found was Simplicity patterns on top of the toilet.

"*¿Quieres ver el álbum?*" Tía Leila asked.

"*Claro qué sí.*"

She struggled to her feet and tottered, cane in hand, into her bedroom coming back with her family photo album, also faded and fossilized. I didn't realize we had that many family pictures, three generations of Nodarse, mostly men.

"You want to see Nenita's apartment?" she asked afterwards. Without waiting for my reply she gripped the rail and painfully climbed up the stairs. I followed her to the master bedroom where she opened the closet to show me her daughter's dresses and her son-in-law's suits and sports shirts. "Everything is as they left it." she said.

"That reminds me, I have something to give you when we get downstairs." She showed me her grandchildren's bedrooms. Same, just as they left it.

Downstairs, she came out of her bedroom cradling a yellow magazine, an issue of *Bohemia* dated November 16, 1952. "*Dáselo a Lorenzo*," she said. The magazine carried my father's open letter to Batista, and I held it with pride.

"We never hurt anybody. We didn't deserve this," I said. And that was God's honest truth. I knew I'd never see Tía Leila again. I was one more person abandoning her, and I thought her heart had to be more wrinkled than her face.

"*No se te olvide la Bohemia.*" she said.

"*Claro que no.*"

I hugged Tía Leila and said, "*Papi se va a poner tan contento cuando la vea.*" And that's how I left her, knowing she would make her brother happy.

I got into the car intending to make one other stop. I wanted to visit the best school in the world. I was afraid this might be my only chance. But time was tight, and I had to accept that I couldn't cram nineteen years into one July afternoon. What if I didn't get back on time and the bus was gone? I had no way to get in touch with them. Didn't even have a passport. I asked my driver to head back to the bus stop. He graciously thanked me as I paid him what to me was nothing, but was over a week's wages for him. I still had about twenty minutes to kill. A cold beer. I'd kill time sipping a cold beer.

I stood in front of the former Havana Hilton. When it was built in 1958, it was the largest hotel in Latin

America. During the first three months of 1959 the Havana Hilton became the revolution's headquarters. The irony had been lost on me then. Of all the hotels in Havana, Fidel chose to commandeer from Hilton, America's most renowned hotel chain. Yes, I'd treat myself to a cold beer at the Hilton bar. I recalled how the hotel's striking façade with its spectacular blue mosaic mural had impressed me when I was thirteen. I could make no sense of it, but the vibrant colors had swept me away. Now that I could see how other artists had influenced the mural I enjoyed the work even more. I walked into one of the rechristened Habana Libre's bars. I was its sole customer. I watched the bartender and only waiter engaged in a lively discussion that didn't look about to end. I waited, hoping they'd acknowledge my presence, but having a New Yorker's tempo, not nearly long enough.

"*Una cerveza por favor,*" I said. They both glared at me like I was just another rude foreigner. If the waiter could have pissed in my beer, I'm sure he would have. The beer was lukewarm at best but I nonetheless sipped it, sucked on a cigarette, and relived my day. Tía Leila all alone. There was a time when I went there every Sunday to visit my grandmother, who was very frail. I don't remember her ever being in good health. Dressed in our Sunday best, Papi would drive all of us over for our weekly ritualistic get together with his mother and other family members. More often than not his brothers and my cousins would be there as well. My brothers enjoyed the visit more than I did since my cousins, all boys, were their contemporaries. I remember my grandmother as bedridden but it wasn't always so. Before being diagnosed with a heart condition she'd join us in the living room or at the porch, wearing a black or black-and-white dress, her long white-yellowish hair coiled in a bun. She smelled of talcum powder, I remember, and was very affectionate. Unfailingly Leila would give the three of us a dollar as we were leaving, saying, "Here, for the movies." As time went by and movie prices increased my brothers joked about it, but never in front of my parents. "Here's a dollar," they'd say, "so you can go to Europe."

It turned out the lousy service I encountered was the rule rather than the exception in today's Cuba. That's what my *compañeros* were talking about when I rejoined them. "Passive counterrevolution," said a member of the old guard. They had a name for everything.

During the long bus ride back to the camp one of my real *compañeros*, José, told me he'd been able to track down the housekeeper who had helped raise him. I was happy for him. "She was wearing a kind of shabby dress," José said, "then she excused herself and came back wearing her Sunday best. We spent some time looking at photos, and I have some to take back to my family."

José had tried visiting his old house, now an embassy, but the guard wouldn't hear of it, wouldn't even let him take a picture. I empathized with his anger but he got little sympathy from those with humbler origins in the group who suspected that if José's house had been turned into an embassy, it had to be a mansion. I felt a different envy. Why couldn't I have come back with stories about Belén, about what she wore, about how she hugged me and how we relived the past? It had been a somber ride back to camp. The pain of a forced separation replaced the elation many had felt when reuniting with friends and family. As for me, I could only think of Leila.

Chapter Thirty Eight

The revolution, they told us, was in the provinces, so we spent our third week crisscrossing the island, sleeping in school dormitories, visiting historical sites or, more precisely, revolutionary museums. Undeniably, *el interior* displayed a revolutionary zeal absent in Havana and I for one didn't find the distinction surprising. Cuban peasants or *guajiros* had always lived in heart-breaking misery, in *bohíos* (that romantic symbol of the Cuban countryside) with dirt floors, without running water or electricity; their lives as stagnant as water at the bottom of an idle well. Exploited by Cubans and foreigners alike, by the owners of sugar mills, *los centrales,* and by multinational corporations, Cuban sugarcane cutters, or *macheteros,* barely survived. There was *la zafra* (the sugarcane harvest), about a four-month season, and *tiempo muerto,* literally dead time.

Macheteros only got paid during *la zafra*. The rest of the year the peasants bought on credit from the company store, did whatever odd job came along to survive or both. Living as they did, with nothing to lose and everything to gain, the peasants backed the rebels in the mountains who guaranteed them food year-round and promised access to public schools and free medical care. And while Havana went to hell, vanishing as a terminal patient in a hospital, people in *el interior* witnessed the construction of hospitals, schools, and new houses with real floors, electricity, and running water.

That said, the revolution's most significant contribution to the Cuban peasantry was literacy. It estimated Cuba's pre-revolutionary literacy at a range of sixty to seventy-six percent, with the *guajiros* or peasants being predominately illiterate. Rural areas had chiefly lacked schools and teachers. It wasn't in the interest of corporations to support education. Reading wasn't a prerequisite for cutting sugar cane.

In January 1961, the government launched a year-long effort to abolish illiteracy in Cuba. Literacy brigades descended upon the countryside, constructed schools, trained new teachers, and taught *guajiros* how to read and write. Education and health-care reform dramatically improved the quality of life among the lowest sectors of Cuban society.

The brigade's steering committee had scheduled our first stop in Oriente, Cuba's furthermost eastern province, roughly 540 miles from Havana. We were in the old colonial city of Holguin, founded by the Spanish in 1545. It was the anniversary of the revolution, July 26, and Fidel

Castro was delivering a speech. We all stood in a big open central plaza surrounded by thousands of local Cubans. No one was allowed to carry anything. Sombreros were prohibited so we were at the mercy of the blistering Cuban sun. As it was commonplace to bus hundreds of factory and field workers to Fidel's speeches the plaza was packed. Listening to *El Máximo Líder* address the crowd I had to admit that while he was no longer the handsome, young revolutionary who had triumphantly marched into Havana in 1959, his melodramatic rhetoric continued to captivate the masses. Nicaragua's President Anastasio Somoza had been recently toppled and leaders of the victorious Sandinistas had flown in to express their gratitude for Cuba's help. Fidel asked the crowd, *"¿Y si Nicaragua necesita mil doctores?"* And if Nicaragua needs a thousand doctors?

"Nosotros le mandamos mil doctores." We'll send them a thousand doctors, echoed the crowd.

"¿Y si Nicaragua necesita mil maestros?" And if Nicaragua needs a thousand teachers?

"Nosotros le mandamos mil maestros."

"Y si Nicaragua necesita..." And so the Supreme Leader went on as we, the people, broiled by the scorching sun and parched by the sweltering heat, had no other choice but to listen to him, intoxicated as he was by the sound of his own voice.

After Holguin we headed to Oriente's capital, Santiago de Cuba. Santiago had been the capital of the Spanish colony of Cuba from 1522 to 1589. There's a long-standing rivalry between the province of Havana and that of Oriente. *Orientales* brag that more *mambises* (patriots) came from Oriente than from any other place in Cuba. Antonio Maceo was born in Oriente, and the Independence War against Spain originated there. Fidel Castro was born in Oriente, and the Granma landed there in 1956 with 82 rebels on board.

Despite benign neglect, Santiago de Cuba didn't disappoint: it still evoked Spain. Santiago had kept its colonial character, much of its original architecture, and an indigenous flavor. I wanted to familiarize myself with the city but we barely got a taste of it before they scurried us off to the port city Cienfuegos, a word that means one-hundred fires. By then, ragged and exhausted from weeks of travel, and overdosed on factories, speeches, and revolutionary museums, about four dozen of us got sick with diarrhea, vomiting, and severe intestinal pain. The earlier bitterness about not having enough free time resurfaced and petty squabbles broke out. Many of us were becoming increasingly irritated by the constant demonstration of the revolution's success. Propaganda has a short life span. Also, it didn't help the group's sinking morale that we weren't used to privations: toilets that didn't flush, lack of toilet paper, absence of air-conditioning, cold-water showers. We were all tired of the living conditions. Ana, a young woman from the California faction, asked the two people sitting next to her if they were willing to take a vote to determine how many of us wanted to see more museums. I didn't really know Ana; few of us did. She stood out, probably because her wardrobe was a vivid reminder of the Age of Aquarius. Ana was very much her own person, and individualists, me included, don't fare well in command-performance communal settings. I suspected she was an environmentalist—maybe a member of the Audubon Society or the Sierra Club. In the bus, whenever she asked for the name of a particular bird she'd spotted, people would either deride her or invent a name for it. "That's a shit picker," I remember our "guide" saying one day. Everyone laughed. It didn't help that Ana's Indian skirts and Haight-Ashbury air made her look like a hippy. It takes one to know one; Ana was a product of the '60s. Asking people if they wanted to take a vote about our itinerary was Ana's second mistake; her first one had been to announce she'd seen shantytowns and whorehouses in Havana.

I was still in the hospital on August 2nd. I remember the date because that's *el dia de mi santo*. I was named after Nuestra Señora de los Angeles, and when I lived in Cuba, it was like having two birthdays.

Everybody else in the group was sufficiently recovered, but the onslaught of vomiting and diarrhea had dehydrated me, and I was on intravenous fluids. When a day or two later I left the hospital, I learned that a member of the steering committee had informed the New York sub-brigade that Ana was attempting to subvert the trip, and that the group needed to vote on whether to expel her. The day after the vote Ana was placed on the first plane out of the county.

The brigade's leaders were eager to get our troops moving again to the next "cultural event" and revolutionary monuments. They had roughly a week left before the trip ended. Since I wasn't recovering as speedily as the others, someone decided—I don't know whom—it was best for me not to travel with my *compañeros* to their next destination. I was to stay in Havana before returning to the States. So I too was separated from the group, and I found it very unsettling. I didn't like being singled out in Cuba, not after all the horrors I'd heard about as an exile. The brigade departed for what was called Isla de Pinos when it was a prison before the revolution. They had renamed it Isla de la Juventud, Isle of Youth. I really couldn't see why I had to leave my country at their command when it would have been simpler for me to catch up with the group in a couple of days. Besides, I'd never been to Isla de Pinos or Isla de la Juventud. But no one asked me.

Like crumbling Havana, I was about to fall to pieces. Weak and exhausted I found no consolation in spending the night at the renowned Havana Riviera, a modernist casino hotel built by the infamous gangster, Mayer Lansky, during the late '50s. From 1956 to 1958 Havana experienced a building boom, the offspring from the arranged nuptials of Batista to the mob. During this period three major hotel/casinos emerged in the capital: the Havana Hilton, the Havana Riviera and the Hotel Capri, fronted by George Raft. The Riviera was purposefully narrow. Like a screen, it partitioned dynamic El Vedado from the white-capped waves of El Malecón. I was escorted there by a member of ICAP, the tourist association hosting our trip. As the official car stopped at the hotel's *porte cochére,* my chaperon told to me to wait while she checked me in. I saw her striding briskly into the lobby, heading to the hotel registry with confidence. I stepped out of the car. I wasn't about to let my weariness prevent me from admiring the sculpture that fronted the entrance. A white marble mermaid and a swordfish intertwined as fluidly as they would have below the surface of the sea.

"Everything's been taken care of," said my *compañera.* "You're our guest for the night."

"Tomorrow morning, at ten, *un compañero de ICAP* will pick you up and take you to the airport. He'll have your airline ticket and passports. *Buen viaje.*"

"Mil gracias y perdona la molestia," I said, apologizing for the inconvenience.

"Para eso estamos."

As I entered the lobby, I faced another astounding work of art: a two-story metal sculpture of two stylized dancers centered the lobby's circular staircase. The sculpture, entitled *Ritmo Cubano,* captured the cadence of my land.

Upstairs I dropped my suitcase on the bed and walked straight to the balcony, certain the sight of the Havana's splendid bay would appease me. I felt shaky; a free-floating anxiety caused my fears to ebb and flow like the waves breaking against the seawall. I wanted to stay, I wanted to leave, I wanted to stay, I wanted a drink. After longing for privacy for weeks, being left alone in this high-rise hotel room gave me the jitters. What scared me was the sense of being at their mercy, of my life not being my own. In fact, it wasn't just a feeling. I had no control over what lay ahead. Throughout the trip I'd known inclusion in a large group—and one under the auspices by the government—had insulated me from experiencing the reality of life in Cuba: long lines, scarcity of food and medicine, constant vigilance, censorship, coerced volunteerism. Now visions of entrapment raced through my mind. Few people in Cuba (and none in the United States) knew where I was. I was unaccounted for. And this awareness led to bouts of paranoia: Am I going to be put on a plane and disappear from the face of the earth as Camilo had? No, I'm not important enough. What if the Cubans (when did they become *"the Cubans?"*) don't give me back my passports? What if they tell me they lost them? Was I about to vanish in a labyrinthine communist bureaucracy where anchored, grim-faced clerks would relish in denying me the mobility they envied? To make matters worse, the stamina to fight these fits of paranoia had been flushed away by my recent illness. I was holding back feelings of hysteria, but I couldn't calm down; soft voices echoed deep in my head, "We told you so!" "We told you not to go!" I couldn't stay still. I had to get out of that room.

The night was like a song, lavender and azure clouds hung low on the horizon, hemming a fiery tangerine sun. A night like this must have inspired Lecuona to compose his much-admired romantic melody *Noche Azul*, "Blue Night." I sat on the edge of the seawall letting my legs dangle, hoping a white-crested wave would splash them. *Noche azul ven otra vez, a que me des tu luz.* Soon a foamy wave splattered my feet, surprising me with its warmth. I gazed upon the shimmering sea with the persistence of memory, and my eyes swelled with tears. I searched my handbag for tissues but found none. When I looked up, I saw the water open wide and swallow the sun in one big gulp—just like that. Then I turned my back to the sea so I could take in Havana one last time: *los novios* readying for a night of courtship, families out for a breath of fresh air, pink Russians promenading down the boulevard, their white socks and sandals a giveaway. Do I even look Cuban? Cuban women weren't wearing washed-out jeans, fashionable sandals, and trendy tops. Nah, I looked like a tourist longing to belong.

Whenever I saw a Russian I felt like a loving wife coming across her husband's mistress: Mine, not yours, goddamn you. *Los rusos* walked about as if they owned the place, which they did. Cuba lost to the Soviets, of all people. The wound of betrayal ran deep. Once I'd been certain that nothing could match the pain of learning I'd entrusted my heart to a cheat. I'd been mistaken.

On September 26, 1960 I had said goodbye to Belén through a glass partition. What had made me think I'd find her alive nineteen years later? Better still, what made me think I'd return to the same country? I wasn't illiterate; I read about Cuba. But self-delusion is indiscernible. Look at the Miami-Cubans; they still thought they had left behind a paradise.

Throughout the trip we Cuban exiles shared stories that told of the pain of separation, stories that hinted of feeling betrayed, being lied to, all because of the promise of a swift homecoming. When, towards the end of the trip I heard someone say "My parents lied to me," I replied, "They didn't know! My mother left behind my birth certificate. She left behind my father's law degree. That's how certain she was we'd be back in no time." No sooner said than a deeply buried memory resurfaced. Not long before leaving, one quiet evening when Mami, Papi, and I were on our porch's rocking chairs, swinging back and forth, my mother said, "Lorenzo, I want to go to Valle de Viñales in case we don't return." I had blocked out not only her statement but our visit to the strikingly lush verdant valley and its monumental limestone bluffs, for it would have been impossible to remember Viñales without hearing Mami say, *"Por si acaso no volvemos."*

Passing back through the hotel's lobby, I saw several new guests checking in. Had they been allowed to keep their passports? Later I realized my fear of entrapment had prevented me from falling for the paradisiacal Cuba sold to us by our brigade leaders. This, my last night in Havana, was no time to reconcile my past, crystallized as it was in the amber of nostalgia, with the present. Something told me I'd have to wait for the present to become the past. It's the exiles' way.

Alone in my room at the Havana Riviera, all those real-life stories I'd heard time and time again about the hopelessness of getting out of Cuba echoed in my psyche with a deafening pitch. They wouldn't let me leave, just like they didn't let them leave. Was it at a cocktail party in New York I'd heard someone say communism was like a cockroach motel: easy to get in, impossible to get out?

The more I contemplated my situation, the more cornered I felt. In retrospect I see myself not so much panicking as building an armor to protect me from revisiting the most harrowing experience of my life: being deracinated at fourteen. For my own good I had been forcefully pulled away from roots, an uprooting that was the cultural shock of my life.

I knew my way around Miami International Airport but on my return to the States I couldn't even find the luggage claim carousel. Disoriented and dispirited, I understood I needed a place to pull myself together. When I finally found my bags, I walked out of the terminal and straight onto the first hotel shuttle bus I saw. I was staying here tonight, too emotionally spent to take another step. My appreciation for the hotel's amenities knew no bounds. Hot shower, TV, air conditioning, room service, the works, But even as I raided the minibar while basking in America's comfort zone, I failed to feel rooted. Free-floating anxiety thrived. I called David. Straightaway he said, "You're not supposed to be back!"

"I know. It's a long story. I'll tell you tomorrow."

I'd believed my true identity waited for me in my native land, not as a vision but as a revelation. You major in literature and you think you can read life. I'd hoped the trip would offer an epiphany straight out of *The Dubliners,* but it hadn't. All that was revealed was that neither my past nor Cuba were what they used to be. Memory is like a palm tree swaying in the wind. My deracination had construed a basic yearning for a place to call home along with a growing hunger to reunite with the girl I left behind. A reunion with Puchita, the girl who was popular, always encircled by friends; the girl who spoke without hesitation, without an accent; the girl who behaved spontaneously because she was on her turf. How was I to know about the fluidity of exile?

Chapter Thirty Nine

When I landed at New York's La Guardia Airport I immediately spotted David's burgundy gingham shirt. He stood tall by the gate and after setting eyes on him my heart grew too big for my chest. Here I was back in New York City, my honey waiting for me, the trip behind me.

So much to tell! I knew I'd lucked out with David; I knew good listeners are hard to find. "Did you write all this down?" asked David when I finally stopped talking.

"Quite a bit. When it was time to leave, I panicked because I was all alone. I thought I'd have problems at the airport. I was sure the *milicianos* would confiscate my journal, but they opened my suitcase, took a look, and closed it again. Piece of cake."

"Look at your notes while everything is still fresh in your mind. You need to make a lot of calls," David said.

Good thing somebody remembered how to be a reporter.

"I can't call anyone, David. Everyone's still in Cuba." I was glad that was the case, I wasn't ready to relive the last few weeks yet; I just got home. "You know how I love to play reporter."

"Nothing's easy," David said. His self-righteousness never failed to turn me off. Before the trip, interviewing people was something I did because I had no choice. In journalism school and even as a public relations writer whenever I interviewed someone I felt I was prying, which of course I was, that's what journalists do. But in this case Cuba had been a shared experience. I'd been a participant. I couldn't wait to hear what my countrymen had to say. They, in turn, were anxious to talk, to be heard as individuals rather than a collective. When Luis told me that if he could get his hands on a boat he'd be gone in a minute, I felt privileged he'd trusted me, and I'd like to think he felt better for getting it out of his system.

It took a few days to recover from the trip. When I thought about my story and tried to shape it, I found myself disjointed, unable to find where to start, forget about putting together a single paragraph. I was all over the place and no place in particular. My thoughts bounced like a ping-pong ball—from Cuba to New York, from the past to the present, from how I felt about the trip to how my family would react to it. I had felt a cold shoulder when I called my parents to say I was back, but then again I've spent most of my life feeling rejected

Being completely out of cigarettes and milk, I sauntered

to the grocery store behind the building. In my head I cataloged everything I encountered under one of two headings: the United States or Cuba. I was repelled by the level of excess and consumerism that surrounded me. American groceries overflowing with a dizzying array of choices versus the naked shelves of Cuban *bodegas*. Cubans wished for a single tube of toothpaste, a roll of toilet paper, a bar of soap, a box of cereal. Here, one could spend hours deciding what brand to choose of any given product. I found the grocery's cereal aisle particularly sickening: cereal with fiber, no-frills cereal, vitamins-and-minerals enriched cereal, Technicolor cereal.

I felt all this guilt about our having so much and their having nothing. It became an obsession that colored all my thoughts, conveniently preventing me from focusing on how desolate I felt. Puchita had stayed behind in Cuba and I, New-Yorker Maria, was nowhere to be found. The country I'd spent all my life treasuring wasn't mine anymore.

What had led David, Michael, and other well-meaning leftists to believe things were now better in Cuba? Was it because they weren't Cuban? Or did they too think we used to walk around barefoot?

A week went by before I picked up my not-so-portable electric Smith Corona, took it out of the case, and set it on the dining table. My secretarial training kicked in and I transcribed my notes with speed and ease. With my journal and my pack of cigarettes I was ready to go. Typing out my notebook entries helped depersonalize them some, allowing a degree of objectivity. I had recorded verbatim *"lo que pasó con Octavio"* and reading my notes felt like stepping on broken glass. Who could have said I'd feel so lonely without my *compañeros?* But wait, Ana was back.

"Hi, Ana, this is Maria from the brigade."

"You're back?"

"Just me. I got really sick, and they sent me back early. How are you?"

"I feel I've been exiled twice," Ana said. Right away I heard the pain in her voice. "The guards at the airport seized my backpack, but that wasn't all. When I picked up my suitcase in Miami, I found the lock broken and the rolls of film gone. I didn't buy anything in Cuba, so I have nothing to remind me of my trip, not even a photo. It's like I was never there. Actually, it's worse because I don't know if they'll ever let me return."

Why would you want to return, I thought but didn't ask.

Several days and a few phone calls later I learned things had loosened up quite a lot after my departure and Ana's expulsion. People were given time to evaluate the trip, give feedback, hang out. The witch-hunt had worked. Manuel from the Boston sub-brigade told me, "I don't know if I'll ever recover from the pain of leaving Cuba. I probably won't. I know I'll never forget saying goodbye to the Grupo Atención, to the journalists who covered our stay, to the people in Cuba. I cried at the airport. I remember thinking this is how we will spend the rest of our lives—saying goodbye and crying."

I said something to the effect that the trip had left an everlasting mark in all of us, and I meant it.

The phone interviews re-energized me. I asked David for feedback. It wasn't smooth sailing. He thought I was overemphasizing Havana's decrepitude. "You have to be

Cuban," I said, "to understand what seeing Havana in ruins does to you."

"All these superlatives..." David said.

"I'm Cuban. That's how we talk." In the end I agreed with him and toned my prose down. Some.

"I think you should leave Belén out," David said.

"No way. I want to pay tribute to her."

"Not here."

"Why not?"

"It doesn't belong here. That's not what this article is about. It's a matter of focus."

Focus is hard to come by when everything in your heart weighs equally heavily. Ultimately Belén was cut out. White-Out speckled the floor in the dining area. The way I remember it I used more Scotch-tape cutting and pasting that article together than during all my Christmases combined. I submitted my fifth draft. It had taken me so long to finish the article I felt I couldn't afford the luxury of individual submissions. So I sent it to every major newspaper. The editor of <u>The Miami Herald</u> Sunday magazine and the editor of <u>The Atlanta Constitution Journal</u> Sunday magazine agreed to publish my article simultaneously. The Sunday it appeared I took the BMT line to Times Square and sprinted to the newspaper kiosk. That day no one could have convinced me that anything in the whole-wide world could surpass the thrill of reading one's by-line on a magazine cover.

David shared my sense of victory, as he should have, since his editing skills were instrumental to the article's publication. That said, the trip affected our relationship. I came back with a clearer view of what it meant to be Cuban in a foreign land, and also Cuban within the land I wanted to be my country. Returning to the Cuba I knew was to never be. It no longer existed, its destruction brought about by the very political system David considered desirable. He was a true believer, and I was increasingly finding his socialist zealotry exasperating. Why couldn't he walk a mile in my shoes?

"But David," I'd say, "I've been there; I've seen with my own eyes the outcome of nearly two decades of communism. Why is it so difficult to believe me when I say repeatedly that Cuba had been wrecked by a communist dictatorship?"

The subject was no longer accessible for discussion. I started to self-censor. David had always been a socialist but confronted with my criticisms he was revealing a doctrinaire side to him that up till now I'd missed.

The trip underscored other significant disparities that had mostly gone unnoticed. I'm led to believe there's some magical thinking lurking underneath the hackneyed "opposites attract." I suspect when you fall for someone who's your counterpart you unconsciously believe he or she will complete you. That's what I think drew me to David. I now realize I'd sought in him the self-control and restraint I lacked, the sense of measure, the level-headedness I so desperately needed. But after my return, David's virtues metamorphosed right in front of my eyes. I saw his caution turn to temerity, his self-control to passiveness. I'd spent a month with fellow Cubans and the closeness that developed between us revealed my own unfulfilled needs. I longed for that communicative shorthand I'd found in Cuba. I longed for David to be more accessible, more emotional, more passionate; I longed for David to be Cuban. Major joint disappointments followed. I could offer a narrative of our parting ways, but it would come up short. Suffice it to say our mutual attraction mutated, and we turned out to be irreconcilably different.

After the article's publication I still had one more gauntlet to run. I called Mami and told her when my plane would land in Houston.

Mami already had dinner ready when the limousine driver dropped me in front of my parents' two-story apartment building in Texas City. I spent the evening describing and explaining my Cuban odyssey, careful not to sound too defensive when questioned about particular events. I wanted them to know what the ability to return to my land, my people, my culture meant to me. The following day Fello stopped by at lunchtime. He kissed me on the cheek, asked me about the flight, the weather in New York, the usual idle chatter. I watched him walk to the kitchenette, open a cabinet, and grab the Italian espresso maker Cubans favor. This was as much his routine in Texas City as stacking his pocket change in a catch-all plate had been in Cuba.

Papi, perhaps the sole Cuban who doesn't like coffee, continued reading the newspaper. Mami approached Fello holding *The Atlanta Constitution Journal* Sunday magazine. "Fello," she said with visible pride, "*Mira lo que escribió Puchita.*" Look what Puchita wrote. The coffee pot whistled, and Fello filled the demitasse cups. He took the magazine from my mother and headed for the empty armchair next to the sofa where Papi usually sat. Within minutes (he couldn't have read over two paragraphs) he got up, threw the magazine on the armchair and said, *"Yo no leo esto."* I won't read this. Mami went after him, asking *"¿Cómo le vas a hacer eso a tu hermana?"* How can you do that to your sister? But he didn't stop to reply, either because he didn't hear her or because he decided the question was not worth answering.

I wasn't surprised; I'd thought my trip to Cuba might turn me into another Mata Hari in my family's eyes. But then I never felt they found much of anything acceptable with how I lived my life. I was certain my brothers believed I should be tending to my folks (after all, it's an unmarried woman's duty) not running about Cuba. What surprised me was Mami being so proud of me. She was thrilled to see her daughter's name on a magazine cover. For that, I felt immensely grateful. I don't know how Papi felt. Uncharacteristically, he made no comments about my trip except to tell me how happy he was I'd visited Tía Leila. Later, on Father's Day, I gave him a bound copy of the Bohemia issue, with an engraved leather cover. My article was never mentioned again in Texas City, Texas. That is, not until 2017. Fello and I were on the phone, talking about Cuba, as usual. "That was a good article you wrote," he said.

"*Gracias*." I said. By then I felt so grateful for his devotion to our parents, looking in on them twice a day, day in and day out, that I was determined to accept him the way he was.

"Yo soy asi," this is the way I am, I'd told Fello when years earlier both our parents were hospitalized at Mt. Sinai

and he had accused me of being overly dramatic.

Like the tides, I've always made waves.

That year, 1979, I believed if the American government's blockade were lifted I could slowly make Cuba my home again. At a time when my identity was a fixation I needed to believe I could go back home, even if the house had shrunk, the club was vacant, the school was no longer American. But as time went on, Cuba, like a bottle cast out to sea, drifted away from me until I lost sight of it altogether. Then I became the drifter. I floated from New York to London, to Madrid, back to New York, then to Texas, and finally to California. In California I called New York home. Home was always defined by the absence of it. I didn't grasp that like all exiles, unwilling immigrants we are, home is the past that persists in our memory, a paradise lost. Many lives later I understood that like the fabled turtle in its shell, I'd been carrying my home with me all along.

Ridgefield Park, New Jersey, Christmas 1960.
Left to right: Fello, Papi, Maria, Mami, Lorenzo

ABOUT THE AUTHOR

Maria A. Nodarse is the daughter of Cuban exiles who migrated to the United States in 1960 fleeing communism. After several years working as a bilingual secretary she obtained a scholarship to Columbia University's School of General Studies in 1968. She was then admitted to Columbia University Graduate School of Journalism, earning a master's degree in 1974. Her student days at Columbia politicized her, and she embraced such liberal causes as the anti-war movement and the feminist revolution. Her ideas and beliefs set her apart from mainstream Cuban exiles.

While living in Manhattan Nodarse worked as a freelance editor, translator, and commercial writer. In 1979 she traveled to Cuba with a group of young left-wing exiles, after which she wrote an extensive article about her experience, a story that was picked up by two major American newspapers. Upon her return from Cuba she worked for New York publishing houses and traveled extensively throughout Latin America. She resided briefly in London and Madrid before returning to New York. She and her husband live in Camarillo, California, with their beloved KC Cavalier, Chloe.

www.ingramcontent.com/pod-product-compliance
Lightning Source LLC
Chambersburg PA
CBHW030300080526
44584CB00012B/386